The Development of
Second Language Proficiency

THE CAMBRIDGE APPLIED LINGUISTICS SERIES
Series editors: Michael H. Long and Jack C. Richards

This new series presents the findings of recent work in applied linguistics which are of direct relevance to language teaching and learning and of particular interest to applied linguists, researchers, language teachers, and teacher trainers.

In this series:

The Development of Second Language Proficiency

Edited by

Birgit Harley
Patrick Allen
Jim Cummins
Merrill Swain

The Ontario Institute for Studies in Education

91-390

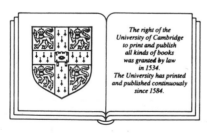

The right of the
University of Cambridge
to print and publish
all kinds of books
was granted by law
in 1534.
The University has printed
and published continuously
since 1584.

Cambridge University Press
Cambridge
New York   Port Chester
Melbourne   Sydney

Published by the Press Syndicate of the University of Cambridge
The Pitt Building, Trumpington Street, Cambridge CB2 1RP
40 West 20th Street, New York, NY 10011, USA
10 Stamford Road, Oakleigh, Melbourne 3166, Australia

First published 1990

Printed in the United States of America

Library of Congress Cataloging-in-Publication Data
The Development of second language proficiency / edited by Birgit
Harley... [et al.].
p. cm. – (The Cambridge applied linguistics series)
Papers prepared for a symposium held at the Ontario Institute for
Studies in Education, November 1987.
Includes bibliographical references.
Includes index.
ISBN 0-521-38410-9 (hardcover) – ISBN 0-521-38795-7 (paperback)
1. Language and languages – Study and teaching – Congresses.
2. Second language acquisition – Congresses.   3. Bilingualism –
Congresses.   I. Harley, Birgit.   II. Ontario Institute for Studies
in Education.   III. Series
P51.D48   1990
418'.007–dc20   89-22247
                                                                                          CIP

British Library Cataloguing in Publication Data
The Development of second language proficiency. –
(The Cambridge applied linguistics series)
1. Schools. Curriculum subjects: Foreign languages.
Learning by students
I. Harley, Birgit
418'.007'1
ISBN 0-521-38410-9 hardcover
ISBN 0-521-38795-7 paperback

Contents

V   THIRTY-FIVE YEARS OF RESEARCH ON BILINGUALISM

CONCLUSION

Contributors

Patrick Allen, Ontario Institute for Studies in Education
Lyle F. Bachman, University of California at Los Angeles
Richard Bourhis, Université du Québec à Montréal
Christina Bratt Paulston, University of Pittsburgh
Jim Cummins, Ontario Institute for Studies in Education
Alison d'Anglejan, University of Montreal
Jean Handscombe, North York Board of Education
Birgit Harley, Ontario Institute for Studies in Education
Wallace E. Lambert, McGill University
Patsy M. Lightbown, Concordia University
Barry McLaughlin, University of California at Santa Cruz
Jacquelyn Schachter, University of Southern California
H. H. Stern, Ontario Institute for Studies in Education
Merrill Swain, Ontario Institute for Studies in Education
G. Richard Tucker, Center for Applied Linguistics

Series editors' preface

For some years now, the Modern Language Centre of the Ontario Institute for Studies in Education (OISE), Toronto, Canada, has played a leadership role internationally in the study of education in and through a second language. Thus, the recent completion of a major five-year OISE study of the development of bilingual proficiency in school-age children naturally attracted considerable interest among researchers and educators alike. We are pleased to publish here the findings of that project, together with expert reaction papers and discussion of the implications for practice.

The Development of Bilingual Proficiency (DBP) project consisted of a series of related studies in three major areas: the components of second language proficiency, the effects of classroom instruction on second language learning, and the relationship of proficiency to age differences and social-environmental factors. The project involved several source and target languages (English, Spanish, French, Portuguese, and Japanese) and a variety of different types of language programs. Along the way, the research team addressed several key methodological issues, including validation of the COLT (Communicative Orientation of Language Teaching) classroom observation scheme.

As the DBP project was nearing completion in November 1987, a symposium was convened at OISE at which experts critiqued the different studies in a series of invited reaction papers. Their contributions also helped relate the project findings to broader issues in second language acquisition and in bilingual and immersion education and went on to consider implications for policy and practice. Those reaction papers are included here, too, along with responses to them by project team members which provide an indication of the lively audience discussions that followed. We think this format makes for stimulating reading.

Drs. Birgit Harley, Patrick Allen, Jim Cummins, and Merrill Swain, the editors of this volume, have done a fine job first as principal investigators on the DBP project and now in making the results of that work available to a wider audience. We think the book enhances the reputation for high-quality, socially relevant research for which the OISE Modern

Language Centre is respected. It is the kind of scholarship we are pleased
to publish in the *Cambridge Applied Linguistics Series*.

Michael H. Long
Jack C. Richards

Acknowledgments

The editors wish to acknowledge the contribution of the many individuals and organizations who have played a role in the Development of Bilingual Proficiency project on which this volume is based. We are grateful to administrators, teachers, students, and their parents in the following Ontario school boards for their participation in the research: the Board of Education for the City of Scarborough, the Carleton Board of Education, the Metropolitan Separate School Board, the North York Board of Education, and the Toronto Board of Education. In addition, we would like to thank the Portuguese Secretary of State for Immigration, the Regional Secretary of Social Affairs for the Autonomous Region of the Azores, and the staff, parents, and students of the Japanese School of Toronto Shokokai, Inc.

We wish to acknowledge the contribution of Ellen Bialystok and Raymond Mougeon, who were principal investigators of the project in 1981–82 and 1981–83, respectively. We would also like to express our appreciation for the role played by project staff and other Modern Language Centre colleagues in conducting the research, administering the project, assisting with the final symposium, and processing text: Sharon Lapkin (project manager); Margarida Aguiar, Glenda Au, Jud Burtis, Susanne Carroll, Christian Ducharme, Maria Fröhlich, Vince Gaudino, Gila Hanna, Mary Lou King, Laurette Lévy, José Lopes, Françoise Pelletier, Bruno Piché, Jorge Ramos, Mireille Tremblay, Virginia Won (Pang) (research officers); Jane Appelt, Eva Bild, Roma Chumak, Patrick Conteh, Giselle Corbeil, Marilou Covey, Antoinette Gagné, Tara Goldstein, Gordon Harewood, Vera Held, Annette Henry, Richard Kruk, Bill Marshall, Josée Mazzilli, Stephanie Paulauskas, Anne Riddle, Emilia Rivas-Arraiz, Mela Sarkar, Kathryn Shred Foley, Nina Spada, Yilin Sun, Tim Tomlinson (graduate assistants); Monica Heller, Janice Johnson, Grace Pung Guthrie (postdoctoral fellows); Ellen Bouchard Ryan, Jan Hulstijn (visiting scholars); Jamshid Etezadi-Amoli (statistical consultant); John Broome, Jeanette Crotty (administrative officers); Ellen Jeske (text-processing specialist); Joyce Hayes, Joyce Howlett, Doreen Panowyk, Donna Schillaci (secretaries).

In all our research at the Modern Language Centre, we have benefited from the vision, scholarship, and enthusiastic encouragement of David (H. H.) Stern, first director of the Modern Language Centre from 1968 to 1981. His sudden death in August 1987 prevented his attendance at the concluding DBP project symposium on which this book is based. We are extremely fortunate, however, to be able to include in this volume the discussion paper he had prepared in advance.

We are grateful to Mari Wesche for presenting David Stern's paper at the symposium and to Fred Genesee, Bernard Mohan, and Lily Wong Fillmore for chairing the discussion sessions.

Finally, we wish to acknowledge the financial support provided in the form of a five-year negotiated grant (No. 431-79-0003) by the Social Sciences and Humanities Research Council of Canada, and the administrative and financial contribution of the Ontario Institute for Studies in Education.

B.H., P.A., J.C., M.S.

Introduction

This book is about a major five-year research project conducted during the 1980s in the Modern Language Centre at the Ontario Institute for Studies in Education. The purpose of the project, entitled the Development of Bilingual Proficiency (DBP), has been to examine a number of educationally relevant issues concerning the language development of school-age children who are learning a second language. Specific issues addressed in the research are: the nature of language proficiency, the effect of classroom treatment on second language learning, the relationship of social-environmental factors to bilingual proficiency, and the relationship between age and language proficiency. The research draws on a variety of minority and majority language learning populations attending schools in the Province of Ontario, including students of Japanese-, Portuguese-, and Spanish-speaking home backgrounds, students attending a French-language school, and students of mainly English-speaking home background learning French as a second language in core and immersion programs.

The aim of this book is not to present the component studies of the Development of Bilingual Proficiency project in all their detail, but instead to place the project in perspective by bringing together short summaries of the research on each issue and a set of discussion papers written by experts in the area of bilingualism and second language education. These papers, prepared for a project symposium held at the Ontario Institute for Studies in Education in November 1987, provide a reflective, and sometimes critical, view of the DBP studies from the outside. They consider the theoretical and practical implications of the research, and point to further research needs. The reader interested in the full details of the research is directed to a series of interim and final reports (Allen, Bialystok, Cummins, Mougeon, and Swain 1982; Allen, Cummins, Mougeon, and Swain 1983; Harley, Allen, Cummins, and Swain 1987) available through the ERIC Clearinghouse for Languages and Linguistics.

The papers in the present volume are organized according to topic in six sections. In Part I, the theme is the nature of language proficiency. In our opening paper, we present the theoretical framework underlying the DBP project and summarize a large-scale factor-analytic study con-

1

ducted in French immersion classrooms. This study was designed to test an educationally relevant model of language proficiency that distinguishes grammatical, discourse, and sociolinguistic competencies, and recognizes the demands of different task conditions for their use. Several other smaller-scale DBP studies focusing on the nature of language proficiency are then outlined: two follow-up studies of the written second language (L2) proficiency of French immersion students, and a study concerned with assessment of oral proficiency in bilingual children. This initial paper summarizing the research is followed by two discussion papers, one by Lyle Bachman and the other by Jacquelyn Schachter, focusing mainly on theoretical and methodological issues in connection with the model-testing study. Part I concludes with a brief response to the papers by Bachman and Schachter.

Part II is concerned with the issue of how classroom treatment affects the development of second language proficiency. The first paper in this section summarizes four DBP studies concerned with instructional practices: the development and validation of an observation scheme, a process-product study using this scheme in core French classrooms, an observational study of language-use patterns in French immersion classes, and a classroom experiment in the teaching of grammar in an immersion context. Again two discussion papers, the first by Patsy Lightbown and the second by H. H. Stern, focus on theoretical and methodological issues raised in the research. A short response by the DBP team to the Lightbown and Stern papers follows.

In Part III, which deals with the theme of social and individual factors in the development of bilingual proficiency, the introductory paper outlines the DBP research on social-environmental variables and age in relation to bilingual development. It incorporates two studies involving Portuguese-Canadian students, one investigating the relationship between language-use patterns, language attitudes, and bilingual proficiency at the grade 7 level, and the other – an ongoing longitudinal study – examining the interactional patterns of young children in relation to later academic achievement. Also included is an ethnographic study of students at a French language school, and several studies examining the relationship between age and language learning, including a study of metaphor comprehension by bilingual Spanish-speaking children, a study of Japanese immigrant students' literacy skills in Japanese and English, and a comparison of the French proficiency of English-speaking students attending three different L2 programs. There are three discussion papers in this section. The first, by Richard Bourhis, focuses exclusively on the study of Portuguese-Canadian students at grade 7 and presents a number of alternative theoretical models for interpreting the results. The second paper, by Alison d'Anglejan, discusses each of a number of the DBP studies in turn. In the next paper, Barry McLaughlin introduces an additional individual factor, language aptitude, that was not investigated in the context of the DBP project but that he considers of major importance. Part III ends with a response to some issues raised in the discussion papers.

The next section of this volume, Part IV, is devoted to the practical and policy implications of the DBP studies. Jean Handscombe, in her paper, discusses the implications of the classroom treatment studies from the perspective of an educational administrator. Christina Bratt Paulston, in the second paper, considers more broadly the practical and policy implications of a number of the DBP studies.

Part V, which consists of a single paper by Wallace Lambert, places the Development of Bilingual Proficiency project in the context of thirty-five years of research on bilingualism. Lambert's paper, presented in connection with the DBP symposium as a public lecture, provides a fascinating account of issues in bilingualism to which he has devoted his remarkably productive career.

In a concluding chapter, Richard Tucker provides an overview of the implications of the DBP project.

PART I:
THE NATURE OF LANGUAGE PROFICIENCY

1 The nature of language proficiency

Birgit Harley,
Jim Cummins,
Merrill Swain,
and Patrick Allen

Theoretical background

Since ancient times, philosophers and psychologists have debated appropriate ways of conceptualizing the nature of language proficiency and its relationship to other constructs (e.g., "intelligence"). The issue is not just an abstract theoretical question, but one that is central to the resolution of a variety of applied educational issues. Educational policies based on hypotheses about how language proficiency develops as a function of different classroom treatments, different experiences in the environment, and different social contexts clearly imply certain conceptions about what it means to be proficient in a language.

The context for our investigation of the nature of language proficiency will be described briefly in relation to the applied, theoretical, and methodological considerations that influenced the conceptualization and implementation of the study.

Applied issues

Several examples will serve to illustrate the point that the conceptualization of the nature of language proficiency has a major impact on a variety of practical and policy issues in education. In the area of language teaching methodology, for example, the predominant emphasis until recently has been on the teaching of grammar. The implicit conception of language proficiency, as it has been operationalized in second language classrooms, has entailed viewing proficiency as little more than grammar and lexis. The recent movement toward communicative language teaching has been associated with a broader view of language that includes not just its grammatical aspects, but also the ability to use language appropriately in different contexts and the ability to organize one's thoughts through language. That is to say,

7

the recent emphasis on communication in language teaching is expressed in attempts to develop students' sociolinguistic and discourse competencies in addition to their grammatical competence. In short, the conception of what it means to be proficient in a language has expanded significantly.

In a very different context, it is clear that in bilingual programs for minority students in the United States, alternative conceptualizations of the nature of language proficiency have played a major role in policy and practice. A characteristic of most of these programs has been the establishment of entry and exit criteria whereby students must be declared of limited proficiency in English to enter the program and of sufficient proficiency in English to follow regular all-English instruction in order to exit from the program. One of the most controversial aspects of the bilingual education policy in the United States has been determining exactly what constitutes sufficient proficiency for the student to survive academically in a regular English-language classroom. In perhaps the majority of bilingual programs, what has been considered as "full English proficiency" amounts essentially to fluency in English; that is, the ability to function adequately in face-to-face situations and use English appropriately in a conversational context. However, the evidence suggests that many children who have exited from bilingual into all-English programs continue to experience academic difficulties in English (see Cummins 1984 for a review). This raises the question of how different aspects of language proficiency (e.g., grammatical, discourse, and sociolinguistic competencies) are related to the ability to manipulate language in academic contexts.

A similar issue arises in the area of psychological assessment. When minority students experience academic difficulties, educators frequently wonder whether the student has some learning disability or simply an inadequate grasp of English. Such students may appear to have overcome difficulties in English since they frequently understand and speak English relatively well. However, when they take IQ and other psychological tests in English, they often show more poorly developed verbal than performance abilities. This has led to many minority students being labeled as "learning disabled" and getting a one-way ticket into special education classes. Ortiz and Yates (1983), for example, report that Hispanic minority students in Texas were overrepresented by 300 percent in the "learning disability" category. Once again, the problem is directly related to the way in which language proficiency has been conceptualized – specifically, the extrapolation from conversational fluency in English to overall proficiency in the language and the judgment that students have sufficient proficiency in English so that verbal IQ tests will not discriminate against them on the basis of language.

Theoretical issues

When we began our investigation of the nature of language proficiency, two stages were evident in the way this issue had been conceptualized and investigated.

The first stage was essentially a continuation of factor-analytic work carried out between 1920 and 1970 by researchers such as Thurstone, Carroll, Guilford, Spearman, Burt, and Jensen, whose aim was to discover the basic structure of mental abilities, including language abilities. John Oller was a principal figure associated with this first stage. What distinguished his work from that of the earlier factor-analytic investigators was that its theoretical basis derived from applied linguistics rather than from psychometrics. Thus, although Oller employed essentially the same analytic methods, namely, variations of exploratory factor analysis, and his results were similar to those of several other investigators (Burt, Spearman, Jensen) in showing a strong general factor that incorporated both language and nonlanguage abilities, his empirical results were interpreted within a coherent framework of relatively sophisticated theoretical constructs (e.g., the pragmatic expectancy grammar) derived from applied linguistics (see Cummins 1984; Oller 1983).

Oller's (1981) provocative claim on the basis of his research and theory that language proficiency was largely indistinguishable from intelligence spurred considerable theoretical controversy and focused further research on the nature of language proficiency. The second stage of research into this issue was characterized by the use of a much more sophisticated form of factor analysis than that used by Oller. Confirmatory factor analysis allowed the explicit testing of theoretical models and was first applied to the field of language proficiency by Purcell (1983) and Bachman and Palmer (1982). Bachman and Palmer's work drew on the theoretical model of communicative competence developed by Canale and Swain (1980). Their results showed clearly that more than just one general factor could be extracted from language proficiency data. In fact, both trait and method factors could be distinguished. Taking into account the work of Bachman and Palmer and also the cogent criticisms of other researchers (see Oller 1983), Oller admitted that his earlier position was overstated and that there probably were nontrivial dimensions of language proficiency in addition to a general factor.

Two frameworks for conceptualizing the nature of language proficiency were particularly influential in the design of our study. The first was the communicative competence framework developed by Canale and Swain (1980). This framework initially distinguished grammatical competence, sociolinguistic competence, and strategic competence. The framework was later refined by Canale (1983) into grammatical, discourse, sociolinguistic, and strategic competence. The framework was designed primarily to facilitate the process of curriculum development and language assessment in second language teaching.

The second framework involved a distinction between the use of language in context-embedded and context-reduced situations (Cummins 1984). The former is typical of face-to-face interactions where the communication is supported by a range of contextual cues, while the latter is typical of many academic contexts and involves primarily linguistic cues to meaning.

The integration of these two frameworks resulted in a 3 × 3 matrix comprised of measures of grammatical, discourse, and sociolinguistic competence assessed in oral and written productive modes and by multiple-choice written tests. Although any testing situation is likely to be less context-embedded than naturalistic, face-to-face interaction, the oral measures were conceived as being relatively more context-embedded than the written measures, which were more typical of academic (context-reduced) assessment procedures.

Methodological issues

Bachman and Palmer's work had clearly demonstrated the utility of confirmatory factor analysis, and this procedure was therefore adopted as a primary means of testing hypotheses about interrelationships among components of language proficiency. We were also aware that hypotheses about the nature of proficiency could be tested through other means than confirmatory factor analysis. For example, comparison between native speakers of a language and second language learners could reveal which aspects of second language (L2) proficiency were acquired most rapidly and help elucidate the ways in which proficiency becomes developmentally differentiated.

Similarly, an investigation of issues such as the relationship between different aspects of first and second language (L1 and L2) proficiency or the relationship between age and L2 acquisition could point to significant implications for the conceptualization of the nature of proficiency. For example, if discourse skills were strongly related across languages but grammatical skills were not, this implies a distinction between grammar and discourse and generates hypotheses regarding the causes of the cross-lingual discourse relationships. For example, it might be that discourse is more strongly related to general cognitive abilities than is true for grammar. Similarly, differential acquisition rates for different aspects of proficiency by older and younger learners can provide evidence relevant to theoretical conceptualizations of the nature of proficiency. Thus, a variety of strategies was employed to investigate the interrelationships among components of the construct of language proficiency.

Large-scale proficiency study

The primary purpose of the large-scale proficiency study (Allen et al. 1983; Swain 1985) was to determine whether the three hypothesized traits, representing key components of language proficiency, could be empirically distinguished. It was hypothesized that grammatical, discourse, and sociolinguistic competence (Canale and Swain 1980; Canale 1983) would emerge as distinct components of second language proficiency which may be differentially manifested under different task conditions. A secondary purpose of the study was to develop a set of exemplary test items and scoring procedures that could be used, or modified for use, in further studies involving the measurement of the hypothesized traits. A final purpose was to examine the target language proficiency of the second language learners tested in relation to that of native speakers.

Sample and design

A total of 198 students was involved in the study, including 175 grade 6 early French immersion students from the Ottawa region, and 23 grade 6 native speakers from a regular francophone school in Montreal. The immersion students had received 100 percent of their schooling in French in kindergarten to grade 2 or 3, after which they had been taught in English for a gradually increasing portion of each day. At the time of testing, about 50 percent of their school subjects were being taught in French, and the other 50 percent in English. This sample of classroom second language learners was selected because of the theoretically interesting and educationally innovative nature of their intensive school-based language learning experience, and because they were at an age where they were sufficiently proficient in the second language to be able to cope with a wide range of language tasks.

A multitrait-multimethod analysis was used to examine the extent to which grammatical, discourse, and sociolinguistic dimensions of the immersion students' French proficiency were distinguishable. To measure proficiency on each trait, three methods were used: oral production, multiple-choice, and written production. A matrix with 9 test cells was created, consisting of 3 tests of grammar, 3 of discourse, and 3 of sociolinguistics (see Table 1.1). The oral production task for each was administered to a subsample of 69 immersion students and 10 native speakers. The next three sections describe how the three traits were operationalized in the testing instruments.

TABLE I.I OPERATIONALIZATION OF TRAITS IN
LARGE-SCALE PROFICIENCY STUDY

Trait / Method	Grammar — Focus on grammatical accuracy within sentences	Discourse — Focus on textual cohesion and coherence	Sociolinguistic — Focus on social appropriateness of language use
Oral	Structured interview Scored for accuracy of verb morphology, prepositions, syntax	Story retelling and argumentation/ suasion Detailed ratings, e.g., identification, logical sequence, time orientation and global ratings for coherence	Role-play of speech acts: requests, offers, complaints Scored for ability to distinguish formal and informal register
Multiple choice	Sentence-level "select the correct form" exercise Involved verb morphology, prepositions, and other items (45 items)	Paragraph level "select the coherent sentence" exercise (29 items)	Speech-act-level "select the appropriate utterance" exercise (28 items)
Written composition	Narrative and letter of suasion Scored for accuracy of verb morphology, prepositions, syntax	Narrative and letter of suasion Detailed ratings much as for oral discourse and global rating for coherence	Formal request letter and informal note Scored for ability to distinguish formal and informal register

Operationalization of grammar trait

The grammar trait was measured in terms of accuracy in French morphology and syntax, with an emphasis on verb and preposition usage. The focus on verbs and prepositions was motivated by their importance as subsystems of French grammar, and also by previous research, which had indicated that these were areas of French grammar where one was most likely to find variability among the immersion students. Note that variability in performance on the measures was a statistical necessity for factor analysis.

The grammar oral production task consisted of a guided individual interview in which the interviewers' questions were designed to elicit a variety of verb forms and prepositions in French, as well as some responses that were sufficiently elaborated to score for syntactic accuracy. The content of the interview questions (e.g., favorite pastimes, trips taken) was designed to focus the subject's attention on communication rather than the code. Scoring was based on the student's ability to produce grammatical forms and structures accurately in the context of particular questions.

The second grammar test was a written, group-administered multiple-choice test. This test also assessed knowledge of the verb system, prepositions, and other forms in sentence-level test items. The student's task was to fill in the gap by selecting the correct response from three alternatives provided.

The third grammar test, written production, consisted of two short compositions – one a narrative and the other a letter of request. In the narrative, the students were given a theme and an opening line which prompted the use of past tense and plural verb forms. The request letter involved persuading an addressee to give the student permission to carry out an action. This composition test was parallel to a discourse written production test, which also involved a narrative and a request letter. All four compositions were scored for grammatical accuracy in verbs, prepositions, and other rules of syntax and morphology.

Operationalization of discourse trait

The discourse trait was defined as the ability to produce and understand coherent and cohesive text. Accuracy of cohesive elements (i.e., specific linguistic realizations of coherence) was included in the assessment because errors in such elements tended to disturb the coherence of a text.

For the individual discourse oral production test, the student was required to retell the story of a silent movie about a mole and a bulldozer. In addition, there was a role-playing task in which the student had to take the part of the mole and convince some addressees not to carry out an action that would have been harmful to the mole. This argumentation-cum-suasion task was designed to parallel a letter of suasion in the discourse written production test. Discourse oral production was rated on a series of five-point scales both globally in detail, focusing, for example, on the student's ability to make clear and accurate reference to characters, objects, and locations; to produce logically coherent text; and to perform the basic tasks required.

The second discourse test was a multiple-choice test consisting of short written passages from each of which a sentence had been omitted. The student was required to select from three alternatives the sentence that best fit the context of the passage.

The discourse written production test, like the grammar written production test, consisted of a narrative and a request letter. All four written production tasks were rated for discourse coherence and cohesion, mostly on the same kinds of features assessed in the discourse oral production test.

Operationalization of sociolinguistic trait

The sociolinguistic trait was defined as the ability to produce and recognize socially appropriate language in context. The individual oral production test involved a set of slides with taped descriptions. The slides represented situations of different levels of formality to which the student had to respond appropriately with a request, offer, or complaint. The objective of this test was to determine the extent to which students were able to shift register, using formal markers of politeness in formal situations and using them less often in informal situations. The selected formal markers were based on what native speakers were found to be using in the formal situations. The final score was a "difference" score; this was arrived at by taking the number of formal markers produced in informal situations and subtracting them from those produced in formal situations.

The items in the sociolinguistic multiple-choice test each involved three grammatically accurate choices for expressing a given sociolinguistic function. The student's task was to select the most appropriate choice in each situation. Scores were weighted according to the responses selected by native speakers.

The final test in the matrix, a sociolinguistic written production task, required the student to write a formal request letter and two informal notes, all of which can be categorized as directives. The request letter written as part of the discourse written production test was also scored for sociolinguistic proficiency. Scores were again difference scores, obtained by subtracting formal markers produced in the notes from those produced in the letters.

Reliability and generalizability of scores

The component within-test scores were combined to produce a single overall score for each of the 9 trait-method cells in the matrix. The composition of each of these overall scores was calculated to maximize validity and reliability. On the multiple-choice tests, the reliability of the immersion students' total scores ranged from .58 on the sociolinguistic test to .75 on the discourse test. Generalizability studies (Cronbach et

TABLE 1.2 CONFIRMATORY FACTOR ANALYSIS – LISREL

	Factor 1 General	Factor 2 Written	Uniqueness
Grammar oral production	.53	—	.72
Grammar multiple-choice	.49	.55	.47
Grammar written production	.68	.39	.38
Discourse oral production	.30	—	.91
Discourse multiple-choice	.41	.42	.65
Discourse written production	.20	.66	.52
Sociolinguistic oral production	.23	—	.95
Sociolinguistic multiple-choice	.47	.24	.72
Sociolinguistic written production	−.03	.49	.76

$X^2 = 14.13$, df $= 21$, p $= .864$

al. 1972) were conducted on those cells for which sufficient data were available: the sociolinguistic oral production test and the three written production tests. G-coefficients for these tests, based on the subsample of orally tested students, were comparable to the multiple-choice test reliabilities.

Testing the model of proficiency

In order to determine whether the three traits – grammatical, discourse, and sociolinguistic competence – could be distinguished empirically, two kinds of analyses were performed: factor analysis, and a comparison of the group means of the learners and native speakers.

The factor analysis based on the 69 orally tested immersion students failed to confirm the hypothesized three-trait structure of proficiency. Instead, confirmatory factor analysis by means of the LISREL program (Jöreskog and Sörbom 1978) produced a two-factor solution. One of these factors was interpretable as a general language proficiency factor (see Table 1.2); it had positive loadings from all cells in the 9-test matrix except for the sociolinguistic written production test. The highest loadings on this general factor were from the three grammatical tests. The second factor was interpretable as a written method factor; it had loadings from the three multiple-choice tests and from all three written production tests. The tests loading on this method factor appeared to be tapping the kind of literacy-oriented linguistic proficiency that is typically learned in classrooms.

A different kind of result emerged from comparisons of immersion and native speaker scores on the various tests. On all three grammar tests, the immersion students' mean score was considerably lower than that of the native speakers, and they also scored generally lower on the sociolinguistic tests than did the native speakers. On the discourse tasks, however, the scores of the immersion students were close or equivalent to those of the native speakers, and there were relatively few significant between-group differences.

Figures 1.1, 1.2, 1.3, and 1.4 provide an overview of the immersion students' scores on the production tasks in relation to those of the native speakers. The immersion students were clearly less proficient on most grammar variables (Figure 1.1), and especially on verbs in the oral grammar test, where they were more constrained than in the written grammar test to produce certain verb forms. Note that the learners and the native speakers were, however, equivalent in the area of homophonous verb endings (e.g., aim*er*/aim*é*) on the grammar written production test, indicating that this is a problem area for native speakers too. Similar results were found on the multiple-choice grammar test, where the average accuracy rate for the immersion students $(\overline{X} = 27.35)$ was significantly lower than that of the native speakers $(\overline{X} = 36.60, p < .01)$.

In contrast, the graphs of immersion and native speaker discourse scores displayed in Figure 1.2 show relatively little difference between the groups on these tasks, particularly in the written mode. At the same time, no significant difference was found between group means on the multiple-choice discourse test. One interpretation of the comparatively strong performance of the second language learners in the area of discourse coherence is that they were able to transfer competence already gained via their first language.

The sociolinguistic oral and written difference scores presented in Figure 1.3 and absolute scores in Figure 1.4 demonstrate graphically that the difference between the informal and formal situations was smaller for the immersion students than for the native speakers. Immersion students tended to produce fewer formal markers in the formal variants of both the oral and written production tasks. Moreover, in the oral production task, they produced more formal markers in the informal situations than did the native speakers. A significant difference between the immersion and native speaker mean scores was also found on the sociolinguistic multiple-choice test.

In contrast to the factor-analytic results, then, the comparison between immersion and native speaker scores showing different results for discourse as opposed to grammar and sociolinguistic tests provides some evidence in support of a distinction between traits. Although the three hypothesized language proficiency traits were not empirically distinguished via the factor analysis, this result may have been dependent on the relatively homogeneous language learning background of the immersion population studied. This did not necessarily mean that the traits would not be distinguishable in a more heterogeneous population. From an educational perspective, it was clear that the analysis of proficiency

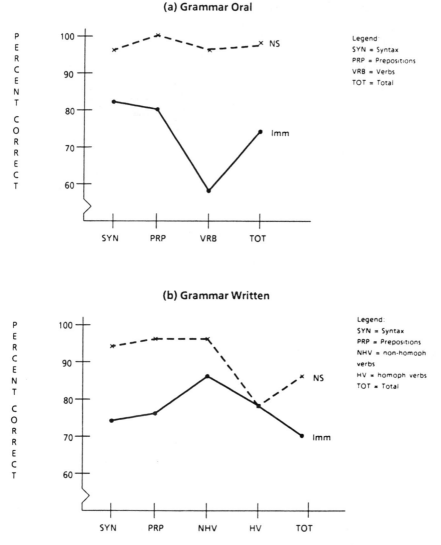

Figure 1.1 Scores of immersion students and native speakers on oral and written grammar production tests

into different components was diagnostically revealing of the second language strengths and weaknesses of the immersion students. Further studies were needed to probe how different dimensions of proficiency develop as a function of the learners' specific language learning experiences.

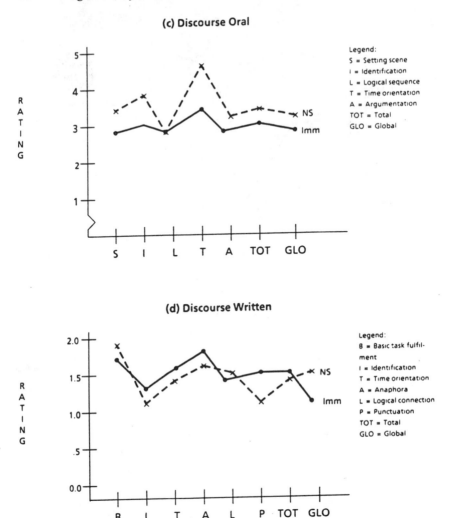

Figure 1.2   Scores of immersion students and native speakers on oral and written discourse production tests

Further analyses of written compositions

In order to obtain a more in-depth understanding of the French proficiency development of classroom learners in the immersion context, two further studies were carried out using data from the written compositions already produced in the main proficiency study. The main findings from these studies are summarized below.

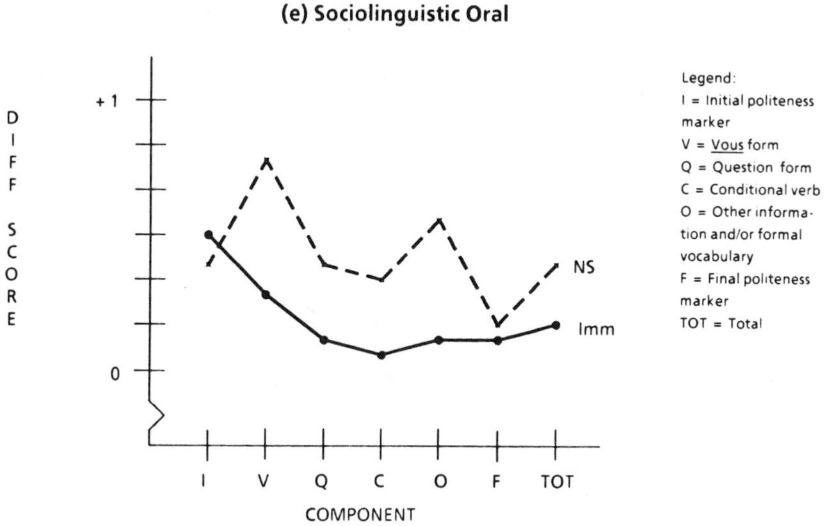
(e) Sociolinguistic Oral
DIFF SCORE
+1
0
I
V
Q
C
O
F
TOT
COMPONENT
NS
Imm
Legend:
I = Initial politeness marker
V = Vous form
Q = Question form
C = Conditional verb
O = Other information and/or formal vocabulary
F = Final politeness marker
TOT = Total

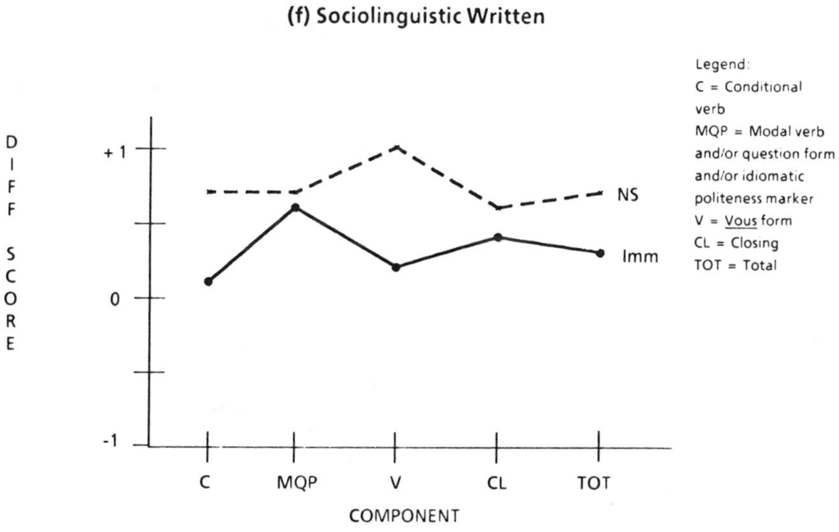
(f) Sociolinguistic Written
DIFF SCORE
+1
0
-1
C
MQP
V
CL
TOT
COMPONENT
NS
Imm
Legend:
C = Conditional verb
MQP = Modal verb and/or question form and/or idiomatic politeness marker
V = Vous form
CL = Closing
TOT = Total

Figure 1.3 Difference scores of immersion students and native speakers on oral and written sociolinguistic production tests

Study of directional expressions

Given the shared mother tongue (English) of the immersion students and the dominance of English in the wider school and outside-school environment of the immersion program, mother tongue transfer was

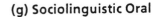

(g) Sociolinguistic Oral

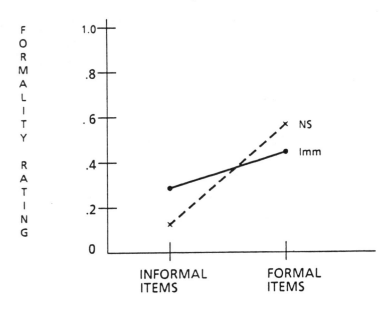

(h) Sociolinguistic Written

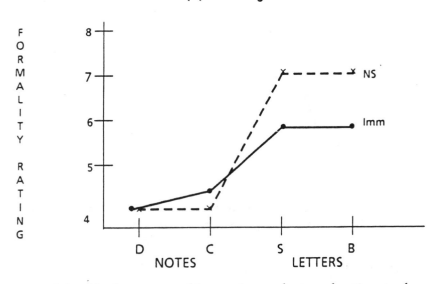

Figure 1.4   Absolute scores of immersion students and native speakers on oral and written sociolinguistic production tests

expected to be a continuing factor in the students' written production at the grade 6 level. In a small-scale study (Harley 1989a) of compositions written by 22 native speakers and 22 of the orally tested immersion students from two randomly selected classes in the larger proficiency study, the hypothesis tested was that mother tongue transfer would be manifested in the way in which the learners were distributing semantic information across syntactic elements in the second language, without necessarily making outright errors.

One of the composition topics assigned in the large-scale proficiency study, *Au secours!*, involved writing a story about the rescue of a kitten from a tree. The students' stories on this topic contained a similar series of events, involving several changes of location. The focus of the present study was on how the immersion students were expressing the location/direction distinction in these stories, given that there are characteristic differences between French and English in this linguistic domain. In English, prepositions generally play an important role in conveying the location/direction distinction (e.g., *at/to, in/into*); in French, there is a general tendency for direction to be expressed in the verb, and for prepositions (e.g., *à, dans, sur*) to be neutral with respect to this distinction. It was hypothesized that the immersion students would rely on prepositions rather than the verb to express the notion of direction.

A comparison of directional expressions in the *Au secours!* stories written by the immersion students and the native speakers showed that, as expected, the immersion students were much less likely than the native speakers to mark direction in the verb. They preferred a nondirectional verb of motion such as *courir* together with a preposition to express the directional notion. At the same time, the immersion students sometimes erroneously used French prepositions unmarked for direction as if they were carrying the directional distinction, and also tended to make more use than the native speakers of prepositional phrases expressing direction, even on the occasions when they also used directional verbs. This tendency did not necessarily lead to error. The findings of the study thus provide support for the hypothesis that the immersion students would show a systematic tendency to rely more heavily on prepositions to express the notion of direction than the native speakers.

Lexical proficiency in a second language

In the large-scale proficiency study described above, there were no measures specifically designed to assess lexical proficiency – not because lexical proficiency was considered unimportant, but because it was assumed to enter into performance on all the tasks assigned. In the present study, the two narratives and three request letters written by 69 immersion students and 22 native speakers in the context of the various written production tests were reanalyzed from a lexical perspective, with verbs being selected as the focus for the study (for details, see Harley, King, and Burtis 1987). The purpose of the study was threefold: to compare different quantitative measures of immersion students' lexical proficiency in their L2 writing; to examine the relationship between written lexical proficiency and other aspects of their L2 communicative competence; and to describe the students' lexical use in relation to that of native speakers.

MEASURES OF LEXICAL PROFICIENCY

Five quantitative measures of lexical proficiency were developed and statistically compared. One of these was a lexical error rate, and the other four were variations on the theme of lexical richness, labeled, respectively, "number of lexical types," "lexical variety," "lexical specificity," and "lexical sophistication." All the measures, except for number of lexical types, were controlled for length of text. For each student, the data from the five written compositions were lumped together. Two of the relatively difficult measures were retained as the most appropriate for further use in a factor analysis. The first was lexical specificity, which consisted of the number of different verb types used by each student, not counting the 20 most frequent verbs in French or those that were used in the instructions to the compositions, divided by the number of verb items produced. The second measure was lexical sophistication, representing those relatively infrequent verbs not found in a basic word frequency list, also divided by the number of verb items produced.

LEXICAL MEASURES AND L2 PROFICIENCY

Three mutually exclusive hypotheses arising from previous work were examined via factor analysis: (1) that lexical proficiency is equally involved in all three components of language proficiency examined in the large-scale proficiency study, grammar, discourse, and sociolinguistics; (2) that lexical proficiency is part of the grammar component; or (3) that lexical proficiency is a separate component, distinct from the other three components of language proficiency.

Confirmatory factor analyses showed that an acceptable solution to fit any one of these three hypotheses could be found, and that there was no conclusive evidence favoring any one of the three hypotheses over the other two. One interesting finding was that in the three- and four-factor solutions corresponding to hypotheses (2) and (3), respectively, a grammar factor and a discourse factor which had not previously been found in the large-scale study emerged where no lexical measures had been included.

LEXICAL USE OF IMMERSION STUDENTS AND
NATIVE SPEAKERS

A comparison of the verb lexis used by the immersion students and the native speakers in their compositions (see also Harley and King 1989) revealed that the immersion students tended to make proportionately more use of relatively high-coverage verbs and less use of some morphologically or syntactically complex verbs such as pronominal and derived verbs. The inflectional complexity of some high coverage verbs did not appear to be a deterrent to their use, although inflectional errors (considered grammatical rather than lexical errors) did occur. Semantic and syntactic incongruence with their English mother tongue (L1) emerged as an important factor in the immersion students' nonuse of some French verb types and in the lexical errors they made. At the same time, the students demonstrated positive L1 transfer in the use of some cognate verbs in French.

Together with the study of directional expressions, this small-scale proficiency study indicates that the mother tongue is a significant factor in the second language development of these classroom learners. Together the two studies suggest that students would benefit from more focused classroom input alerting them to lexical characteristics of French that are different from English, and from more classroom activities designed to increase their lexical resources. These issues are taken up again in the context of the classroom treatment studies in Part II.

Communicative skills of young L2 learners

Another small-scale exploratory study (Hulstijn 1983) involved a detailed investigation of methods of scoring oral L2 performance and of the interrelationships among various aspects of L2 proficiency. The study was based on a subset of data previously collected in the context of another Modern Language Centre project (Cummins et al. 1981). It consisted of oral tasks in English with 22 Japanese immigrant students in grades 2, 3, 5, and 6, together with academic tests of reading and vocabulary in the L2.

A comparison of global rating scales and detailed frequency scores as measures of specific aspects of oral L2 performance indicated that the two kinds of measurement were substantially correlated where there was sufficient variability in the data. An exploratory factor analysis of 26 variables, including measures of oral performance and academic test scores, yielded 3 orthogonal factors, interpreted as general English proficiency (including all the academic tests), vocabulary, and communicative style (consisting of interview variables). No separate factor was found for measures of fluency. Both the general English proficiency factor and the vocabulary factor were affected by length of residence in the L2 community, and general English proficiency was also affected by the students' age. Neither length of residence nor age was related to communicative style.

It was concluded that language proficiency results are strongly affected by the testing method (e.g., academic reading test, oral interview, storytelling task), and that an inherent difficulty in validating models of L2 proficiency is that measures faithfully reflecting a particular construct may not have adequate psychometric properties, while other psychometrically acceptable measures may fall short of representing the construct.

Conclusions

These studies provide support for the idea that different methodologies are useful and important in investigating language proficiency. It is not sufficient to rely exclusively on confirmatory factor analysis, partly because of the difficulty of operationalizing constructs, and partly because of the fact that different groups of learners will have had a different array of language learning experiences. The relationship between different components of proficiency is likely to be a function of these different experiences. Particular factor structures that emerge with adult second language learners are not necessarily applicable or replicable within a sample of young students who have had a different pattern of experiences.

The first conclusion to emerge from the studies was that, despite the fact that confirmatory factor analysis did not strongly support the hypothesized distinctions, other ways of looking at the constructs and at the relationship between the constructs did provide some support for the hypothesis that these constructs are distinguishable and also educationally relevant.

Another pattern to emerge from the various studies was that written language tests, or academic tests, tended to be strongly related. It was found in several other studies, notably in two studies of Portuguese and Japanese immigrant students (see Part III), that academic skills were significantly related *across* the two languages in use. These findings are suggestive of an interdependence or commonality across languages with respect to context-reduced or academic types of proficiency. Weaker support for relationships across languages for some kinds of oral skills were also found in the Portuguese study (see Part III).

A point that will be taken up again in Part III is that different aspects of proficiency seem to be differentially related to attributes of individuals. Cognitive variables appear to be more strongly related to discourse aspects of proficiency and to written aspects of proficiency than they are to oral grammatical skills.

An overall conclusion from the studies of the nature of language proficiency is that language proficiency must be conceptualized within a developmental context as a function of the interactions that students or learners experience in their languages. Although the trait structure that we had hypothesized did not receive unequivocal support from the results, the evidence leads us to conclude that the concept of traits is something that should be maintained; even though they may not always be empirically distinguishable in certain samples, they are conceptually distinct and relevant to educational contexts.

2 Constructing measures and measuring constructs

Lyle F. Bachman

One of the primary areas of research in the Development of Bilingual Proficiency (DBP) project was the investigation of the nature of language proficiency, which was the focus of a large-scale study conducted during the first two years of the project. This question was also examined in studies of lexical proficiency and metaphor comprehension conducted during the later years of the project. While the results of these and some of the other studies conducted as part of the project have implications regarding the nature of language proficiency, this discussion will center on the large-scale study.

This study quite appropriately took the form of construct validation, in which both the hypothesized constructs of language proficiency and putative measures of those constructs were subjected to empirical scrutiny in what is essentially a special case of theory verification (or falsification). The *process* of collecting evidence in support of the construct validity of test score interpretations and hence of the constructs themselves is perhaps as complex as the very constructs it examines; its *logic,* on the other hand, is quite simple:

1. Define theoretical constructs and hypothesize relationships among them
2. Define these constructs operationally (as measures or as observable characteristics)
3. Make predictions about how performance on these measures should or should not be functionally related, or how the performance of different groups of individuals should or should not be different
4. Observe performance
5. Determine the extent to which predicted relationships or differences are observed in the data

Two of the large-scale study's stated objectives are directly related to the question of construct validity:

Determine the extent to which our theoretically hypothesized traits ... are empirically distinguishable.
The description of the target language performance of the students tested ... relative to native speakers of the target language. (Allen et al. 1983:14–15)

The first objective implies examination of the extent to which performance on putative measures of the hypothesized traits is consistent with relationships predicted by a theoretical framework of language proficiency; the second objective implies the examination of predicted differences between native and non-native speakers on the measures of the hypothesized traits. In either case, the empirical part of the investigation begins with constructing measures and leads to some statement about the degree to which we have measured constructs. It is these two aspects of the process of construct validation that I will address.

In this discussion, I will attempt to convey my perceptions of how the results of this study contribute to advances in both applied linguistic theory and research methodology. I will do this by considering two types of findings: (1) the wide variation in correlations observed among the various measures of language proficiency, and (2) the differences in performance across measures in both immersion students *and native speakers.* Some of the correlations reported in the study are among the lowest I have ever seen, and some are among the highest. Given the nature of multitrait-multimethod matrices, however, this in itself is not alarming. What is intriguing is the probability that these variations in correlations are not due entirely to differences in errors of measurement, but are indicative of a much richer complexity of traits than the analyses have revealed. The second finding, varied profiles of performance of native speakers on different components of language proficiency, as well as the wide variations in differences between the performance of native and non-native speakers, are equally remarkable. Indeed, few studies have so convincingly demonstrated the fact that native speakers vary greatly in their control of different aspects of language proficiency. And while we may find some explanation, as have the investigators, by looking at patterns of prior language learning, I believe these variations must also be seen as indicative of the complexity of these abilities themselves.

If we are to begin to fathom the complexity of language proficiency, we must be prepared to embark on the detailed, careful, and lengthy exploration of multifaceted observations, as this study has so aptly demonstrated. The data to be examined are necessarily complex, as are the analytic tools that are required. And while this study is exemplary in its attention to detail and care in analysis, the investigators have, in my opinion, only begun to examine the patterns of relationships and differences that have been so fully documented in the reports. They began with a relatively fixed set of hypotheses about the nature of language proficiency, examined these quite thoroughly, found them essentially unsupported by the data, and then proceeded to other aspects of the research agenda. Given the other research questions to be examined in the project as a whole, for which a set of usable measures of language proficiency was required, this is entirely justified. However, it has, in my opinion, left unresolved the essential issues of construct validation to which the study was addressed, and it is my hope that there will be time and resources to continue the investigation of these issues in the future.

Constructing measures: models and operationalizations

The study used the ex post facto correlational approach, and incorporated a multitrait-multimethod (MTMM) design (Campbell and Fiske 1959). This design demands that each of several different hypothetical traits be measured by several distinct methods of observation, and each measure thus constructed can be seen as a trait-method unit. The number of measures or trait-method units required for a given study will be the product of the number of traits and methods hypothesized. This design makes it possible to identify and quantify the differential effects of traits and methods on test performance, with evidence of validity being found if the effects of traits are greater than those of test methods.

The investigators utilized Cummins's distinction between context-embedded and context-reduced language use for distinguishing test methods (Cummins 1980, 1981a). This resulted in the identification of three methods: (1) oral production, which was hypothesized to be relatively context-embedded; (2) multiple-choice, which was seen as a relatively context-reduced receptive task type; and (3) written production, a relatively context-reduced productive task. Within the oral and written production test methods, variations in two other test method facets that were not controlled may have affected performance. These include the topic (rescue of a kitten, bicycle, bank robbery, dog, favorite pastimes, trips taken, mole's fear of bulldozer, social situations) and the illocutionary act (descriptive narration, request, answering questions, retelling story, persuading, description of pictures).

The theoretical framework that provided the basis for defining traits was that of Canale and Swain (1980). While this model is, I am sure, quite well known, I would like to outline briefly its salient components in order to facilitate the discussion of how these components were realized as measures. The Canale-Swain framework consists of three components: grammatical, sociolinguistic, and strategic competence. Grammatical competence includes lexis, morphology, sentence grammar, semantics, and phonology; sociolinguistic competence includes sociocultural rules and rules of discourse; strategic competence consists essentially of communication strategies that "compensate for breakdowns in communication due to performance variables or to insufficient competence" (Canale and Swain 1980:30). This model was refined by further distinguishing discourse competence as an independent com-

TABLE 2.1 COMPONENT ABILITIES (TRAITS) INCLUDED IN
DBP PROFICIENCY MEASURES

Grammatical competence
Ability to use the rules of morphology and syntax
1. Prepositions
2. Verb forms
3. Miscellaneous

Discourse competence
Ability to use (produce and recognize) coherent and cohesive text, oral
or written
1. Basic task fulfillment
2. Identification of characters, objects, and locations
3. Time orientation
4. Anaphora
5. Logical connection
6. Punctuation
7. Setting the scene

Sociolinguistic competence
Ability to produce and recognize socially appropriate language in context
1. Conditional verb forms
2. Modal verbs
3. Direct and indirect questions
4. Politeness expressions
5. Formal vocabulary
6. *Tu/vous*
7. Formal closings

ponent comprising rules of cohesion and coherence. In their plan for
operationalization, the investigators recognized that developing and administering measures of all these subcomponents would not be feasible
in this study, and decided to narrow the focus. They chose not to attempt
to measure strategic competence separately at all, and included only the
subcomponents shown in Table 2.1.

It is my contention that one of the reasons for the wide variations in
correlations observed in the study is that the actual measures themselves
consist of a mixture of diverse abilities. This is most questionable, I
believe, in the measures of discourse competence. Recall that in the
hypothesized model, this competence consists of the ability to use coherent and cohesive text. The problem I see with this definition is that
it conflates formal and functional aspects of discourse. Widdowson
(1978) makes a distinction between cohesion, which consists of *explicitly*
marked relationships among propositions, on the one hand, and coherence, which comprises *implicit* relations among illocutionary acts, on
the other. Whether one accepts Widdowson's definitions or not, a close
examination of the tasks themselves indicates that both formal and

functional aspects of language use are grouped together in the various operational definitions (measures) of discourse competence.

Consider, for example, the trait category "basic task fulfillment," from the written production method, which includes the following characteristics:

To qualify as a narrative, for example, the compositions...needed to include a series of events. To qualify as suasion, the letters...had to contain an exhortation to the addressee along with at least one supporting argument. (Allen et al. 1983:23)

Narration, suasion, exhortation, and argumentation must surely be considered illocutionary acts that can be distinguished, for example, from description, consolation, and classification. Another category in this test method is "identification of characters, objects, and locations." While I would consider identification itself as an illocutionary act, the definition of this component includes reference to specific formal markers of new information (nonspecific noun phrases), as well as to the amount of prior knowledge on the part of the reader that was assumed by the writer. (It is not clear to me exactly where presupposition falls; perhaps in strategic competence.) Along with these components, which appear to include a mixture of formal and functional characteristics, we find the components "time orientation" and "anaphora," which focus quite clearly on formal markers of discourse. Finally, in the oral production method we find the component "setting the scene," which is described as follows:

The student's establishment of the atmosphere of the story was assessed. This was important for the coherence of the story, in that it was the idyllic habitat and lifestyle of the mole...that were at risk throughout the story. The student then was assessed for the attention that was given to (a) the initial idyllic state, (b) the fear and urgency engendered by the approaching bulldozer, and (c) the ultimate return to a peaceful state of affairs. (Allen et al. 1983:27)

I would argue that what is being assessed here is primarily the illocutionary force of the writing; that is, the ability to capture the affective meanings of the story, and to highlight these particular aspects, as opposed to, say, the literal description of the mole's habitat or the simple narration of events in the story.

While these examples are particularly salient, I believe a similar mixture of abilities can be seen in the measures of sociolinguistic competence, where the emphasis is on formal markers of register. The point I would like to make here is simply that the actual measures that were constructed appear to be much more complex than the model on which they were based. The measures include a wider range of test method facets, and may well tap a richer variety of language abilities, than were hypothesized by the theoretical model. It is this unplanned complexity that may

TABLE 2.2 COMPOSITE SCORES USED IN PRIMARY DATA ANALYSES

	Traits		
Methods	*Grammatical*	*Discourse*	*Sociolinguistic*
Oral production	Percent correct	Subjective, global	Total difference
Multiple-choice	No. of items correct	No. of items correct	Sum of weighted item scores
Written production	Percent correct	Subjective, global	Total difference

Source: Adapted from Allen et al. 1983.

explain, to some extent, why attempts to fit the data to the model were not successful.

Measuring constructs: Analysis of data

The two methods of statistical analysis used in the study were factor analysis (both exploratory and confirmatory), for examining patterns of correlations among measures, and significance tests for differences between native and non-native speaker means. Although correlations among individual measures within components of language proficiency and group mean differences for individual measures are reported, these individual measures were combined to form nine overall scores, corresponding to the nine cells in the MTMM design, as illustrated in Table 2.2.

Differences in native and non-native performance

The comparison of group means, which reveals an overall pattern of superior performance of native speakers, also reveals differential patterns across traits and methods. If we simply look at the rank order of magnitude of the ω^2 statistic, for example, we can see that differences between native and non-native speaker groups are clearly ordered with respect to both trait and method.

By trait:
Grammar (.34) > Sociolinguistic (.25) >> Discourse (.03)
By test method:
Oral production (.32) >> Written production (.19) > Multiple-choice (.12)

From these orderings it is clear that native speaker performance was not equally superior to that of non-natives across all measures, and that differences in group performance were a function of both traits and methods. Differential patterns across traits and methods can be seen even more clearly at the level of individual measures by inspecting Figures 1.1, 1.2, and 1.3 in this volume. While the investigators provide an extensive discussion of the reasons for differential performance across *traits,* they do not consider similar differences across *methods.* The conclusion that variations in differences across traits "provides some strong validation at least for the model's distinction between grammatical and discourse competence" (Allen et al. 1983:50) must therefore be taken with caution.

Relationships among measures

The factor analyses of the nine component measures generally support the conclusion that the three traits and three methods hypothesized are not distinct. However, a number of questions must be raised about technical aspects of the factor analyses used (for a general discussion of the statistical issues involved, see Harmon 1976). The first question has to do with the number of factors extracted and the method of factor extraction. There were three factors with roots greater than unity, and the default of the statistical package (SPSS), MINRES, was used in the initial extraction. One potential problem here is that with an adjusted correlation matrix (communalities, rather than unities, on the diagonal), the criterion of roots greater than one often results in underfactoring. An error in underfactoring will be compounded by the MINRES extraction, which only examines the matrix defined by the number of principal axes, or factors, that have been specified. This problem is particularly worrisome when there are large uniquenesses, as is the case with these data. While specifying two- and four-factor solutions will tend to minimize this potential error, the MINRES extraction will still ignore a substantial proportion of the covariance in the original adjusted matrix. An alternative approach would be to identify the number of factors initially by the scree test (Cattell 1966), or by parallel analyses (Humphreys and Montanelli 1975; Montanelli and Humphreys 1976), using squared multiple correlations as communality estimates and then extracting principal axes without iteration.

The second question has to do with the method of rotation. Although orthogonal solutions (uncorrelated factors) have historically been preferred because they tend to yield more interpretable solutions, researchers who deal with abilities that they expect to be related are increasingly turning to oblique solutions (correlated factors). The reason is quite straightforward: orthogonal solutions force factors to be uncorrelated, and thus may actually distort underlying relationships. Given the number of studies in the field of language testing that have found either a general factor or correlated factors to underlie test scores, it would seem unreasonable to use an orthogonal rotation, as was done in this study. A preferable alternative is to obtain an oblique solution and then transform this to an orthogonal solution with a general factor, as described by Schmid and Leiman (1957) and advocated by Carroll (1983).

My main concern with the confirmatory factor analysis is that this procedure should not be inappropriately used in an exploratory manner. One question that must be addressed in model testing is whether the models that are tested can be justified on the basis of substantive theory. But since this is ultimately a matter of subjective judgment, it is not, in my opinion, a resolvable issue. A second question is related to the nature of hypothesis testing in general: One does not generally reject one hypothesis and then use the same data set to attempt to confirm or reject another. That is, if one tests one or more models with a set of data and then modifies these models on the basis of the fit statistics, the goodness of fit of the resulting models cannot be tested without recourse to a second set of data. (Extensive discussion of the problems related to model specification and specification search in causal modeling can be found in references such as Blalock 1964, James, Mulaik, and Brett 1982, Pedhazur 1982 and Dillon and Goldstein 1984, while Jöreskog, 1971, discusses the requirements for congeneric model comparison.)

Reconstructing constructs

In my view, further analyses of the data could be well worth the effort, because even though the reliabilities of many of the measures are quite low, I believe the main problem with the data is not measurement error, but rather inconsistencies among the individual measures, and the fact that these inconsistencies were aggregated in the composite scores that were used as the basis for the factor analyses.

One source of inconsistency may be in the test method facets. Earlier I suggested that test method facets not specifically examined in the factor analyses may have affected performance. Some evidence for this can be seen in the comparisons of native and non-native speakers discussed above, where there was a distinct ordering of difference by test method. Inconsistencies in performance within methods can be seen in the profiles for discourse written production (Figure 2.1), in which there appears to be an interaction between trait and genre, with both native speakers (N) and immersion students (I) performing much better on the identification trait (IDENT) for narratives than for letters, but generally performing worse on the time trait (TIME) for narratives than for letters.

A second source of inconsistency may be in the traits measured. I have

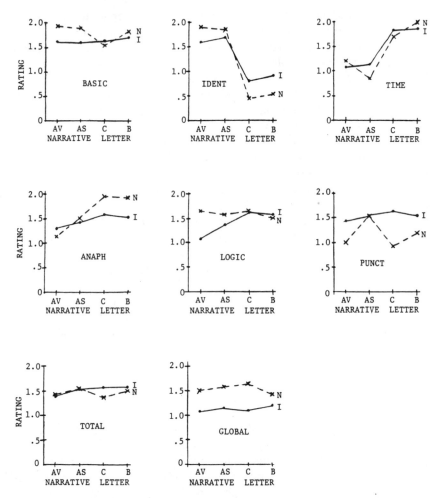

Figure 2.1   Discourse written production (from Allen et al. 1983, Figure III:4)

argued earlier, on the basis of applied linguistic theory, that the specific measures whose scores were combined to form composite scores for the factor analysis in fact tapped a variety of abilities. Evidence for inconsistencies among individual measures within trait-method units can be seen by examining the correlation matrices provided in Tables III:8, III:13; III:15, III:19 and III:23 of Allen et al. 1983. Rather than attempting to discuss these in detail, I have extracted the lowest and highest correlations that are reported, both among component tests and between component tests and total tests. These are given in Figure 2.2. The inconsistencies here are quite self-evident. It would appear, for example,

TRAITS METHODS	GRAMMATICAL		DISCOURSE		SOCIOLINGUISTIC	
Oral Prod. # of cmps	3		5		6 (18/36)	
cmp r's: (L - H)	-.10	.04	.03	.74	-.14	.37
cmp-T r's (L - H)	.37	.67	.49	.78	.24	.61
M-C # of cmps	4		1 (?)		1 (?)	
cmp r's: (L - H)	NA		NA		NA	
cmp-T r's: (L - H)	NA		NA		NA	
Written Prod. # of cmps	4		6		7 (14/28)	
cmp r's (L - H)	.04	.45	.11	.45	NA	
cmp-T r's: (L - H)	.45	.74	.47	.76	NA	

Figure 2.2   Number of component scores (# of comps) and low and high correlations (L-H) among component scores (comp r's) and between component and total scores (cmp-T r's).

that the individual component measures that make up the grammar oral production measure have almost nothing in common (high = .04), while in the discourse oral production cell correlations among component measures range from virtually zero (.03) to high (.74).

In determining how best to combine component scores within trait-method units, the investigators started with the intention of constructing the total scores as the simple mean of the component scores. They adjusted these total scores to maximize the reliabilities and tried eliminating components with low or negative correlations with other components. There apparently was no thought of recombining the component measures across trait-method cell boundaries. While such recombining would have been problematic for the confirmatory factor analysis, it is exactly this type of recombining, based on careful analysis – both qualitative and quantitative – of the component measures, that I believe may provide deeper insight into the nature of the traits actually measured in the study.

What I would like to suggest is that the initial research question be extended by reanalysis of the existing data. The original research question was: "Do these tests measure these traits?" The follow-up question is: "If these tests do not measure these traits, what traits (if any) do they measure?" This reanalysis should begin with a detailed task/ability analysis of the component measures based on more highly differentiated frameworks of language abilities and test methods, such as those I have proposed (Bachman 1990). There are approximately 37 component measures in the study, but within the sociolinguistic oral production and written production cells there is a nested design, so that rather than difference scores, absolute scores for formal and informal contexts could be used. And within these, separate scores for requesting, suggesting, and complaining, in the oral production method, and for the letter and the note, in the written production method, could be used. A task/ability analysis might also permit the identification of subsets of items within the multiple-choice discourse and sociolinguistic cells, so that component scores could be computed for these cells as well.

Following this qualitative analysis of test tasks and abilities, the full array of component measures could be analyzed through exploratory factor analysis, using the procedures outlined above. This may seem an unreasonable suggestion, but it is one that the researchers themselves tantalized us with in their discussion of four years ago:

We are currently continuing to investigate the factor structure of the present data by examining the correlations among the full set of 40 component scores. ...It seems that if there are distinguishable trait factors in the data, they are weak relative to the two factors that emerged in the main analysis, and will be seen only if a successful factor analysis of at least four or five factors can be done. The inclusion of all 40 of the component scores, or at least a large subset of them, may allow such factor analysis, which seems to be blocked by the small number of variables when total scores are used. (Allen et al. 1983:54–55)

Whether such analyses have, in fact, already been carried out and the results are equally inconclusive would certainly be of interest to the field. All too often, so-called negative results are deemed unworthy of publication, and the valuable information they contain is lost. If such analyses have not yet been carried out, I would hope that the investigators will be able to find the time and resources to make good on their promise.

While the results with respect to differences between native and non-native performance are intriguing, the paucity of data does not warrant, I believe, further analyses. However, should time and resources permit, the investigators might consider administering the tests to a larger sample of comparable native speakers to permit more powerful analytic procedures, such as multivariate analysis of variance.

Conclusion

The investigation of language proficiency that was part of the Development of Bilingual Proficiency project was certainly one of the largest and most ambitious of its kind, on almost any measure you might choose – number of subjects, range of abilities examined, number of measures used, or number of person-hours logged (by both investigators and subjects). And although the initial results may seem inconclusive, in that a particular "model" of language proficiency has not been supported, the results must be seen from the broader perspective that the investigators themselves provide in their concluding statement, a perspective that I find both insightful in its characterization of past research and encouraging in the agenda it sets for the future.

In their conclusion to the second-year report, the investigators distinguish three stages of development in the history of empirical research into the nature of language proficiency (Allen et al. 1983:55–58). The first stage was characterized by the use of exploratory factor analysis as the primary statistical tool, beginning with John Carroll's work on verbal abilities in the 1940s, and culminating in the g-factor studies of John Oller and his students in the 1970s. The major development during this stage was the change in applied linguistic theory regarding the nature of language proficiency. While early researchers focused primarily on the formal characteristics of language, Oller's research was based on the axiom that the functional, or pragmatic, dimension of language is fundamental.

The second stage, toward the end of which the DBP study falls, has been characterized not only by increasingly complex and comprehensive frameworks of language proficiency, but also by sophisticated (and exhausting) research designs and statistical analyses. As the investigators correctly observe, this was the state of the art when they designed their study over six years ago. During that time several other studies have also demonstrated what, it seems to me, is one of the major outcomes of this study: that both background characteristics of language learners (e.g., Hansen 1984; Chapelle and Roberts 1986; Sang et al. 1986) and test method effects (e.g., Bachman and Palmer 1982; Fouly 1985) can influence test performance as strongly as the traits we wish to examine, and that there are thus limitations on the analysis of test performance as a paradigm for research into the nature of language proficiency. While there may still be a researcher or two out there who secretly hopes for the opportunity to conduct a "really big" MTMM study, the DBP MTMM study may have marked the passing of a paradigm, much as did the Pennsylvania (Smith 1970) and Göteborg (Lindblad and Levin 1970) studies for large-scale quasi-experimental method comparison research in applied linguistics.

The third stage, whose onset has been spurred on in no small degree by the DBP study, will be marked, according to the investigators, by the interpretation of language performance "explicitly in terms of how different aspects of communicative competence have developed as a function of specific language acquisition/learning experiences" (Allen et al. 1983:58). This stage will draw on both abstract models of language use and theories of language acquisition/learning. This stage will also be marked by the use of a much wider range of research approaches and analytic procedures. I would further speculate that this stage will see the marriage of language testing research and second language acquisition research in designs that will permit the full application of the tools of multivariate analysis. The usefulness of such designs and analyses has already been demonstrated in studies such as Bachman and Palmer (1983), Gardner et al. (1983), Fouly (1985), Bachman and Mack (1986), Sang et al. (1986), and Wang (1987), which have examined the complex relationships among learner characteristics and different aspects of language proficiency.

It is in this perspective that the results of the DBP investigation of language proficiency can be properly evaluated. They have provided us with a sobering reaffirmation of the complexity of language proficiency at a time when overly simplistic views have gained ground in both second language acquisition research and in language testing. More important, however, this study, in its relationship to other studies in the project, points the way to a broader agenda for research into the nature of language proficiency, an agenda that promises to further enrich our understanding of both this ability and its acquisition.

3 Communicative competence revisited

Jacquelyn Schachter

Large-scale proficiency study

I understand the goals of the language proficiency component of this large project to have been threefold: (1) to determine the extent to which the model of linguistic proficiency developed by project members could be found to be empirically justified, (2) to illuminate the nature of the second language proficiency of grade 6 immersion students as compared with their native speaker peers, and (3) to facilitate the accomplishment of these goals, to develop an appropriate set of tests and scoring scales and procedures. The model to be tested was a composite one of the nature of linguistic proficiency in native speakers that tied together three schemes: the communicative competence model of Canale and Swain (1980), which was adopted and modified, overlaid with Cummins's (1980, 1981) model of linguistic skill grouping involving those used in basic interpersonal communication (BICS) and those used in cognitive/ academic tasks (CALP), and the characterization of implicit and explicit linguistic knowledge of Bialystok (1978). This was quite an ambitious undertaking, and probably a premature one, since the theoretical constructs underlying these models are, I believe, neither fully delineated nor even sufficiently understood for us to feel confident in attempting to devise tests to validate them empirically. In particular, I believe that the overall state of knowledge of communicative competence beyond the level of the sentence (in isolation) is fragmentary, and that the interaction between the linguistic system and other conceptual systems involved in the communication process is insufficiently understood.

The model of communicative competence

This model needs to be isolated and examined carefully since, in my view, it constitutes the most basic of the three models used for the study, at least when viewed from the perspective of a serious attempt to clarify the nature of the language proficiency of immersion students.

First proposed by Hymes (1970), the notion of communicative competence provided great impetus to those linguists frustrated by the then-

39

current major focus on grammatical competence alone. It was felt and is still felt by many linguists that there is much more to linguistic competence than knowledge of phonology, morphology, syntax, and semantics and that this knowledge in fact plays a major role in determining what forms are used and in what ways they are used in production.

Hymes maintained, furthermore, that the Chomskyan distinction between competence and performance was valid not only for grammar, but also for rules of language use, and as Canale and Swain (1980) point out, almost all linguists dealing with the notion of communicative competence subsequently have done the same (including Chomsky 1980). We can therefore safely view this competence in the Chomskyan manner as a system (or systems) of constitutive rules that provide the speaker with criteria to decide what is grammatical, acceptable, and appropriate, and what is not.

There is still much confusion and disagreement, however, on what constitutes competence beyond the level of the grammar. This is not surprising, since the gap between knowledge of the structure of a sentence studied in isolation and knowledge of what is conveyed in uttering that sentence in a particular setting is a wide one. Exploration of that gap occupies the attention of a large number of linguists these days. Particularly relevant in the context of this project is the question of what the major constitutive components of communicative competence are and whether and to what extent they can be clearly delineated.

The framework within which project developers are working was originally that of Canale and Swain (1980), with subsequent modifications during the course of the project itself. The final decision was to claim that there are four major components, only three of which were chosen for validation: (1) grammatical competence, (2) discourse competence, and (3) sociolinguistic competence. I have concerns about these, both about their constituting the major components of communicative competence and about the conceptual definitions provided by project members. Let me attempt to weave my understanding of these notions together with my criticisms of the ways in which they have been defined within the project. My ultimate concern is that if these theoretical notions are not well founded, the items chosen to instantiate them in the tests will be confounded, and thus the tests themselves will not provide the kinds of evidence that will either justify *or* disconfirm the proposed constructs.

Grammatical competence would appear to be the most clearly delineated trait. One current approach to characterizing grammatical competence is to say of it that it involves the "computational aspects of language," the rules or formulations or constraints that allow us to pair sound with meaning, the rules that form syntactic constructions or phonological or semantic patterns of varied sorts. But even here problems exist at what may be called the periphery of such knowledge. In some formulations, for example, grammatical competence may not include lexical knowledge, if by lexical knowledge we mean the pairing of certain sound sequences with objects, actions, and events in the world and also such notions as "agent," "goal," and "instrument." This latter knowledge may form part of what Chomsky calls a conceptual system, which constitutes "part of some other faculty of mind that provides common sense understanding of the world." Involved in this system, Chomsky suggests, are "such 'generative' factors as origin, function, material constitution, and the like" (Chomsky 1980:55). These two systems are said to interact, of course, but the conceptual system "will have a central role in all sorts of mental acts and processes in which language plays no special part" (Chomsky 1980:54–55). If Chomsky's suggestion is correct, a great deal of work must go into the delineation of what properly belongs to conceptual knowledge and what to linguistic, and to the question of how these interact. This seems an enormous task, one in which work has only begun. But it remains as a quite possibly significant confounding factor in the determination and detection of grammatical competence.

In terms of this project, it must be noted that the Canale and Swain characterization of grammatical competence *includes* knowledge of lexical items, but it is not clear just what this is intended to mean. Much more controversial is the characterization of what has traditionally been called pragmatic knowledge, which is nowadays often assumed to be the ability of language users to pair sentences with the contexts in which they would be appropriate. This is a particularly appealing characterization from the perspective of those working within a Chomskyan framework, since it allows them to make the same distinction within pragmatics between competence and performance that is made for other aspects of linguistic inquiry (cf. Levinson 1983:24). Pragmatics, thus viewed, is concerned with the recursive assignment of appropriateness conditions to an infinite set of well-formed sentences. Let us take it as a working hypothesis that there is such a thing as pragmatic competence, and that it is characterized by "a certain system of constitutive rules represented in the mind" which underlie the ability to use grammatical knowledge along with the conceptual system to achieve certain ends and purposes (Chomsky 1980:59).

What do these rules deal with? As Levinson points out, characterizations abound, each differing somewhat from the others. Among those he discusses, there are two he prefers. One is a characterization whereby pragmatic knowledge is defined in terms of a boundary-drawing exercise between semantic knowledge on the one side and sociolinguistic knowledge on the other, such that in the distinction between semantics and pragmatics, the latter would be viewed as meaning minus truth-

conditional semantics. Furthermore, in the distinction between pragmatic and sociolinguistic knowledge, the former would be viewed as
providing the meaning of linguistic items, whereas the latter would be
seen as providing detailed characterizations of the *usage* of these same
terms (but cf. Levinson 1983:28 for some objections to this characterization). The other characterization he favors is an ostensive one which,
he says, might run as follows: "Pragmatics is the study of deixis (at least
in part), implicature, presupposition, speech acts, and aspects of discourse structure" (1983:27).

Where does pragmatics fit into the Canale and Swain framework? Is
it assumed not to exist? Or is it thought to be coextensive with discourse
competence? On some readings of the content of the report one would
be led to say that project members have chosen a very circumscribed
characterization of pragmatic knowledge and decided to label it "discourse competence," which they define as being composed of rules of
coherence (speech acts) and cohesion (deixis) (Allen et al. 1983:22). On
other readings, however, one suspects they have in mind some of the
kinds of textual knowledge that are focused on in discourse analysis –
that is, certain aspects of discourse structure (Allen et al. 1983:23).

There is, of course, a burgeoning field of discourse analysis whose
practitioners view it as a tool for the exploration of this vast area between
knowledge of linguistic structure and knowledge of culture. It is characterized by Stubbs this way:

> ... attempts to study the organization of language above the sentence or above
> the clause, and therefore to study larger linguistic units, such as conversational
> exchanges or written texts. It follows that discourse analysis is also concerned
> with language in use in social contexts, and in particular with interaction or
> dialogue between speakers. (Stubbs 1983:1)

If "discourse competence" is to be viewed as knowledge of the structure
of text (in the larger sense of the meaning of *text*, subsuming both written
and oral text), then it would be more appropriate to view it as part of
sociolinguistic competence. And this brings us directly to a consideration
of the kinds of knowledge involved in such competence.

In some conceptualizations, sociolinguistic knowledge has been
viewed as a continuum, with microsociolinguistic knowledge at one end,
and macrosociolinguistic knowledge at the other, the former having to
do with knowledge of text (viewed broadly as either written or spoken
text), the delineation of text types, how these are put together, what
speech acts are required and what are prohibited in a particular text
type, what grammatical forms co-occur frequently in a text type and
what forms are rare in that type, the effect of the displacement of the
hearer on the text, the effect of the cognitive content on the text, and
so on. The latter has to do with the influence on text of group mem-

bership, participant roles, degrees of formality, of politeness, and so on. The continuum thus ranges from strictly linguistic knowledge to strictly cultural knowledge, with no obvious dividing line between discoursal and sociolinguistic knowledge (cf., for example, Heath 1983; Kochman 1981; Philips 1983; Shieffelin and Ochs 1986).

The earlier Canale and Swain (1980) conception of sociolinguistic competence viewed it as being composed of two sets of rules: sociocultural rules of use, and rules of discourse. These appear to correspond roughly to the notions of macrosociolinguistic and microsociolinguistic knowledge described above. In the current model, these have been separated into two distinct components on the basis of a paper by Canale (1983) in which he characterizes sociolinguistic knowledge as knowledge of "the extent to which utterances are produced and understood *appropriately* in different sociolinguistic contexts depending on contextual factors such as status of participants, purposes of the interaction, and norms or conventions of interaction" (p. 7) and discourse knowledge as "mastery of how to combine grammatical forms and meanings to achieve a unified spoken or written text in different genres" (p. 9). What is unclear to me is the conceptual justification for the separation of discoursal and sociolinguistic knowledge into distinct components. Surely unity of a text involves appropriateness and depends on contextual factors such as status of the participants, purposes of the interaction, and norms or conventions of interaction.

In a Bachman and Palmer (1982) study referred to in the DBP report, three traits were posited: grammatical, encompassing morphology and syntax; pragmatic, encompassing vocabulary, cohesion, and organization; and sociolinguistic, encompassing register, nativeness, and non-literal language. Only two traits were isolated, which Bachman and Palmer labeled grammatical/pragmatic competence and sociolinguistic competence. If nothing else, this study points out the difficulties involved in distinguishing coherent and theoretically separable competences. Project members decided, nevertheless, that the conceptual distinction between the hypothesized discourse and sociolinguistic traits was sufficient to outweigh the Bachman and Palmer results. But it is just this conceptual distinction which is unclear to me.

Discoursal knowledge viewed as knowledge of text seems to be more clearly microsociolinguistic knowledge; viewed as cohesion and coherence, it seems more clearly pragmatic knowledge. Discoursal knowledge clearly involves both cultural conventions and appropriate grammatical choices. Whether or not it constitutes a separate kind of knowledge from either will come, I expect, not from tests attempting to validate it, but rather from more clearly delineated theoretical models than are currently available.

Last, but not least, I am not even sure if there is a *conceptual* distinction to be made between pragmatic and sociolinguistic competence. It seems we must always resort to talking in terms of "more or less" – more meaning-oriented phenomena lean toward the pragmatic, more culturally determined phenomena lean toward the sociolinguistic. It seems at least possible that communicative competence is best viewed as consisting of two kinds of competence – grammatical and pragmatic – and that sociological phenomena interact with these two components at all levels. Is it not the case that cultural or sociological criteria influence all levels of a grammar, from phonological to syntactic to pragmatic? Why should we want to claim that they constitute yet a third component?

Operationalization of theoretical constructs

Let us put these questions aside, crucial though they are, and consider the decision-making process at the next lower level of abstraction, that of choosing the appropriate items to test one's theoretical constructs. Even if we were to have an adequate theoretical model within which core characterizations of each type of competence could be made, we would still have difficulty deciding in many particular instances whether or not a particular aspect of language was or was not an exemplification of one kind of competence or another; that is, peripheral delineation would still cause problems. An example comes to mind which demonstrates this difficulty (drawn from Chomsky 1980:63). If I say, "It was Dickens who wrote *Moby Dick*," you can appropriately respond, "No, it was Melville," but not "No, it was David Copperfield."

If you were to give the second response, I would understand you to mean that David Copperfield wrote *Moby Dick*. As Chomsky points out, this can be described in terms of focus and presupposition, and relates to the position of main stress. But is this truly a matter of grammatical knowledge (i.e., semantic knowledge) or pragmatic knowledge (sociolinguistic or discoursal)? Chomsky's point here is that we need to develop coherent and integrated theories with explanatory power and see where examples such as this fall; we should let the theories decide for us. I agree with his claim and further wish to suggest that at the level of features chosen for testing in this project, some of the features chosen involved examples such as the one above, for which it is (and will continue to be) difficult to say which component they exemplify.

With this cautionary statement in mind, let us turn to the question of how the hypothesized traits were operationalized in this project.

The grammatical trait was said to be operationalized as "rules of morphology and syntax, with a major emphasis on verbs and prepositions." Yet I see little evidence here of morphological rules (the *a* + *le* = *au* is one), and no evidence of syntactic rules. Furthermore, in this trait alone, what seems to have counted as proficiency was lack of error production rather than evidence of the existence of specific kinds of syntactic knowledge (how questions are formed, how negation is dealt with, whether or not relative clauses, clefts, etc., occur). Such evidence presumably remains available in the data but was untapped for this study. Error analysis allows an analyst to pick up some limited kinds of knowledge of grammatical proficiency, specifically in the area of morphology, but remains inherently limited as a tool for getting at fundamental aspects of syntactic knowledge (see Schachter and Celce-Murcia 1977).

Four error categories were established: syntactic errors, preposition errors, nonhomophonous verb errors, and homophonous verb errors. I am pleased to see that homophonous verb errors were separated from nonhomophonous verb errors, but I would have expected not to have them count as errors at all. Surely the ability to spell correctly is not to be viewed as part of grammatical competence, however it is ultimately defined.

The ability to use verb forms accurately fits squarely into the area described above, since it is very difficult to decide whether or not, say, in the elicitation of such forms (in the oral production task) an error in production has to do with whether the subject has a form and doesn't know yet when to use it appropriately (a pragmatic error for these forms) or whether the subject has not yet acquired that form (a grammatical error). The distinction between the passé composé and the imparfait (two forms elicited in the study) illustrates this nicely. Since they are both used to indicate past time, the choice of one over the other is very often a pragmatically based decision (see Waugh and Monville-Burston 1986; also Comrie 1976).

The discourse trait was defined for this study as the ability to use coherent and cohesive text, whether written or oral. The major problem in the operationalization of this component was that the trait itself was not well defined, so the list of items chosen for testing is an odd one. The list is as follows: (1) basic task fulfillment; (2) identification of characters, objects, locations; (3) time orientation; (4) anaphora; (5) logical connection; (6) punctuation; and (7) scene setting (in the oral production measure only). Items 1, 2, 5, and 7 seem to fit best into sociolinguistic knowledge, and items 3 and 4 into pragmatic. Item 6 does not fit at all. A confounding factor for both the composition and the oral production task is that of memory if, as is my understanding, students did not invent the narratives themselves, but rather retold them. It would seem that scores on 1, 2, and 3 would be based in part on how well a subject could remember a story, not on whether s/he had the requisite sociolinguistic or pragmatic ability.

Sociolinguistic competence was defined for the project as the ability to produce and recognize socially appropriate language in context. In my opinion, the sociolinguistic tests were the best designed of the three sets of tests, and also the most limited. The tasks were appropriate and the items chosen for analysis fall squarely within what anyone would reasonably identify as part of the core of sociolinguistic knowledge. I was particularly impressed with the effort, in this case, to test the tests on native speakers before using them on the immersion subjects.

Consequences

In sum, my concerns are that the three hypothesized major components of the communicative competence model used in this project are neither well defined nor clearly understood. The discourse component is particularly suspect, since the characterization and discussion of it give rise to two interpretations: (1) textual knowledge, and (2) a limited concept of pragmatic knowledge. Furthermore, in part because of this conceptual confusion and in part because peripheral questions are always vexing, a number of items chosen to test the traits exhibit the borderline problem, in that it is difficult to decide which trait they actually represent.

In view of these concerns, it is not surprising that factor analysis failed to confirm the project's hypothesized three-trait model of communicative competence. The final project report suggests that the fact that the hypothesized trait structure did not emerge from the analysis "may have been due to the homogeneity of the immersion student sample" (Harley, Allen, Cummins, and Swain 1987, Vol. I:4). My perception is that this was *not* the cause, and that the real cause is that the traits themselves were not sufficiently distinguished conceptually. This may in fact be the underlying cause of part of the two-factor solution produced by LISREL, the first of these being interpretable as a general language proficiency factor. If many of the test items were ambiguous and if the three traits were poorly defined, it makes sense that factor analysis would produce such a factor. Each item in the set of tests would be contributing to knowledge of the language, but not necessarily to knowledge of a trait. To claim that there *is* a general language proficiency factor (as Oller 1976 does) would be to miss the point. The problem lies at the conceptual end.

The primary goal of this proficiency study – to find empirical support for the hypothesized three traits composing communicative competence – was not realized. But valuable information was collected, much of which could be used to further the second purpose of the study, that of providing a broadly based description of the target language proficiency of the second language learners tested and of comparing their proficiency with that of native speakers of comparable age. With this purpose in mind, the analytical work would not focus on the extent to which subjects reached criterion (or failed to reach criterion in the case of the grammatical written and oral tasks), but rather on the actual linguistic forms they have incorporated into their grammars and how these are being put to use in communicative tasks. Comparable analysis of the production of native speakers would allow critical comparative work to be carried out. And this in turn would lead to implications for improvement of educational practices as they relate to second language learning and teaching.

Communicative skills of young second language learners

I found this study (Hulstijn 1983) intriguing for several reasons. The study used a different population type than the immersion subjects of the large-scale proficiency study: These subjects were Japanese learners of English, and furthermore they were immigrant children whose exposure to their target language was presumably much wider and more intensive than that of French immersion students.

The study adds interesting data to the ongoing debate over the question of whether and to what extent older second language learners are more efficient as language learners.[1] According to the results of this study, amount of L2 exposure (for which length of residence is an index) is a more important factor in determining the level of linguistic skill than is cognitive development (for which age is an index). This would indicate that second language learners may simply need an extended period of time for the acquisition process to take place. Particularly crucial here is a third factor, age at first exposure. Given the ages of the students tested (11 grade 2/3 and 11 grade 5/6), it is clear that all of these individuals began the second language acquisition process *during* what is called the critical period for first language acquisition, generally thought to be from birth to puberty (cf. Scovel 1988 for an extensive discussion of this issue). What is required here is further exploration of the possibility that the critical period for first language acquisition extends to second language acquisition as well. Needed are Japanese immigrant children who have arrived just at the end of or after the close of the critical period (ages 11 to 13), who have the same range of exposure to English as exhibited by the children already tested (15 months to 5½ years). It is quite possible that for post-critical-period

1 For more information on this study, see Part III, Chapter 9, page 131.

language learners, cognitive maturity is at least as important as amount of L2 exposure.

Studies of transfer and lexical use in immersion students' writing

Here we have two fascinating small studies on the ongoing problem of the extent to which transfer exhibits itself in the course of second language acquisition (Harley 1989a; Harley, King, and Burtis 1987). The immersion students are learning French in a largely naturalistic manner (i.e., via communication more than by overt teaching) and yet subtle indications of transfer have been detected in the area of the interaction between the lexicon and the grammar. In the context of directional expressions, the students were observed to produce verb and prepositional phrase sequences in situations in which native speakers would use single, lexically specific verbs, in which direction was marked within the verb itself. This did not necessarily result in error (although occasionally it did), but it no doubt provides part of the flavor of immersion student French, marking them as non-native in a very subtle way.

This is quite similar to the phenomenon observed in the lexical proficiency study whereby native speakers were noted to make more use of conditional verb forms (*j'aimerais, je voudrais*) to indicate politeness in requests than did immersion students, who tended to use *pouvoir* + verb (in combination with *s'il vous plaît*).

The former appears to be a case in which L2 learners infer that comparable syntactic phrases (verb + prepositional phrase) in the L1 and L2 carry the same function. The latter seems to be a case in which the function of a set of inflectional forms in the target language is not perceived because no such inflectional forms exist in the native language. Both kinds of inferences will have a negative impact on the learning of the grammar of the L2. For example, if I assume that modals are the indicators of politeness in the target language as they are in my native language, I will not necessarily discern from the input that a certain verb inflection (the conditional) carries that function in the target, nor will I see much need to learn the set of forms associated with the conditional. If I assume that the way to express movement and direction is via a nondirectional movement verb plus a prepositional phrase, I will not discern that simple verbs can carry that function in the target, nor will I see the need to learn such verbs.

This apparent learner tendency to assume translation equivalence in both semantic and syntactic co-occurrence constraints may be an indication of how non-native grammars get built up in the minds of the learners. It is possible that conscious intervention in the classroom in the form of *comparisons* of features of the two languages and how they carry the same or different functions might break this cycle and allow learners to redirect their own grammatical development. I would support the recommendation (Harley, Allen, Cummins, and Swain 1987, Vol. I:40) that this be attempted.

4 Response by DBP Project members to the discussion papers of Lyle Bachman and Jacquelyn Schachter

Let us briefly summarize the two main points Lyle Bachman made in his discussion paper. The first was that he was concerned about the variety of abilities, or as he put it "inconsistency" of subscores, that make up the overall score in each cell of the multitrait multimethod matrix; second, he wondered whether this lack of consistency in the subscores might account for the factor analyses in the large-scale proficiency study not revealing the traits we were looking for, and whether it might not be useful to look further at the detailed correlations among the 40 + subscores and try to find more consistent factors that would perhaps cut across the three traits we had originally proposed. As he noted, we even hinted in the second-year report (Allen et al. 1983) that we were going ahead with something like the factor analysis of the detailed scores that he is proposing.

To take the second point first, the reason we did not pursue the analysis of the detailed scores was simply that the subscores did not appear reliable enough to warrant such an analysis. Actually, what we had planned to do was slightly different from what Bachman is proposing – we were going to try to find evidence for our original constructs in the detailed analysis, whereas Bachman is suggesting that we might look for evidence of a new, more consistent set of constructs that would cut across our original set. But in either case reliability would be a problem. In particular, the large correlation matrix of the component scores, which would form the basis for any further analysis, was not interpretable at an intuitive level, presumably because of low reliabilities. In fact, one of the things we learned from this project is just how difficult it is to achieve reliability with the kinds of protocol data we have been using. One needs a large amount of material on which to base the score, and when one starts examining subcomponents based on just some of that material, it is very hard to get high reliability. (But see Swain 1988a for a theoretical/language acquisition argument for why we did not get high

The editors are grateful to Jud Burtis, on whose reply to Lyle Bachman at the DBP symposium much of this written response is based.

reliabilities.) So we did not proceed along those lines simply because the reliabilities of the subscores did not appear to warrant it.

However, we did pursue the factor analysis along some of the other lines that Bachman has suggested – notably oblique rotations. And in so doing, we did obtain factors that represented grammatical and discourse traits, although not a sociolinguistic trait. These findings are reported in the lexical proficiency study (see Chapter 1).

With regard to Bachman's first point, we would like to respond in some detail, because it involves the fundamental purpose of the study and the issue of whether the goals of the study have been properly addressed by the data analysis. We are concerned here with the variability of subscores within cells, the "unplanned complexity," as Bachman puts it. The subscores within a cell – Bachman's examples are subscores in the discourse cells – often do not correlate with each other or correlate inconsistently with each other; moreover, the performance levels on the different subscores are different, as if the subscores are all measuring different abilities. And yet, within each cell we have proceeded to average the subscores in order to construct a global score for each cell. The issue then is whether this procedure is justified (especially in view of our intention to do a multitrait multimethod factor analysis), or whether the lack of homogeneity of our measures is evidence in itself that we have not properly identified some of the traits we are trying to measure.

This issue is one we have thought about often during the course of the project, and our current thinking can be summarized as follows. The concern seems to arise because it is natural to suppose that the validity of a trait or a factor depends on the consistency of its constituent parts. Certainly, factor analysis is often used to break a test down into its homogeneous components in exactly this sense. But in the present case, the traits being proposed – sociolinguistic, discourse, and even grammatical proficiency – are not meant to be unitary or pure. They are examples of what the testing literature refers to as heterogeneous, as opposed to homogeneous, traits (intelligence is a prime example of a heterogeneous trait). As such, each trait may be made up of many different components, and there is no reason why all components within a trait must correlate. Among the components of the sociolinguistic trait, for example, there may even be a grammatical subcomponent – a grammatical form that is needed in order to express politeness or familiarity. But that does not mean that the grammatical subcomponent should be taken out of the sociolinguistic trait in an effort to refine the trait further. Instead, this subcomponent should be kept with the sociolinguistic trait on the grounds that sociolinguistic proficiency is a heterogeneous trait.

Perhaps what we should think of as holding traits together – what makes them theoretically meaningful units – is not the consistency of their subcomponents, but the uniformity of the effect of those subcomponents, the fact that there are situations where the various subcomponents work together to contribute to success, or proficiency. There may be situations where, for example, sociolinguistic proficiency, including all its components, is needed, or where discourse proficiency is needed, or where grammatical proficiency is needed. And there are presumably also learning situations and language experiences that contribute specifically to one or another of these proficiencies.

If these traits are heterogeneous, as they appear to be from the within-cell correlations, is a factor analysis appropriate, or is it undermined by the heterogeneity of the traits? We would argue that it is appropriate because of the particular nature of a factor analysis carried out on a multitrait multimethod matrix. In particular, the purpose of such a factor analysis is not to analyze traits or measures into internally consistent parts, as is more commonly done in factor analysis, but rather to demonstrate the existence of the global traits and to validate them. That is, the consistency at issue in this type of factor analysis is the consistency of traits (whether homogeneous or heterogeneous) across methods, not the consistency of subscores within the traits themselves. It asks, for example, whether "discourse proficiency," however heterogeneous it may be, is the same trait regardless of method of testing. Therefore the averaging of uncorrelated components within a cell should not adversely affect the outcome of the factor analysis, which remains appropriate even if the components within the cell do not correlate, and even if there are large variations in performance across these components. What the variability shows is that we are looking at heterogeneous rather than homogeneous traits.

One last point with reference to Bachman's paper: We would like to highlight, for ourselves as much as for others, the difference between native speakers and immersion students on different test methods that he mentioned. We had noticed and reported that native speakers were better than immersion students on grammatical measures, but not on the discourse measures, and that this provided some evidence for the existence of those traits (see Chapter 1). But as Bachman has pointed out, there are also test method differences whereby native speakers have a greater advantage over immersion students on oral measures of proficiency than on multiple-choice or written measures, which is another interesting finding, showing the existence of the method factor.

In her discussion paper, Jacquelyn Schachter takes issue with the theoretical framework underlying the DBP proficiency studies and with the way in which some of the theoretical constructs were operationalized. Observing that there is still considerable confusion and disagreement concerning what communicative competence beyond the level of grammar consists of, she concludes that the time is not yet ripe for carrying out an empirical study to validate a construct like discourse competence. Schachter believes that the question of whether or not discourse competence in the DBP framework constitutes a distinct kind of knowledge will come not from tests attempting to validate it but rather from more clearly delineated theoretical models than are currently available.

We fully agree that more detailed and clearly delineated theoretical models are a high priority. But we see empirical studies going hand in hand with theorizing in the abstract, and serving an important function in helping to clarify theoretical concepts. If we waited until everyone was satisfied with the theory, then in our opinion, no empirical studies would ever be done. We believe that model building and model testing are, and should be, mutually supportive activities.

It should perhaps be emphasized that the grammar, discourse, and sociolinguistic constructs as operationalized in the DBP studies were not claimed to represent everything that is involved in communicative competence. Rather, our intention was to isolate aspects of communicative competence that we considered of educational significance and to test the hypothesis that these would emerge as distinct components and would be differentially manifested under different task conditions and in different learning settings.

Schachter's criticisms of the operationalization of the grammar component seem to bear mainly on the multiple-choice test in the large-scale proficiency study, where we agree that, due to the nature of the task, there was little emphasis on sentence syntax. We did score for syntactic accuracy on the open-ended oral and written production tasks, however, focusing, for instance, on word order rules. We did not look at amount of use of relative clauses, cleft sentences, and so on, since our impression was that such measures would not distinguish among the immersion students in our sample. Note that in order to obtain satisfactory statistical reliability for the purposes of factor analysis, it was necessary to use measures that would capture variability among the students. Hence our choice of accuracy in French morphology and syntax, with a special emphasis on verbs and prepositions. In further DBP studies (e.g., Cummins, Lopes, and King 1987), we did use measures of syntax in English that went beyond accuracy, reflecting the fact that the English of some minority groups was virtually error-free.

A further issue Schachter raised concerns the difficulty, in operationalizing constructs, of achieving a clean dividing line between different constructs – for example, between grammar and discourse. We were aware of this as a potential problem, and made every effort to avoid overlapping scores. In the area of French verbs, for example, we scored under grammar for usage *within* written sentences and *within* oral exchanges where obligatory contexts had been created; under discourse we rated for appropriateness and consistency of tense use *across* sentences. While one might object that this kind of division between grammar and discourse cannot always be scrupulously upheld, we would argue that there were a sufficient number of clear-cut differences to render the traits adequately distinct in operational terms.

Finally, in responding to Schachter's paper, we would like to reiterate that although the factor analysis in the large-scale proficiency study did not provide evidence for a separate discourse trait of the kind we had hypothesized, other evidence did support the separation between discourse and grammar traits, first in the comparison of native and non-native scores (see Chapter 1) and second in two of the subsequent factor analyses that included lexical measures (see Chapter 1).

PART II
CLASSROOM TREATMENT

5 Aspects of classroom treatment: toward a more comprehensive view of second language education

Patrick Allen,
Merrill Swain,
Birgit Harley,
and Jim Cummins

In an influential paper published in the early eighties, H. H. Stern distinguished between learning a language through use in the environment (i.e., functionally) and through processes of language study and practice (i.e., formally). As Stern (1981) pointed out, this aspect of language behavior can be characterized as a psycholinguistic/pedagogic continuum, or P-scale. There is nothing inherently good or bad about activities at either end of the scale, and in organized language teaching we often find an interplay between formal and functional approaches. In this paper the term *experiential* is used to refer to activities at the functional end of Stern's P-scale, while *analytic* refers to activities at the formal end. The experiential-analytic distinction is analogous (although not necessarily identical) to distinctions made by other investigators with regard to general pedagogic orientation. Barnes (1976), for example, discusses *interpretive* versus *transmission* teaching; Wells (1982) distinguishes between *collaborative* and *transmission* orientations; while Cummins (1984) uses the labels *reciprocal interaction* and *transmission* to refer to these two dimensions.

The relationship between experiential and analytic activities in the classroom has recently emerged as one of the key issues in second language pedagogy. According to some authorities (e.g., Krashen 1982) analytic or grammar-based activities are of minimal benefit, since conscious "learning" cannot be converted into the central process of unconscious L2 "acquisition." Others (e.g., McLaughlin, Rossman, and McLeod 1983) have argued that "controlled" processes may precede the development of "automatic" processes. If this is so, there is no reason to exclude grammar teaching from the L2 classroom, so long as it is appropriate to the communicative goals and the maturity level of the students. The investigation of a number of issues relating to the analysis-experience option is a common theme that draws together the five treat-

57

ment studies in the DBP project. The purpose of this paper is to provide a summary discussion of the treatment studies which, we believe, are leading us to a more comprehensive view of what constitutes effective second language teaching.

Although recent approaches to L2 instruction, such as communicative language teaching, emphasize the need for a more meaningful and natural use of language inside the classroom, it is still not clear what precise differences in methodology and outcome distinguish these from more traditional approaches. The first task, then, is to establish a conceptual distinction between analytic and experiential activities.

As a result of our review of the literature, we decided not to attempt a definition of experiential language teaching as a general global concept, but rather to compile a list of indicators of communicative behavior, each of which could be separately observed and quantified. It is important to emphasize that the pedagogic orientation of classrooms is not determined by any one feature, but by a cluster of interrelated features. For example, it would not make sense to take the single feature "group activity versus whole-class activity" and to use it as the basis for distinguishing between experiential and analytic classrooms. However, if we find classes where relatively more time is spent on a combination of activities marked by group work, broad range of reference, use of extended text, reaction to message rather than code, and so on, it is possible to characterize these as having an overall experiential profile. Similarly, classes that spend relatively more time on whole-class activities, form-focused practice, use of minimal text, reaction to code rather than message, and so on, can be described as having an overall analytic profile.

As Stern points out in his discussion paper (Chapter 7), it is important to be objective about both types of activity, and not to prejudge the issue by comparing experiential teaching at its best with analytic teaching at its worst. Although the extremes of Stern's P-scale are clearly distinct, in practice many teachers draw selectively upon the two approaches in order to develop composite or mixed methodologies that are tailor-made for particular instructional settings. Consequently, in comparing analytic and experiential teaching, we are often concerned with relative degrees of emphasis, rather than with absolute differences between classrooms.

The remaining sections of this paper will be organized as follows. First we will discuss the development and validation of the COLT observation scheme (Allen, Fröhlich, and Spada 1987), and the employment of this instrument in a core French process-product study at the grade 11 level (Allen, Carroll, Burtis, and Gaudino 1987). Second, we will describe the immersion observation study (Swain and Carroll 1987), which examined vocabulary instruction, *tu/vous* input, opportunities for student talk, and error treatment at the grade 3 and grade 6 levels. Third, we will discuss the French immersion experimental study (Harley 1989b), which was designed to investigate the effect on proficiency of functionally focused materials at the grade 6 level. Finally, we will consider the pedagogic implications for core French and immersion, and draw a number of conclusions for second language education.

Development and validation of the COLT observation scheme

Although a number of observation instruments have been developed for the L2 classroom (Moskowitz 1970; Fanselow 1977; Bialystok et al. 1979; Ullmann and Geva 1984), we found that none of the existing schemes could be adapted in its entirety for the purposes of our project. We therefore decided to develop our own scheme – known as COLT (communicative orientation of language teaching) – which would contain categories to measure features of communication typical of classroom discourse, as well as categories to measure how closely these interaction patterns resemble the way language is used in noninstructional settings (see Appendix).

The COLT observation scheme was derived from the DBP communicative competence framework and from a review of current issues in communicative language teaching. The scheme is divided into two parts. Part I, filled out by observers during the class, identifies different types of classroom activity and categorizes them in terms of (a) participant organization; (b) the content, or subject matter, of the activity; (c) student modality; and (d) materials in use. Part II, which is coded from a tape recording of the class on a time-sampling basis, analyzes the communicative features of teacher-student interaction. Seven main categories are identified: (a) use of target language, L1 or L2; (b) information gap; (c) length of utterance; (d) reaction to code or message; (e) incorporation of preceding utterances, or how the participants react to each other's contributions; (f) discourse initiation by teacher or student; and (g) relative restriction of linguistic form.

The COLT was piloted in 13 classes, mainly at the grade 7 level. The sample included 4 core French classes, 2 extended French and 2 French immersion classes, and 5 ESL classes. The study was begun with a number of tentative expectations about the main characteristics of the four types of program. Core French is taught as a subject within a limited time frame, and classes in this program were expected to contain a relatively large proportion of form-focused, teacher-centered activities.

Since extended French involves the presentation and discussion of subject matter in addition to core French instruction, the teaching in this program was expected to be somewhat less structural and more meaning oriented. Of the three types of French program, French immersion was expected to provide the greatest opportunity for authentic discourse and for the negotiation of significant meaning.

ESL teaching in Toronto differs from French language instruction, since many more opportunities exist for acquisition outside the classroom. As a result, it was expected that ESL teachers would tend to use class time to practice various aspects of the language code, but that they would also seek to introduce communicative enrichment material from the real world outside the classroom. Expectations about the distinguishing characteristics of each program were largely supported by the observation data. The core French classes turned out to be the least "communicative" in terms of the COLT categories and the immersion classes the most, while the ESL and extended French classes occupied a position in between.

The ability of the COLT observation scheme to capture differences in instructional orientation in a variety of programs was seen as an indication of its validity. We were now in a position to suggest what the differences were between programs, but we were not yet able to say which characteristics might be most beneficial for developing which aspects of language proficiency. Therefore, we took the third and final step in the series of COLT studies, which was to use the observation scheme along with appropriate testing instruments in a study which would compare instructional differences within a program and relate them to learning outcomes.

The core French observation study

The core French program was selected for the process-product study because the students' L2 proficiency could be assumed to derive largely from the classroom. Eight grade 11 classes from the metropolitan Toronto area were selected with the help of school board personnel to represent a range of L2 teaching practices. Early in their grade 11 year, the students were given a series of pretests: (a) a multiple-choice grammar test; (b) two written production tasks (a formal request letter and an informal note), which were scored for both discourse and sociolinguistic features; (c) a multiple-choice listening comprehension test requiring the global comprehension of a series of recorded texts; and (d) an individual oral interview administered to a subsample of students from each class and scored for proficiency in grammar, discourse, and sociolinguistics. During the school year, each class was visited four times for observation

TABLE 5.1 RANK ORDER OF SCHOOLS (EXPERIENTIAL
TO ANALYTIC) BASED ON COLT PARTS I AND II

School	Score
5	534 Experiential
2	509
3	400
7	390
6	383
1	358
8	356
4	309 Analytic
Mean	408

with the COLT scheme. In May the classes were posttested with the same tests, and those students interviewed at the time of pretesting were interviewed again.

On the basis of the Part I and Part II categories of the COLT observation scheme, it was possible to rank-order the eight classes on a bipolar composite scale from "most experiential" to "most analytic." We grouped the COLT features into binary oppositions (experiential vs. analytic, or "high" vs. "low" communicative feature) in order to arrive at a score that would permit ranking of the classes. We took the total percentage of time spent on each of the high communicative features in COLT Parts I and II and summed the figures. This gave us two classes in the high communicative group and six classes in the low communicative group, with the mean score being used as the dividing line (see Table 5.1).

To give some idea of what the labels experiential and analytic mean in terms of classroom behavior, consider some examples. In the two most experiential classes, there was proportionately significantly more topic control by students, more extended written text produced by the students, more sustained speech by students, more reaction (by both teacher and students) to message rather than code, more topic expansion by students, and more use of student-made materials than in the other classes. These two classes were labeled Type E classes, in contrast to the remaining Type A classes, where significantly more analytic features were in evidence, including a higher proportion of topic control by teachers, minimal written text by students, student utterances of minimal length, student reaction to code rather than message, and restricted choice of linguistic items by students. The COLT analysis revealed at the same time that none of the classes were prototypically experiential or analytic, but rather all were intermediate along the bipolar scale. The COLT findings were supported by teacher questionnaires providing information about classroom activities throughout the year.

Three analyses were carried out on the data. First, it was hypothesized that the Type A classes would score significantly higher on both written and oral grammatical accuracy measures than the Type E classes, but that the Type E classes would score higher on all other proficiency measures, including discourse and sociolinguistic measures, and scores on global listening comprehension. In fact, when pretest and posttest scores were compared, no significant differences were found between the Type E and Type A classes, although a near-significant difference ($p < .06$) emerged in favor of the Type A classes on the grammar multiple-choice test. When the two Type E classes were compared to the two most analytic Type A classes (labeled Type A*), the Type A* classes did significantly better on the grammar multiple-choice test (and specifically on agreement rules), but few other significant differences were found.[1] These results were both surprising and somewhat disappointing in that they suggest either that the similarities between the two groups of classes outweighed the differences, or that overall pedagogic orientation has no real effect on proficiency as measured by our particular tests.

The next step was to find out whether some classroom features were more important than others for the development of second language proficiency. To this end, we performed a detailed correlational analysis relating the use of all the individual observation variables to learning outcomes. The purpose of this analysis was to explore the empirical relationships between COLT categories and proficiency measures without any a priori assumptions about their relative pedagogic value. The results of the correlational analysis suggest that core French students benefitted from a generally experiential approach in which relatively more time was devoted to such features as information gap, reaction to message, and topic incorporation. At the same time, there were positive correlations between various form-focused, teacher-directed activities and adjusted posttest scores. These results lead us to the conclusion that the analytic focus and the experiential focus may be complementary, and that they may provide essential support for one another in the classroom.[2]

1 Group A* scored significantly higher than Group E in the use of the conditional verb tense in the letter-writing task ($p < .001$). Also Group A* scored significantly higher in providing a rationale ($p < .01$) and a closing ($p < .01$) for the letter.

2 This should not be interpreted as an argument for returning to a structurally graded syllabus. It may be, however, that we should explore the possibilities for developing appropriate types of focused input within the context of meaningful task-based activities.

One unexpected result merits further discussion. When we calculated the total gain in proficiency for each school over the year, we found that of the two experiential classes, one (class 2) made the greatest gain in overall proficiency and the other (class 5) made the least gain. A possible explanation for the difference in proficiency results may be found in the suggestion by Ellis (1984) that it is not the quantity of interaction that counts, but the quality. Ellis formulates two hypotheses: (a) L2 development is fostered by consistency and accuracy of teacher feedback; (b) communicatively rich interaction that affords opportunities for the negotiation of meaning may aid development, where more structured forms of interaction do not. To examine these ideas, we undertook a qualitative analysis of the transcripts for classes 2 and 5.

The qualitative analysis provided evidence that the high-scoring experiential class engaged frequently in communicatively rich interaction involving feedback and the negotiation of meaning, while the low-scoring class received less feedback and spent more time on stereotyped routines that lacked the quality of spontaneous discourse. For example, class 2 spent 66 percent of observed time on activities that involved a focus on formal features of language, but this was usually done in the context of meaningful tasks such as whole-class discussion of the errors in student compositions. Class 5 spent 24 percent of observed time in form-focused activities, but in this case the activities often consisted of decontextualized grammar practice, such as asking questions clearly lacking in genuine communicative intent. According to the quality interaction hypothesis, the class 2 procedure appears to be pedagogically more effective in its emphasis on meaning negotiation and the development of metalinguistic awareness.

The immersion observation study

Whereas core French is traditionally oriented toward the analytic end of the scale and has potential for developing an experiential component, the situation in immersion teaching is the reverse. Immersion programs are mainly experiential because of their emphasis on substantive content. It has been suggested, however, that too much emphasis has been placed on the concept of "comprehensible input." If it is the case that students can understand discourse without precise syntactic and morphological knowledge, it is possible that at least part of the content lesson needs to be taken up by activities which encourage the production of "comprehensible output," precisely conveyed messages demanding more rigorous syntactic processing than that involved in comprehension (Swain 1985).

In the immersion observation study, classroom observations were carried out in nine grade 3 and ten grade 6 early total immersion classes for the purpose of obtaining information about various aspects of classroom treatment. In our report (Swain and Carroll 1987), four aspects of the classroom environment were examined: vocabulary instruction, *tu/vous* input, error correction, and restricted/sustained talk by students.

Vocabulary instruction

The analysis of L2 vocabulary instruction in grade 6 early total immersion classes was based on a classification scheme that focused on various pedagogic distinctions (e.g., planned/unplanned instruction, written/oral activities, control of vocabulary selection) and also on the linguistic aspects of vocabulary knowledge (e.g., phonology, morphology, syntax). Analysis of the classes in the light of these descriptors indicated that most planned vocabulary teaching occurred during reading activities organized around particular themes. Students learned to pronounce words that they read aloud and to interpret passages, and the meanings of unfamiliar words were explained. The focus of both planned and unplanned vocabulary teaching was mainly on the interpretation of meaning in a specific context. There was little attempt to provide instruction about the use of words in other contexts and, with few exceptions, the presentation of structural information about vocabulary was limited to a separate grammar lesson. Because of its association with reading activities, the teaching of new words emphasized written varieties of French; few attempts to teach words unique to the spoken mode were observed. Furthermore, there was no evidence that teachers were focusing on sociolinguistic or discourse-related aspects of vocabulary. We conclude that vocabulary teaching in the immersion classes occupied a rather narrow place in the overall teaching plan, and that it mainly involved meaning interpretation, with little planned attention to other aspects of vocabulary knowledge.

Tu/vous *input*

In the analysis of *tu/vous* input, all uses of these pronouns by ten grade 6 teachers were counted, as were the uses of the same pronouns in the public talk of the students. The pronouns were classified according to the functions they served: singular, plural or generic; formal or informal. Teachers were found to use *tu* and *vous* about equally often, with *tu* generally used to address individual students and *vous* the class as a whole. Occasionally, however, *tu* was used to the class and *vous* to individual students, leaving room for potential confusion. There was scarcely any use of *vous* by the teachers as a politeness marker, and its infrequency in this function in the classroom context was seen as a reason for its underuse as a politeness marker by early immersion students. Although *vous* plural was used relatively frequently by teachers, it was noted that very few opportunities appeared to arise for student production of *vous* plural in the classroom context.

It appears, then, that the classroom environment was functionally restricted in two ways. First, opportunities for students to observe the sociolinguistically motivated use of *tu* and *vous* were limited. Second, opportunities for students to produce the grammatically motivated use of *vous* also appeared to be infrequent in regular classroom discourse. In view of this we hypothesize that, at this age and with the knowledge that students already possess, the provision of relevant grammatical and sociolinguistic rules in context, together with adequate opportunities for appropriate use, would benefit learning.

Restricted/sustained talk

The comprehensible output hypothesis (Swain 1985) has two parts: (1) Students need to produce language as well as listen to it if they are to move toward native-speaker proficiency; (2) feedback needs to be provided so that learners can develop their knowledge of linguistic systems. In order to determine the opportunities the immersion students had to talk in class, transcripts based on 90 minutes of French class time in each of the nine grade 3 and ten grade 6 classes were analyzed, as well as the English portion of the day in the grade 6 classes. Each student turn was categorized according to length (minimal, phrase, clause, and sustained) and source (teacher or student initiated, planned or unplanned, linguistically restricted or unrestricted).

Table 5.2 indicates that in the French portion of the day, student turns were less than two-thirds as frequent as in the English portion of the day. Sources of student talk in French were very similar for grade 3 and grade 6 students, the most frequent source being teacher-initiated student talk where the student's response was linguistically controlled. Constraints of this type appeared to encourage minimal responses from the students. Extended talk of a clause or more was more likely to occur when students initiated an interaction and when they had to find their own words. However, less than 15 percent of student turns in French were found to be sustained (more than a clause in length) when reading aloud was not included. These results suggest that greater opportunities for sustained talk by immersion students are needed, and that this might be accomplished through group work, the provision of more opportunities for student-initiated talk, and teachers' asking more open-ended questions.

TABLE 5.2 LENGTH OF STUDENT TALK IN FRENCH FOR GRADE 3 AND 6 IMMERSION AND IN ENGLISH FOR GRADE 6 IMMERSION

Grade	Language	Total no. of utterances	Minimal (% of total)	Phrase (% of total)	Clause (% of total)	Sustained (% of total)	Sustained minus that read from text (% of total)
		$\overline{X}$	$\overline{X}$	$\overline{X}$	$\overline{X}$	$\overline{X}$	$\overline{X}$
3	French[a]	223.2	38.5	10.9	34.4	16.2	12.9
6	French[a]	226.7	39.5	11.7	30.1	18.7	14.9
6	English[b]	358.4	35.1	10.6	34.9	19.4	16.7

Minimal: One or two words (includes spelling)
Phrase: A nominal, adverbial or verb phrase
Clause: One clause
Sustained: More than one clause

[a]Based on 90 minutes of tape per class.
[b]Based on an average of 88 minutes of tape per class.

Error correction

The second part of the comprehensible output hypothesis refers to the need to provide students with useful and consistent feedback about errors (Swain 1985; see also Ellis 1984). In order to determine what error-correction strategies were used by teachers, we undertook a further analysis of the complete French transcripts of the ten grade 6 early total immersion classes. The analysis focused on the grammatical and pronunciation errors corrected by the teachers, the proportion of such errors corrected, and how systematic the error correction was. The highest proportion of error was observed in frequently used (i.e., unavoidable) grammatical features such as gender, articles, and verbs. Only 19 percent of grammatical errors overall were corrected, and corrections were often made in a confusing and unsystematic way.[3] There was little indication that students were being pushed toward a more coherent and accurate use of the target language. It seems reasonable to conclude that the lack of consistent and unambiguous feedback is likely to have a detrimental effect on learning.

To summarize, the immersion observation study suggests that content teaching would benefit language learning more if it were integrated with the right kind of focused input. In particular, there appears to be a need for a more systematic approach to word study and error correction, and for carefully planned activities to enable students to produce extended discourse and to experience language in its full functional range.

Functional grammar in French immersion

Most discussions of L2 curriculum have tended to assume two basic approaches to classroom treatment, corresponding to the analytic and experiential ends of Stern's P-scale.[4] It has been suggested, however, that there is room for a more flexible, variable-focus approach to curriculum incorporating three essential aspects or components: a structural-analytic component in which the focus is on the formal features of language and medium-oriented practice, a functional-analytic component in which the focus is on discourse and in which practice is both medium- and message-oriented, and an experiential component in which the focus is on the natural, unanalyzed use of language for personal,

---

3 A useful review of recent work on L2 error correction is provided by Chaudron (1988), pages 141–52.
4 Although this statement is broadly true, it should be noted that a number of authors have pointed out the difficulty of identifying different approaches in practice. See Chaudron (1988), Long and Sato (1983), Swaffar, Arens, and Morgan (1982).

social, or academic purposes (Allen 1983). The aim of the functional-analytic component is to provide an element of carefully planned, guided communicative practice that will enable students to focus on the meaningful use of particular grammatical forms, and to practice the productive use of such forms.

The advantage of incorporating such a component into the curriculum is that it provides opportunities for focused input, error correction, and guided production within the context of purposeful, task-based learning. The three instructional approaches can be considered complementary rather than mutually exclusive. Depending on the participants in, and circumstances of, a particular program, one of these approaches will be the primary focus, but this does not mean that another approach will not be the focus some of the time.

The immersion experimental study was designed to investigate the effect on students' L2 proficiency of functional-analytic materials that involved the provision of focused input in a problematic area of French grammar and provided students with increased opportunities for productive use of the target forms. Following a workshop with teachers, a set of classroom materials aimed at teaching the meaning distinctions between the imparfait and the passé composé verb tenses was introduced for an eight-week period into six early immersion classes in six schools. These experimental classes were compared on pretests, immediate post-tests, and delayed posttests with a comparison group of grade 6 immersion students in six other schools who had not been exposed to the materials. The tests consisted of a narrative composition, a cloze test with rational deletions, and an oral interview administered to a subsample of students in each class. All the tests were designed to assess the students' ability to make appropriate use of the two past tenses and were scored accordingly.

The classroom materials used in the study provide an opportunity to see what functional-analytic curriculum materials might look like, and how they could be incorporated into a mainly experiential French immersion program. A general introduction to the materials explained their purpose to the teachers, gave some linguistic background on the imparfait/passé composé distinction, and briefly outlined the content of each week's activities. The purpose of the materials was described in terms of the need for L2 teaching in an immersion context to bridge the gap between form-focused grammar exercises and natural, communicative subject-matter teaching. It was argued that there was room for a functional-analytic approach that would provide opportunities for students to use specific forms in communicative contexts. Specific goals were: (1) to establish the different meanings of the imparfait and the passé composé; (2) to integrate this grammar teaching with the teaching of worthwhile content and with the personal experience of students; and (3) to demonstrate a functional approach to grammar teaching in an immersion context that could be applied to other linguistic content.

The materials, oral and written activities divided into eight units, included the following: reading a simplified French-Canadian legend, discovering how the imparfait and the passé composé served different functions in the legend, illustrating contrasting sentences, applying proverbs to the legend and to the students' own experiences, miming the progressive function of the imparfait, working in small groups to create new legends, and producing albums of childhood memories.

Figure 5.1 indicates that there were some immediate benefits to the students exposed to the experimental treatment. Three months later, however, at the time of delayed posttesting, there were no significant differences between experimental and comparison groups on any of the tests; both groups had improved their test performance over time. The fact that there were no significant long-term differences between the groups might be construed as support for the view that comprehensible input is all that is needed by immersion students (Krashen 1982, 1984). This hypothesis, however, rests on the assumption that this is all the comparison students were getting, whereas it is clear from the teachers' questionnaire responses that students in the comparison classes spent a considerable amount of time focusing on the code in grammatical activities, and on the passé composé and imparfait tenses in particular.

The interpretation here assumes, moreover, that the experimental treatment the students received fully realized the potential of the teaching approach. This may be questioned. In the first place, some of the teachers' comments suggest that organizational inadequacies in certain activities needed to be overcome. Second, the materials were designed to provide a wide variety of activities, and yet it was clear that some kinds of activities appealed to particular teachers (and presumably to their students) more than others. This suggests that a greater range of options might have led to greater benefits. Third, it appears from teachers' comments on some weekly evaluation sheets that the content of the material did not necessarily promote a simultaneous focus on the code. And from the classroom observations that were conducted during week 4 of the study, it appears that only one of the four teachers observed was focusing on the verb forms that students were using during the proverbs activity. In three of the classes, students producing the present tense remained uncorrected. It is worth noting in this connection that the experimental class with a teacher who consistently corrected the students in content-oriented activities was, of the four classes observed, the one with the largest difference score on the composition task from pretest to either posttest.

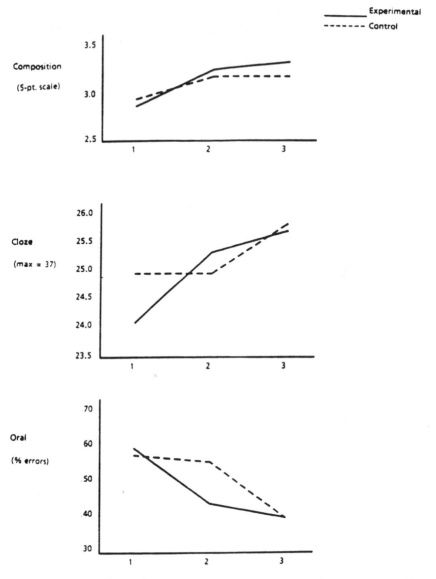

Figure 5.1   Unadjusted means on pretest (1), immediate posttest (2), and delayed posttest (3) for experimental and control groups on each measure, with the student as the unit of analysis

The results of the experimental study suggest that the use of motivating, functional-analytic materials attuned to the age level of students can accelerate grammatical development. The experiment did not attempt to isolate specific aspects of the input or interaction that may have had a key role in the results, on the assumption that factors such as increased frequency and salience in the input, greater and more focused opportunities for output, goal-directed interaction in small group contexts, and appeal to students' metalinguistic awareness will all have combined to produce the initial enhancing effect. It remains to be seen, based on further discussions with teachers, adjustment of materials in line with their comments, and the possible use of age-adapted materials at earlier grades, whether a more long-lasting effect can be achieved in an early immersion context.

Pedagogic implications

In the DBP treatment studies, we undertook a detailed analysis of core French and immersion classrooms. The two programs provide an interesting contrast, since core French is traditionally analytic, with potential for moving in an experiential direction, whereas French immersion has a strong experiential focus that, however, does not rule out the use of grammar-based activities where appropriate. In our conclusion we will discuss these programs in turn, starting with core French.

Implications for core French

The results of the core French observation study support the view that there may be a need for the core curriculum to move in a more experiential direction. Although there were significant differences between our Type A and Type E classrooms, there is no doubt that the core French sample, considered as a whole, was biased toward the analytic end of the scale. If we examine the mean percentage of observed time spent on various activities for all the core French classes combined, we find that teachers spent about half the time addressing the whole class or individual students, while students addressed the whole class or other students for just over a quarter of observed class time. Teachers were in control of the topic being discussed for 82 percent of the time; students selected the topic only 5 percent of the time. With regard to subject matter, 54 percent of observed class time was characterized by an explicit focus on form, compared with 15 percent devoted to substantive content with a broad range of reference.

A teacher questionnaire devised to obtain information about teaching/learning activities throughout the year, including occasions when the observers were not present, also indicated an analytic bias in the sample as a whole. For example, the following analytic activities were noted as having occurred "quite often" or "very often" during the year by all the teachers in the sample: Students do grammar and/or vocabulary exercises either orally or in written form; the teacher focuses on spelling, grammar and/or use of vocabulary in correcting written work (as distinct from focusing on stylistic appropriateness or logical organization of text); the teacher focuses on pronunciation, grammar and/or use of vocabulary in correcting oral work (rather than focusing on the message being conveyed); the teacher assigns grammar and vocabulary exercises in a single-sentence format for homework. All the teachers in the sample, with one exception, used a basic, structurally graded textbook (e.g., *Vive le Français* or *Passeport Français*) supplemented by a variety of other material.

Although it may be true that core French teachers need to devote more time to experiential activities, this does not mean they should abandon the grammar-oriented, transmission mode of instruction. When we performed a detailed correlational analysis in the core French study relating the use of all the individual observation variables to L2 proficiency outcomes, we found that the profile of a successful classroom that emerged from COLT Parts I and II was as follows: The teacher does relatively more talking compared with individual students to the class as a whole; relatively more time is spent on classroom management; more time is spent on form-focused activities than on general discussion; the students themselves spend relatively little time speaking; and visual aids and L2 materials are used relatively often. The analysis based on combined COLT categories showed that focus on form, extended writing, information gap, reaction to message, and topic incorporation were positively related to improvement. In other words, the most successful activities in our core French classrooms appeared to involve a mixture of analytic and experiential features.[5]

Whereas the eight core French classes spent 54 percent of total observed time on activities marked by an explicit focus on form, less than 1 percent was assigned to activities focusing on functional, discourse, or sociolinguistic aspects of language. When we compared pretest scores for Type A and Type E classes, we found that both groups showed evidence of improvement during the year on written/ oral grammar and listening comprehension measures. However, neither group showed much improvement on written/oral discourse or

5 At first sight, it may appear that these results lend support to a modified or conservative version of communicative language teaching, according to which experiential activities go hand-in-and with form-focused activities, rather than to a stronger or more radical version, according to which comprehensible input is both necessary and sufficient. It should be pointed out, however, that our analysis was based on a sample of only eight classrooms, and few of the correlations reached significance. There is no doubt that much more research will be needed before we can come to any definite conclusion about the role of focused input in a communicative classroom.

sociolinguistic measures. We attribute these results to the virtual absence of instruction on discourse and sociolinguistic aspects of language in both types of classroom. In the absence of explicit instruction, we cannot assume that knowledge of these aspects of language will be inferred from more general features of classroom interaction. We suggest, therefore, that there is a need in core French for activities that focus explicitly on functional, discourse, and sociolinguistic aspects of the target language in order to ensure that students gain a knowledge of the relevant rules.

The qualitative analysis of transcripts for the highest-scoring and lowest-scoring core French classes showed the importance of distinguishing between stereotyped routines and quality interaction that emphasizes meaning negotiation and the development of metalinguistic awareness. In the case of the high-scoring class 2, the most striking examples of jointly negotiated meaning occurred in a lesson devoted to a philosophical discussion of *Le Petit Prince*. In this discussion the teacher insisted students use the target language to develop and express their own ideas, thus helping them to establish links between the text and the world of their own experience. The communicatively rich interaction that resulted contrasted with the stereotyped nature of student presentations in the low-scoring class 5.

In one class 5 lesson, several groups of students gave presentations on topics of general interest, such as videos, abortion, and popular TV programs. The students had prepared the topics themselves, and the activity was potentially a valuable one. Unfortunately, however, the students addressing the class articulated so badly it was difficult to hear what they were saying; the discussion that followed each presentation was generally in English rather than in French, and the teacher provided virtually no feedback concerning students' use of the target language. In view of the quality interaction hypothesis, it seems likely that these factors must have seriously detracted from the effectiveness of the activity. Nevertheless, in terms of the quantitative analysis, the classroom presentations received credit for such experiential features as extended speech, broad range of reference, and content control by the students.

It appears, then, that a statistical analysis based on schemes such as COLT cannot be depended on to distinguish between pedagogically effective communicative activities and pedagogically ineffective ones. One problem is that the COLT observation scheme was designed to provide a broad picture of the types of activities that characterize L2 classrooms. As a result, it does not enable us to pay sufficiently close attention to the exchange structure of discourse, particularly to the way in which conversations are jointly negotiated by means of various topic incorporation devices. The importance of topic incorporation in facilitating mother-child interaction has been clearly demonstrated (Wells 1982), and there is reason to believe that it plays an equally important role in second language acquisition (Pica 1987). In any future study, therefore, it is important that the observation procedures based on COLT be supplemented by a more detailed discourse analysis, with a view to obtaining additional information about the way meaning is negotiated in the classroom.

Implications for immersion

According to Krashen (1984), the success of immersion programs is due to the fact that comprehensible input, which he sees as "the only true cause of second language acquisition" has been provided via subject matter teaching. In this type of teaching, comprehensible input – defined by Krashen (1982) in terms of "$i + 1$," or input that is slightly in advance of a student's current level of competence – is provided automatically in the natural, roughly tuned talk of teachers as they focus on conveying interesting and relevant messages in the target language. However, other researchers (Harley and Swain 1984; Schachter 1983; White 1987a) have questioned the assumption that the teachers' message-focused input automatically provides the "$i + 1$" that students need in order to make continued progress in the L2. It may be, as Harley and Swain (1984) have argued, that student opportunities for output have to be planned from a linguistic point of view, in that the speech acts which occur naturally in the classroom context may provide little opportunity for students to produce the full range of target language forms.

In other words, whereas an overemphasis on the teaching of grammar may lead to certain undesirable effects, such as lack of transfer from organized practice to language use in real life settings, it is possible that typical content teaching – focusing exclusively on the message rather than the code – also fails to provide the most favorable conditions for second language acquisition. If this is the case, it may be necessary to look for ways of combining experiential and analytic activities in the hope that we can find the right kind of balance between the two. In his discussion paper, Stern (Chapter 7) suggests two main ways of establishing links: one in which "an analytic strategy is dominant and the experiential in a supporting role," and another in which the relationship is reversed, that is, "the experiential is dominant and the analytic is supportive."

From this point of view, immersion can be seen as an experientially focused program that might benefit from additional analytic support. Observations conducted in grade 6 immersion classrooms show that grammar is already being taught. However, the main emphases in these activities appear to be more on manipulating and categorizing language forms than on relating forms to their meaningful use in communicative contexts. It is a relatively rare occurrence for teachers to refer to what has been learned in a grammar lesson when they are involved in content teaching, and even more rare for teachers to set up content-based activities for the purpose of focusing on problematic language forms. It appears, then, that in immersion classes, where language and content learning are equally important goals, the question of how to achieve a closer relationship between the teaching of structure and the teaching of meaning is a topic that deserves serious consideration.

We would like to suggest, contrary to Krashen's (1984) claim, that not all content teaching is necessarily good language teaching (see also Swain 1988). Typical content teaching focuses on meaning comprehension, whereas what L2 learners need is to focus on form-meaning relationships. An ability to do this is encouraged through the production of language, whether in written or spoken form. Because the typical question/answer sequence found in content lessons tends to elicit short responses of minimal complexity from students, at least part of the content lesson needs to be devoted to activities designed to elicit longer and more complex utterances that will be both grammatically and semantically coherent. As Swain (1985) has pointed out, L2 learners need at least as many opportunities to use the target language as native speakers. Yet the grade 3 and grade 6 data show that immersion students are not only getting fewer opportunities out of class; they are getting fewer opportunities in class as well. This raises the question of what can be done to increase the opportunities for students to produce language. The observation results show a considerable similarity between grades 3 and 6 with respect to the sources of student talk. The most frequent source is "selecting from limited choice," which appears to encourage minimal responses. The second most frequent source is "finding their own words," which appears to encourage extended responses, as does self-initiated student talk. These results suggest that if teachers provide more opportunities for student-initiated discourse and ask more open-ended questions that require students to find their own words, the amount of sustained student talk will increase.

Another way of increasing the opportunities for comprehensible output is to involve students in group activities. However, almost no group work was observed in the immersion classes. For teachers who claim that group work is counterproductive because students tend to revert to their mother tongue, a number of pedagogic strategies can be employed. One solution is to make sure that students are provided with a task that requires the outcome to be a spoken or written text in French. Examples include the preparation of materials for use in the classroom, the production of a class newspaper, and the preparation of a radio show to be recorded on tape. The assumption underlying group work is that conscious reflection on form-meaning relationships is encouraged when students use the target language as a medium for conveying their own meanings as precisely as possible. However, this process should not be left to chance. Students have the right to expect some help as they struggle to express their ideas in French. This is the point at which we see a role for carefully planned, guided communicative practice that will push students toward the production of comprehensible output. One form of guidance is to engage students in activities contrived by the teacher to focus attention on potential problems, that will naturally elicit particular uses of language. Another form of guidance is to develop activities that make use of functions which would otherwise rarely be encountered in the classroom.

Observations made in immersion classes suggest that content teaching, with its strong focus on meaning, may result in unsystematic, possibly random feedback to learners about their language errors. Within the context of experiential language teaching, we are confronted by a dilemma: If teachers correct student errors, there is a danger that the flow of communication will be interrupted, or even halted completely. However, if teachers do not correct errors during the flow of communication, opportunities to make crucial links between form and function are reduced. We would like to suggest that the solution lies in providing students with a motivation to use language accurately, coherently, and appropriately by writing for, and speaking to, real audiences. Preparation for such activities will normally involve a process of editing and revision, and a commitment to an error-free final product. The concept of error-free does not mean that we have to return to a rigid, authoritarian, transmission mode of teaching. It does mean that we will try to ensure that students are fully committed to whatever communicative task they have set themselves, and that they will not be satisfied until they have conveyed their intended meaning as fully and as accurately as possible.

The implication is that error correction derives its consistency from the stage in an activity where it occurs. Students will come to understand that there is a stage of spontaneous production during which they generate texts which will have to go through further stages of revision and editing before they can be presented in public. During the revision stage, self and peer monitoring are as important as teacher feedback. At the same time, there will be a major role for the teacher, since consistency in error correction also derives from the questions that initiate the process. We suggest that the type of teacher response likely to motivate successful error correction is not "Wrong! repeat after me," but "Do you mean this or do you mean that? It's not clear from what you've said." Or: "It's not clear from the way you've written this. Could you write it more clearly?" In the immersion study, teachers spent only minimal amounts of observed time asking students what they intended in producing a specific utterance or written text. Yet surely there is pedagogic value in systematically encouraging students to reflect on what they want to say and then helping them to make an appropriate choice of language forms. One advantage of this type of instruction is that it does not require any special training or materials; it simply requires that teachers understand that one of their main functions is to provide students with the grammar and vocabulary they need to express the ideas they have in mind.[6]

Summary and conclusions

Our classroom treatment findings from different program settings lead to three main overall conclusions. First, there is a suggestion arising from both the core French and the immersion observation studies that the analytic focus and the experiential focus may be complementary, and that they may provide essential support for one another in the L2 classroom. Second, the quality of instruction is clearly important in both analytic and experiential teaching. Analytic teaching will be successful in developing L2 proficiency only if it is appropriately matched to the learners' needs, while experiential teaching should involve communicatively rich interaction that offers plenty of opportunities for production as well as global comprehension on the part of the student. Third, learners may benefit if form and function are more closely linked instructionally. There is no doubt that students need to be given greater opportunities to use the target language. But opportunities alone are not sufficient. Students need to be motivated to use language accurately, appropriately, and coherently. In all these respects, the how and when of error correction will be a major issue for future investigation.

It seems reasonable to conclude that in all the programs currently under investigation – core French, heritage languages, French immersion, and ESL – much more work needs to be done in the area of curriculum design. Such work should include research to determine what combinations of analytic and experiential activities are most effective for different types of student. Another comparatively neglected area from the research point of view is teacher training and

---

6 For further discussion of the role of feedback in L2 classrooms, see Chaudron (1988).

professional development. This area is likely to become more important at a time when more and more teachers are breaking away
from a dependence on prescribed pedagogic formulas and are increasingly making their own, more flexible, decisions about what can
be done in the classroom.

Appendix

COLT Observation Scheme: Definition of Categories
Part I: Classroom events
  I. Activity
     The first parameter is open-ended; that is, no predetermined descriptors
     have to be checked off by the observer. Each activity and its constituent
     episodes are separately described: drill, translation, discussion, game (sep-
     arate activities); teacher introduces dialogue, teacher reads dialogue aloud,
     students repeat dialogue parts after teacher (three episodes of one activity).
 II. Participant organization
     This parameter describes three basic patterns of organization:
     1. Whole class
        a. Teacher to student or class, and vice versa (One central activity
           led by the teacher is going on; the teacher interacts with the whole
           class and/or with individual students.)
        b. Student to student, or student to class and vice versa (Students talk
           to each other, either as part of the lesson or as informal socializing;
           one central activity led by a student may be going on, such as a
           group of students acting out a skit and the rest of the class being
           the audience.)
        c. Choral work by students (The whole class or group participates in
           the choral work, repeating a model provided by the textbook or
           teacher.)
     2. Group work
        a. Groups all work on the same task.
        b. Groups work on different tasks.
     3. Group and individual work
        a. Individual seat work (Students work on their own, all on the same
           task or on different tasks.)
        b. Group/individual work (Some students are involved in group work,
           others work on their own.)
III. Content
     This parameter describes the subject matter of activities – that is, what
     the teacher and the students are talking, reading, or writing about or what
     they are listening to. Three major content areas have been differentiated,
     plus the category topic control:
     1. Management
        Procedural directives and disciplinary statements.
     2. Explicit focus on language
        a. Form: Explicit focus on grammar, vocabulary, or pronunciation.
        b. Function: Explicit focus on illocutionary acts such as requesting,

apologizing, and explaining.

c. Discourse: Explicit focus on the way sentences combine into cohesive and coherent sequences.

d. Sociolinguistics: Explicit focus on the features of utterances that make them appropriate to particular contexts.

3. Other topics

This is a tripartite system which deals with the subject matter of classroom discourse apart from management and explicit focus on language.

a. Narrow range of reference.

Topics of narrow range involve reference to the immediate classroom environment, and to formulaic exchanges such as "Good morning" or "How are you?" which have phatic value but little conceptual content. Included in this category are references to the date, day of the week, weather, and so on that go beyond the classroom environment but are formulaic in nature.

b. Limited range of reference.

Topics of limited range necessitate information that goes beyond the classroom while remaining conceptually limited: concrete personal experiences involving movies, hobbies, holidays, school topics including extracurricular activities, and topics that relate to students' personal and family affairs, such as place of residence, number of brothers and sisters.

c. Broad range of reference.

Topics of broad range go well beyond the classroom and immediate personal experience and involve reference to public issues, world events, abstract ideas, reflective personal information, and other subjects, such as math or geography.

Topic control

Who selects the topic that is being talked about – the teacher, the student, or both? If the teacher selects the topic, this may be done in conjunction with a textbook.

IV. Student modality

This section identifies the various skills that may be involved in a classroom activity. The focus is on the students, and the purpose is to discover whether they are listening, speaking, reading, or writing, or whether these skills are occurring in combination. The category "other" is included to cover such activities as drawing, modeling, acting, or arranging classroom displays.

V. Materials

This parameter introduces categories to describe the materials used in connection with classroom activities.

1. Type of materials

a. Text (written).

b. Audio.

c. Visual.

2. Length of text

a. Minimal (e.g., captions, isolated sentences, word lists).

b. Extended (e.g., stories, dialogues, connected paragraphs).

3. Source/purpose of materials

    a. L2 (specifically designed for L2 teaching).
    b. L1 (materials originally intended for L1 or nonschool purposes).
    c. L1-adapted (utilizing L1 materials or real objects and texts, but in a modified form).
    d. Student made (materials produced by the students themselves).

Part II: Communicative features

Seven communicative features have been isolated:

  I. Use of target language
    a. Use of first language (L1)
    b. Use of second language (L2)
  II. Information gap
    This feature refers to the extent to which the information requested and/or exchanged is unpredictable (not known in advance). The two categories designed to capture this feature are:
    1. Requesting information
      a. Display request (The speaker already possesses the information requested.)
      b. Information request (The information requested is not known in advance.)
    2. Giving information
      a. Relatively predictable (The message is easily anticipated in that there is a very limited range of information that can be given. In the case of responses, only one answer is possible semantically, although there may be different correct grammatical realizations.)
      b. Relatively unpredictable (The message is not easily anticipated in that there is a wide range of information that can be given. If a number of responses are possible, they can provide different information.)
  III. Sustained speech
    This feature is intended to measure the extent to which speakers engage in extended discourse, or restrict their utterances to a minimal length of one sentence, clause, or word. The categories designed to measure this feature are:
    1. Ultraminimal (utterances that consist of one word – coded for student speech only).
    2. Minimal (utterances that consist of one clause or sentence – for the teacher, one-word utterances are coded as minimal).
    3. Sustained speech (utterances that are longer than one sentence, or that consist of at least two main clauses).
  IV. Reaction to code or message
    Explicit code reaction (a correction or other explicit statement that draws attention to the linguistic incorrectness of an utterance).
    Explicit message reaction (a correction or other explicit statement that draws attention to the factual incorrectness of an utterance).
  V. Incorporation of preceding utterances
    To allow coding for a limited selection of reactions to preceding utterances, six categories have been established.
    1. Correction: Correction of previous utterance/s.
    2. Repetition: Full or partial repetition of previous utterance/s.

3. Paraphrase: Completion and/or reformulation of previous utterance/s.
4. Comment: Positive or negative comment (not correction) on previous utterance/s.
5. Expansion: Extension of the content of preceding utterance/s through the addition of related information.
6. Clarification request: Request for clarification of preceding utterance/s.
7. Elaboration request: Request for further information related to the subject matter of the preceding utterance/s.

VI. Discourse initiation

This feature measures the frequency of self-initiated turns (spontaneously initiated talk) by students.

VII. Relative restriction of linguistic form

Two categories have been proposed to examine the degree of restriction placed on student talk:

1. Restricted: The production or manipulation of one specific form is expected, as in a transformation or substitution drill.
2. Unrestricted: There is no expectation of any particular linguistic form, as in free conversation, oral reports, or personal diary writing.

6 Process-product research on second language learning in classrooms

Patsy M. Lightbown

Doing research on how instructional variation affects learning in class-room settings is one of the most frustrating endeavors known. When the classroom setting is one in which a second language is being taught and learned, the researcher is immediately faced with a major theoretical problem: There is little agreement among theorists about the relationship between the actual samples of the language that learners are exposed to (whether in or out of classrooms) and the rules and systems that eventually characterize their knowledge of the language (see White 1985b). Beyond this very fundamental theoretical controversy, all the uncertainty associated with educational research must be added: the impossibility of identifying comparable control groups or ensuring random selection for treatment groups; the influence of unmeasured variables such as momentary motivation and attentiveness; the problem of knowing what happens in the classroom environment when no observer is present; the fact that in second language situations, learning continues outside the classroom.

Some classroom-centered research is done by the blissfully uninformed. The researcher carefully counts the occurrences of some seemingly interesting phenomenon in one teacher's speech or behavior and compares it to that of another teacher and confidently infers that any differences in student performance are related to these observed teacher behaviors. Indeed, some researchers do not even go so far as the second step (correlating some instructional difference with differences in outcome). They go directly from observation to recommendation, having concluded in advance that more (or less) error correction, more (or less) simplified syntax, more (or fewer) information questions facilitate learning. For researchers who are aware of the pitfalls at every step, it takes courage, commitment, and a great tolerance for ambiguity to pursue classroom-centered research. Those who do so with this knowledge are convinced that something as important as finding research evidence which can lead eventually to the improvement of second language instruction cannot be abandoned simply because it is so difficult.

The classroom-centered research carried out within the Development of Bilingual Proficiency project – not only the work reported in Volume

II of the final report (Harley, Allen, Cummins, and Swain 1987), but in student theses and published papers as well – has been done by researchers who are sensitive to all the ways in which Murphy's law can apply to such studies. The reports almost always acknowledge threats to validity, problems of generalizability, and the tentativeness of the conclusions. The research ranks among the very best studies of the effects on learning of what actually goes on in second language classrooms, and many researchers have benefited greatly from the ideas and procedures developed here.

In this discussion paper, I will restrict my focus to the four chapters in Volume II of the DBP final report: the Allen, Fröhlich, and Spada report on the development and validation of the COLT observation scheme; the Allen, Carroll, Burtis, and Gaudino study of core French; the Swain and Carroll observation study of French immersion; and the Harley experimental study of French immersion. The four studies are summarized in Chapter 5 of this volume.

The four studies reported in Volume II represent the three stages in research in teaching effectiveness outlined by Rosenshine and Furst (1972:122):

1. Development of procedures for describing teaching in a quantitative manner
2. Correlational studies in which the descriptive variables are related to measures of student growth
3. Experimental studies in which the significant variables obtained in the correlational study are tested in a more controlled situation

The first step is exemplified by the first treatment study, the development and validation of the COLT (communicative orientation of language teaching) observation scheme. Characterizing classroom interaction is not a straightforward exercise, and the range of variables one might choose to describe is very great. The COLT scheme, significantly, starts from a theoretical perspective that makes possible predictions about the characteristics which will distinguish classrooms from each other in ways that will make a difference in learner outcomes. From the outset, however, it was intended that the COLT would eventually be used in studies which combined the study of learner outcomes with systematic observation of classroom interaction. In this way the development of COLT differed from that of some classroom observation schemes developed on the assumption that we already knew what was good for learners, and that the observation schemes would make it possible to see which teachers and classrooms were providing these advantageous features to a greater or lesser degree. Such schemes tended to be used for teacher training rather than in process/product research, and they stopped at stage 1 of the teacher effectiveness research loop proposed by Rosenshine and Furst.

COLT was developed at a time when attitudes toward communicative language teaching (CLT) had hit a very high peak – or to put it another way – when CLT had reached a point high enough that it became a fine target to be knocked down by the inevitable sticks and stones of criticism. Even though COLT was based on the hypothesis that CLT would be an improvement over traditional teaching approaches, the COLT research itself has provided some of those sticks and stones which, if properly assembled, may be used to rebuild a higher target for future constructive criticism.

The core French observation study

As described in Chapter 5, the grade 11 core French study is a process/product study of eight classes in which students received French instruction for about one hour a day. Classes were chosen for detailed observation (on the basis of consultation with school board personnel and preliminary observation) to represent a range of classroom interaction types from analytic to experiential. The initial selection and labeling create something of a problem in terminology. That is, the classes being observed and compared are, at the outset, labeled as experiential (E) and analytic (A) on the basis of information obtained prior to beginning the detailed observation study. Results of the detailed study make it clear that, although the labels are partly confirmed by the summed COLT scores, only a few features distinguish E classes from A classes, and furthermore, that the differences are not always in the predicted direction.

For example, although class 8 rather than class 1 is grouped with class 4 as representing the extreme analytic end of the experiential-analytic continuum, classes 1 and 8 had virtually identical cumulative COLT scores (356 for class 8; 358 for class 1 – see Chapter 5, Table 5.1). A slightly less arbitrary decision might have combined classes 1 and 4 as the most analytic, or concluded that, as there was no difference between 8 and 1, both classes could have been retained in the analytic group. Such a decision would appear to be amply motivated by results such as the following: class 1 is more like class 4 than is class 8 on focus on form, a variable that would appear to merit a stronger weighting than some other variables – for example, topic selection by teacher. That is, even if the cumulative scores are virtually the same, form focus seems to be more likely to be a truly distinguishing feature than topic selection.

Furthermore, it is disconcerting that one of the two E classes spends virtually as much time on form focus as the most extreme A class. For this E class, almost two-thirds of observed class time is spent focused on form. For two of the three extreme A classes, the figure is about 70 percent. Although these issues are acknowledged and numerous discussions are devoted to showing how other classroom variables do show differences in the predicted direction, one remains troubled by the thought of labeling as experiential a class in which two-thirds of teacher-student interaction is focused on language form.[1]

The feeling of disquiet continues when we learn that there were in learner outcomes (posttest scores) few significant differences between E classes and the most extremely analytic of the A classes. The difference between A and E classes on the written multiple-choice grammar test is indeed significant, but the classes were different on only one subtest, and one may well ask whether the difference is meaningful. There were two other differences: on the subtests of the written sociolinguistic measures.

The core French study serves most of all to raise the question of whether statistically significant differences are pedagogically significant. As the authors themselves say, in reality, "[t]he most striking aspect of the results...is the extent to which Groups A/A* and E are indistinguishable" (Allen, Carroll, Burtis, and Gaudino 1987:86). Differences, even those posttest results sufficiently consistent to lead to statistical significance, show one group of students outperforming another group on three of eleven measures, and that by a matter of three or four percentage points on scores in the general vicinity of 50 to 60 percent. This suggests that it is on the *similarity* that one should focus and for which one should seek explanations. One explanation of the findings is that in one hour a day at the end of many years of core French instruction, progress may be minimal or at least difficult to measure. The between-group differences on the posttest scores are generally of the same magnitude as the pretest/posttest differences within groups. Indeed, on some measures, there is a decline from pretest to posttest scores.

In the light of such minimal differences between analytic and experiential classes – on both observed classroom interaction and posttest results – one is resistant to statements, even those couched as suggestions, such as "a relatively strong analytic focus may lead to a certain level of mastery of grammar which is not replicated by a more experiential approach" (Allen, Carroll, Burtis, and Gaudino 1987:87).

It is important to point out that the researchers do not limit their analyses to comparisons between the pre-identified E and A classes or to analyses based on single cumulative scores. Further analysis is based

---

1 During the symposium it became apparent that much of the form-focused discussion in this class was actually in the context of meaningful discussion of form/function relationships, rather than decontextualized exercises on form out of a meaningful context. As Nina Spada pointed out in the discussion, the original COLT does provide for such combination of categories and it's not clear why, in this study, the combination of categories is not used.

on correlations between individual COLT categories and posttest performance by all classes. These correlations are clearly much more interesting because they are based on systematic observation rather than on a priori classification. Some problems of interpretation do arise, however. For example, it is reported that "focus on form tends to be positively related to improvement, while the discussion of general topics with limited and broad reference tends to be detrimental" (Allen, Carroll, Burtis, and Gaudino 1987:85). In contrast, a further comparison shows positive correlations between both oral and written measures of proficiency and teachers' and students' reaction to message (as opposed to reaction to code). It is difficult to imagine that reaction to message would be a principal feature in focus on code classes as opposed to classes where there are discussions of general topics.

Also of concern is the fact that, in general, little or no mention is made of the possible interaction between individual learner variables and classroom interaction variables. That is, an instructional program that meets the needs of one group or individual may fail to do so for another (Strong 1983; Wong Fillmore 1985). Thus inferences about the application of findings are particularly questionable.

The immersion observation study

In the immersion observation study, a number of issues that have grown out of previous research on learning in immersion classes are examined in light of observations of grade 3 and grade 6 immersion classes. This chapter, by Swain and Carroll, is an exploratory study of classroom interaction looking at four issues: vocabulary instruction, the use of the *vous/tu* distinction, the frequency and amount of student talk, and the treatment of error. The three papers included as appendixes are Harley's (1985) overview of immersion students' strengths and weaknesses in French and a proposal for an experimental study, Swain and Lapkin's (in press) study of the sociolinguistic performance of immersion students in secondary school, and Swain's (1988) paper on the apparent limitations of content or subject matter teaching as language teaching.

The exploratory study responds to the often-heard complaint that we don't really know what goes on in immersion classes, and while there certainly have been studies dealing with some aspects of immersion classroom interaction (e.g., Chaudron's 1977 study of teachers' reaction to error, and the COLT development and validation study by Allen, Fröhlich, and Spada 1987), this is both the most comprehensive and the most focused. It is comprehensive because it is based on reasonably good samples of instruction at two grade levels and includes observation of

English instruction, permitting important comparisons. It is focused in the sense that four areas are selected for intense scrutiny.

Results of the exploratory study certainly show the source of Swain's claim that immersion students get little practice in speaking, and confirm Chaudron's earlier finding that error correction is meaning-based and quite unsystematic. The *tu/vous* study offers an explanation for students' unfamiliarity with the formal use of *vous:* they almost never hear it.[2] The vocabulary study appears to show that teachers rarely take advantage of opportunities to equip students with certain kinds of strategies that would permit them to refine and expand vocabulary on their own. Swain and Carroll conclude with the recommendation that immersion teachers be involved in experimental studies seeking to test some of the hypotheses generated by this and other observation studies. This, in a sense, is what the experimental study of French immersion does.

Functional grammar in French immersion

Harley's experimental study of French immersion did not grow out of the observation and correlation studies in an absolutely direct way. That is, there was no specific evidence from the previous observation and correlation studies that students who received more functional practice in the past tense forms of French verbs were more accurate in using these verbs than those who received less. There was, rather, evidence of a relative rarity of past tense forms in the classroom language that learners heard and an inference that more focused exposure to these verb forms could improve performance.

In the experimental study, the contrasting use of the French past tense forms, passé composé and imparfait, is investigated. This aspect is a favored domain for an experimental study not only because it is an area of known weakness, but also, as noted above, because classroom observation data show that these forms are not as frequent in the input as

---

2 An anecdote that gives an example of immersion students' problems with making the *tu/vous* distinction comes from one of my sons. He had three years of French schooling, then switched to an English school with extended French in grades 4 and 5 and full immersion in grade 6. In grade 7 (a partial immersion follow-up year) he was preparing for a test on the imperative. He was giving me an example of what he might say in the oral component of the test: "Eh bien, Monsieur, prenez la rue Ste. Catherine jusqu'à la rue Berri. Puis tourne à droite et continue..." I interrupted, "Don't you mean *tournez, continuez?*" "No, he said, *"tournez* and *continuez,* that's *vous."* "Right," I said, "aren't you using vous?" "No," he said, "this is the imperative. *Vous* is *plusieurs personnes."* You may be assured that he quickly got a thoroughly metalinguistic explanation of the use of *vous* as a politeness marker.

might be expected – even in contexts such as a social studies or history lesson (Harley 1989c; Swain 1988). There seemed good reason to assume that a series of lessons designed to focus on these verb forms in meaningful contexts would be useful. The results of the experiment were encouraging in the immediate posttesting, but the delayed posttesting showed no differences between students who received the special lessons and those who did not. Why didn't the experimental program "work" over the longer term? That is, why didn't the students receiving the special materials get better and stay better than the comparison groups on the past tense forms?

It has been suggested (by Manfred Pienemann,[3] if not by others) that if these verb forms are part of a developmental continuum, the lack of long-term effect of the experimental teaching program on learners' performance is merely a quantitative quibble. That is, if learners *ever* show signs of using the passé composé and imparfait, then absence of these forms in many obligatory contexts is simply a matter of gaps (Pienemann's term) within a developmental stage where the simple presence of a form entitles it to be called acquired. If these forms are not part of a developmental continuum but are instead a variational feature, they should be more amenable to instruction but will continue to be supplied with variable accuracy according to the situation in which the speaker is performing or the speaker's personal orientation to the target language and its speakers. Although some morphological features of German and English have been tentatively assigned places on a developmental continuum, there is no research regarding where the passé composé/imparfait contrast would be placed on a French developmental continuum. (See Pienemann 1985 for discussion of developmental and variational continua.)

In addition to Pienemann's (and perhaps – as Harley suggests – Krashen's) developmental explanations, there are several possible explanations which Harley points to: the fact that comparison groups also got instruction that focused on French past tense forms; the relatively small amount of time (less than 12 hours over eight weeks) actually spent on the experimental materials; the manner in which the materials were actually used by the teachers. It has occurred to me – as to others perhaps as well – that the focused instruction was, in fact, not focused enough and that students missed the point of the instruction. Certainly, the experimental study is based on a meaning-based, nonexplicit approach to language teaching. On the other hand, if teachers and students had been aware of the exact purpose of the

---

3 At the 1987 AILA congress in Sydney, Australia, following Harley's presentation of her results.

study, there would have been considerable risk of their engaging in some teaching techniques that overemphasized the past forms of French verbs while neglecting other important content. We know that intensive drill on a form can lead to relatively long-term changes in performance but may not reflect a genuine integration of the form into the learners' interlanguage system (see, e.g., Lightbown 1983). Further, their behavior might have been so atypical of their usual teaching practice as to render any recommendations or conclusions invalid. Nevertheless, in a future study, ensuring more explicit metalinguistic teaching might be worthwhile.

There is increasing evidence that, even when it is amply available, learners can fail to see the disconfirming evidence in the input. This is true not only of learners at a too early developmental stage to use certain information, but also of advanced learners who have achieved fluency and, as Carlos Yorio suggested in his comments at this symposium, successful comprehensible output. In their widely quoted article, Higgs and Clifford (1982) argue that learners who are communicatively successful early in their second language acquisition (SLA) may not progress to accurate use of language. Clearly this suggests that, under certain conditions, learners will need more explicit guidance. Recent articles by Lydia White (1985a, 1987b), Jacquelyn Schachter (1985), Robert Bley-Vroman (1986), and others explore some theoretical bases for determining where learners may need explicit guidance, and Michael Long has made some suggestions about how such guidance might be provided (Long 1988).

Moreover, Swain (1985) refers not only to evidence from the large-scale proficiency study on immersion (see Chapter 1), but also to examples from research by VanPatten (1985) which show that language learners who are focusing on meaning may not be able to attend to form at the same time.[4] This would be in keeping with a cognitive psychological orientation to language learning which suggests that learners have limitations on the number of "controlled" operations they can engage in (see McLaughlin 1987 for discussion). If understanding meaning requires "processing space," then linguistic forms cannot be focused on (or attended to or noticed) at the same time. Thus both classroom evi-

---

4 Again a confirming anecdote from one of my children, showing the extent to which what Swain and Carroll (1987:220) refer to as "overwhelming graphic, phonetic, morphological, and semantic information" may be missed. My son recently read an adventure novel in French about two boys and a karate master. Only when I was proofreading his final report on the book did I discover that one of "les garçons" was a girl. A twelve-year-old boy's life experience of same-sex friends was more powerful than scores of feminine pronouns, adjective agreements, and even one – slightly ambiguous – illustration.

dence and theoretical underpinning suggest the need to include form-focused teaching as part of a program for language learning – even one based largely or principally on content instruction.

Conclusion

We all seem to feel the need to restore form-based instruction and error correction as part of the language teaching/learning context. But it is very important to acknowledge that our research to date shows only that learners who don't get it tend to plateau or fossilize or, in any event, fail to reach mastery of the language. We do not have research evidence to show convincingly that those who *do* get it *do* reach mastery. That research remains to be done. (Studies such as Carroll 1975 and Long 1983 address this issue only indirectly and do not deal with mastery, only with relative success.)

We must not forget how hard we worked to convince teachers to try CLT and, if it has now turned out that in some contexts CLT has been interpreted as rather too extreme a rejection of *any* form-based teaching, we might do well to proceed with caution when we seek to restore what we think is an equilibrium between form-based and meaning-based instruction. I hope we won't be so successful as to tip the balance too far in the other direction. If we were not convinced by the experience of seeing the results of years of exclusively grammar-translation teaching, SLA research has surely taught us that not everything can be taught or corrected on a convenient schedule of instruction. And, although I fear this may be a most unpopular thing to say, I don't believe that all learners have or should have as their objective full mastery of the target language. I think that CLT (including immersion) offers a chance for fluency to learners who, under the old analytic systems, got neither fluency nor accuracy.

What I'm suggesting is that we must warn constantly against the misinterpretation of some of the COLT research and related studies. There is nothing in any of this research to suggest that a return to teaching which is *principally* form-based, teacher-centered, metalinguistic, and decontextualized will be better than teaching which is *principally* meaning-based, learner-centered, experiential, and contextualized.

We know that language acquisition, if it is to be successful, takes thousands of hours of contact, interactive use, and – for learners with literacy and metalinguistic knowledge in their first language – study. French immersion, extended French, intensive courses, and exchange programs are successful mainly because they provide more time than traditional courses, and do so in contexts where learners' attention can be engaged and held for extended periods. To say that this may not be enough is not to say that it is not necessary. Conversely, one cannot conclude that analytic teaching is enough on the basis of studies showing that within contexts where both experiential and analytic teaching and learning opportunities exist, there is an advantage to learners who receive a greater proportion of analytic instruction.

It is noteworthy that, just as research in immersion, hailed by Krashen and others as the ultimate in communicative language teaching, is turning its attention to the necessity for form-focused activity *within* a communicatively oriented program, ESL teaching in Quebec, particularly at the elementary level, is in the throes of a reorientation toward communicative language teaching, with a virtually exclusive focus on meaning and a high tolerance for error, at least in the elementary school programs. For those schools – by far the majority – where students get less than two hours a week of English starting in grade 4, such an approach may be ideal. It can serve to encourage students to try to speak and understand so that, when they come in contact with English outside school, they will have enough confidence to take advantage of the opportunity to continue learning. In programs where students have more time and more meaningful contact with the language, more form-focused instruction may be both necessary and desirable.

In my own research in Quebec (with Nina Spada, one of the developers of COLT, as co-investigator), we are following the development of English by francophone students in grade 5 or 6 who are receiving five months of intensive all-day instruction in English (Spada and Lightbown 1989). The programs we are observing follow the communicative language teaching approach very closely, and there is very little explicit language teaching. Planned, systematic grammar teaching is virtually nonexistent. When there is form focus, the focus is overwhelmingly on the vocabulary necessary for a particular thematic content unit. Correction of student errors in most classes is extremely rare. Preliminary results from our ongoing research suggest that students develop high levels of fluency, a rich vocabulary, and good discourse skills. However, their accuracy on a number of features leaves rather a lot to be desired. What explanations for the results might be suggested by the findings of the classroom treatment studies?

The DBP treatment studies all appear to show that whether students have many hours of contact with the language (as in immersion) or few hours (as in core French), it is important that some attention be given to teaching the language itself, to providing some formal, analytic teaching that can help students see where their use of the target language differs from that of native speakers. Such findings tend to be supported by other research, both empirical and theoretical, that in the absence of such guided instruction, learners may develop fossilized interlanguage when they become able to communicate fairly successfully. I agree with

Christina Paulston, who said at the DBP symposium, "It's time to get the baby back." But I don't think there's any evidence, here or in any other research I've seen, to suggest that, to get the baby back, we also have to take the bath water.

7 Analysis and experience as variables in second language pedagogy

H. H. Stern

The two concepts in the title of this discussion paper, experience and analysis, present in my view the common theme of the treatment studies in the DBP project (see Chapter 5). The central problems are: Which of these two concepts is more important for proficiency development? How should they manifest themselves? What is the most effective relationship between them? The DBP researchers discuss these issues and conclude:

> The analytic focus and the experiential focus may be complementary, and... they may provide essential support for one another in the L2 classroom. (Chapter 5:77)

The COLT studies (Allen, Fröhlich, and Spada 1987; Allen, Carroll, Burtis, and Gaudino 1987) deal directly with the relationship between analytic and experiential activities. The two immersion studies (Harley 1989b; Swain and Carroll 1987) also deal with this issue, but perhaps more indirectly. They seem to be based on the assumption that immersion is largely experiential anyway, and that it is now timely to pay more attention to vocabulary, grammar errors, and other aspects of the immersion student's proficiency development. The broader issues of content teaching and language teaching in immersion programs are discussed in more general terms in Harley (1989b) and Swain (1988). The immersion experimental study questions Krashen's theoretical position that we should avoid grammar teaching of any kind, and deliberately experiments with analytic materials which "are attuned as closely as possible to the primarily experiential focus of an immersion program" (Harley 1989b).

By dealing directly or indirectly with the analysis-experience option, I believe the DBP project is making a significant contribution to one of the major issues in pedagogy today. I do not think that the treatment studies have resolved the issue, nor do the researchers claim they have, but they have dealt with it from a number of interesting perspectives and have laid a good foundation for further work on this question.

Trends of development

As Allen et al. point out (Chapter 5), the analysis-experience issue has gradually come to the fore in second language teaching during the past twenty years or so, until today it has become one of the key issues of pedagogy. Language teaching methods in the past have always been mainly analytic, in the sense that they have based themselves on some kind of analysis of the language, with an emphasis on grammar. As recent debates on syllabus design have shown, most language teaching syllabuses are grammatical: Grammar is the organizing principle, whether the method of teaching is referred to as grammar-translation, audiolingualism, the cognitive approach, or whatever. A great deal of L2 classroom practice is also analytic, in that one grammatical feature after another is practiced through drills and exercises.

Systematic objections to analytic techniques as the main standby of language teaching were raised in the mid–1960s by several language educators, ranging from Newmark and Reibel (1968), Jakobovits (1968, 1972), Macnamara (1973) to Krashen and Terrell (1983) and Krashen (1984). Since the early 1970s, there has been increasing consciousness of the need to complement or substitute conventional language teaching and its grammatical-analytic drill techniques with communicative-experiential procedures or some form of transition to natural language use. Communication, communicative competence as an objective, or communicative teaching, as it became increasingly known, was adumbrated in several well-known articles and studies such as Paulston (1970), Rivers (1972), and Savignon (1972).

The immersion movement further strengthened the belief in communicative-experiential teaching by its emphasis on content and "message-oriented" teaching, as Dodson (1978) called it, in contrast to "medium-oriented" (analytic) approaches. Krashen's SLA theory lent additional support to an experiential communicative orientation by providing concepts and a terminology, and by boldly claiming the absolute superiority of experiential procedures over the older analytic approaches. Provided the subject matter input is comprehensible, so Krashen has argued, "subject-matter teaching *is* language teaching" and *that* is "what immersion has taught us" (Krashen 1984:62). Interestingly enough, this view is echoed and countered in Swain (1988) where she warns: "Typical content teaching is not necessarily good second language teaching."

From the late 1970s until now, the interest in communicative language teaching has grown and spread. Communication or communicative competence has come to be viewed as the main objective of language teaching; at the same time, communication has increasingly been seen as the instrument, the method, or the way of teaching. Simultaneously with this growing and somewhat uncritical acceptance of communicative teaching, however, a number of voices of caution and criticism have begun to be heard. Among the immersion researchers, there have for several years been some, particularly among the Modern Language Centre team, who have drawn attention to both the positive and negative aspects of proficiency development in immersion students. These include earlier studies by Harley and Swain (e.g., 1978, 1984) and Harley (e.g., 1984). The DBP immersion treatment studies continue these previous efforts to identify problem areas in the development of the proficiency of immersion classes. The experimental study, too, builds on this critical appraisal of immersion classes and attempts to find a rational solution for one such problem area.

A few applied linguists have taken a much more negative view of communicative teaching in general (Higgs and Clifford 1982; Swan 1985) and in Canada of immersion education (Bibeau 1984). Higgs and Clifford, for example, regard the early push toward communication as premature and unproductive in the long run, and Bibeau takes a skeptical view of immersion; in his opinion, the immersion solution is too drastic a measure for the meager results in language proficiency it yields. He believes much better results could be achieved by a different pattern of planning second language education. Swan questions many of the pretensions of communicative teaching and offers a very salutary dose of skepticism about some of the concepts and principles that underlie it.

Such, then, is the context in which the treatment studies deal with the analytic-experiential question. Besides the different strands of opinion for or against experiential teaching that have to be taken into consideration, we should also take note of three main problems of communicative-experiential teaching that have become crystallized since the early 1980s.

Three problem areas of experiential teaching

The first question is how a communicative methodology becomes reality in the classroom. Teachers are often vague and confused about communicative language teaching. They would like to implement it but don't know how to, or they are not clear whether the kind of teaching they are doing is communicative or not. The question of classroom implementation has prompted a very impressive classroom observation study in Britain (Mitchell et al. 1981), which attempted to find out how in fact communicative teaching is being realized. This study has quite rightly influenced the design of COLT, although COLT has gone much further in the definition of the characteristics of communicative teaching than the British study did. But the uncertainty about how to pinpoint communicative teaching has been a concern until today. Of the many efforts that have been made to state precisely what features make up communicative teaching, COLT is the most comprehensive, the most detailed, and the clearest. The publication of the earlier COLT studies (e.g., Allen, Fröhlich, and Spada 1984) has already been very helpful to students of communicative language teaching. The COLT studies in the DBP project make a valuable contribution to sorting out the distinction between a more analytic and a more communicative approach in language classes.

The second issue, which has also contributed to this uncertainty, arises from the origins of communicative teaching. Its development has been strongly influenced by the mixing of two different concepts of communicative teaching: One is teaching *about* communication (i.e., the analysis of communication through the study of speech acts, discourse analysis, and sociolinguistics). This analytic treatment of communication derives mainly from the work of European linguists such as Widdowson, Wilkins, Brumfit, and others, and the Council of Europe project. The other is the concept of communicative teaching as teaching *through* communication by involving the learner as a participant. In North America this approach is mainly represented by Savignon and Krashen and the advocates of immersion education; in Britain, Candlin and Breen have adopted this point of view.

That learning about communication and learning through communication are different, although they may well be complementary, has been pointed out repeatedly since the late seventies – for example, by Stern (1980) and also in Allen's well-known curriculum design model, which distinguished three components: structural-analytic, functional-analytic, and experiential (Allen 1983).[1] In spite of this well-recognized differentiation, the confusion of these two approaches to communicative teaching (functional-analytic and experiential) persists.[2] As we shall see below, even within the DBP treatment studies, we find indications of some confusion between these two ways of dealing with communication.

A third issue has been the problem of balance and of the relationships between experiential and analytic teaching. Can language teaching perhaps dispense with analytic teaching and become entirely experiential? Are analytic procedures unnecessary or even harmful? I think one can interpret Krashen's theory as a positive answer to both questions, with the further addition that analytic teaching, in Krashen's view, is superfluous because it never leads to an intuitive, acquisition-type command

1 This model is specifically referred to in the experimental study (Harley 1989b) as guiding its curriculum approach.
2 In order to avoid confusion in terminology, it has become customary to refer to language learning *through* communication as experiential and to reserve the term functional for the analysis of communication as it occurs in discourse analysis or the teaching of speech acts (notions and functions).

of a language. This extreme position has not been accepted by other theorists, who have operated with combinations of analytic and experiential approaches and believe there is a possibility of a fruitful interplay. The question for this group of applied linguists is one of finding a balance between the analytic and the experiential, of discovering productive ways of combining the two approaches, and of integrating the experiential with the analytic. This is also the position that not only the COLT studies, but all the DBP treatment studies seem to adopt. They provide varied data and discussion on this issue, and this is why they should be so useful for coming to grips with it.

The conceptual distinction between analytic and experiential strategies

In order to appreciate the contribution of the various studies, it may be helpful to make clear the conceptual distinction between the analytic and the experiential orientations.

The analytic strategy

THE RANGE OF ANALYTIC TECHNIQUES

Analytic teaching is very familiar, but it is not clearly formulated. In the treatment studies too, the views about it are implicit or stated in asides rather than being specifically defined. The analytic approach does not have the excitement of novelty that is offered by the experiential or the communicative approach. Hence we tend to be negative or at least ambivalent about it. COLT as a scheme, for example, was designed to identify the characteristics of communicative teaching, while those of noncommunicative analytic teaching were more or less taken for granted. This ambivalence toward the analytic is also noticeable in other DBP treatment studies.[3]

Because analytic teaching is well established, it is also for many teachers the natural way of teaching, including its good and bad features. Critics of analytic teaching have usually focused on its negative qualities

---

3 For example, we read in Swain (1988) that for language production, we need "syntactic and morphological knowledge." This means the teacher should "help learners undertake the sort of form-function analysis needed to be effective communicators in their second language," unquestioningly a demand for functional-analytic teaching. This is hedged in by a remark that shows clearly the ambivalence we so often find toward analytic procedures: "This does *not* imply teaching rules, although it may well be an effective strategy for some aspects of language and for some learners."

and have tended to dismiss it as teaching with incomprehensible grammar rules, senseless exercises, and boring drills. If we want to consider the analytic strategy as equivalent to an experiential one, we have to be clear about what its essential attributes are and not mix them up with accidental features associated with it because of its historical development. It is also important that we do not compare experiential teaching at its best with analytic teaching at its worst. In other words, we will have to make a qualitative distinction between productive and unproductive analytic procedures.

The analytic strategy covers a very wide range of teaching-learning techniques designed to promote the learning of the L2 outside a situation of actual use. The learner stands away, so to speak, from the language in use, examines it, or rehearses and practices it in some way. The language item or usage, presented and practiced through an analytic technique, makes no pretense of being real communication. Analytic techniques point to, identify, observe, explain, compare, illustrate, and practice an L2 feature or an aspect of language use. The training of any of the four skills or a component of the four skills can also be subsumed under the analytic strategy. Through the analytic strategy, the learner is enabled to focus on the code.

The range of analytic techniques can be summarized in terms of the main divisions of linguistic analysis: phonology, morphology, syntax, lexis, semantics, discourse, and sociolinguistics. The first four cover the structural-analytic component and the last three the functional-analytic component of Allen's (1983) curriculum scheme. The analytic strategy is not confined to grammar; it includes grammar teaching, but also refers to any other aspect of the language that can be identified and isolated, phonological, lexical, semantic, discoursal, and sociolinguistic.[4] It is therefore rather surprising to find that the functional-analytic aspects in the COLT scheme appear under the experiential heading and not under the analytic one.[5]

---

4 COLT, for example, divides the explicit focus on language into form (grammar, vocabulary, and pronunciation), function (illocutionary acts such as requesting, apologizing, and explaining), discourse (cohesion and coherence), and sociolinguistics (appropriateness to particular social contexts) (Allen, Fröhlich, and Spada 1987:27–28).

5 See, for example, the list of experiential activities (Allen, Carroll, Burtis, and Gaudino 1987:68) which includes such functional-analytic activities as "students are taught aspects of paragraph and text structure." See also Table 11, p. 115 (experiential activities): items 5 (Students were taught aspects of paragraph or text structure) or 6 (Students were taught the social and cultural rules how to make polite requests, etc.) should be classed as analytic rather than experiential, and item 4 (Students listened to authentic spoken French material) might be either, depending on how the spoken text is treated. If it is treated within a context as subject matter, it would be experiential; if it is treated as text to be studied for its vocabulary or

The four sections of the immersion observation study are analytic: the first focuses on vocabulary instruction; the second, on a sociolinguistic point (the *tu/vous* distinction); the third, on discourse length; and the fourth, on the treatment of grammatical errors. The immersion experimental study too has an analytic theme – the distinction between two French past tenses.

FEATURES OF THE ANALYTIC STRATEGY

The most obvious characterization of an analytic approach to language teaching and learning is that it is an approach to the language as an object of study and practice. In detail, this involves the following:

1. The analytic strategy focuses on specific language features and by isolating them makes them salient for the learner. These include features that might otherwise be overlooked, like pronouns, word order, affixes, intonation patterns, or sociolinguistic distinctions. The immersion studies, as we just noted, are especially geared to observations on lexical, grammatical, and sociolinguistic features. The experimental study is specifically concerned with one grammaticosemantic aspect, the difference in function of the imparfait and the passé composé tenses.

2. An analytic strategy of necessity decontextualizes linguistic features. In the current communicatively oriented literature there is a great deal of emphasis on "language in context" (Omaggio 1986), but an essential feature of language analysis is to decontextualize and of course also recontextualize language features.

3. As objects of study, language items are examined, observed, explained, compared, and put into some order within a system. Language rules are a consequence of the lawfulness of languages.[6]

4. A further characteristic of an analytic strategy is that it provides an opportunity for the learner to come to grips with a specific language feature through practice. The mode of practice has somewhat changed over time, but practice of language features or of language skill aspects (listening practice, reading practice, and so on) have been a mainstay of the analytic strategy. They offer something we should not despise, the

grammatical or stylistic features, it is analytic. Table 12, no. 5 (listening to extended spoken text) might also be either, depending on how students listen to it.

6 For example, the lexical section of the immersion observation study advocates a much more systematic approach to word study in the immersion program. It proposes: "The idea would be to explicitly draw the learner's attention to the rule-governed nature of this relationship" (Swain and Carroll 1987:218), and with regard to sociolinguistic rules, Swain and Lapkin (in press) make this suggestion: "[the] solution...is that teachers are needed to provide both sociolinguistic rules *and* examples of language used in a variety of contexts."

opportunity to try out a language feature safely outside the pressure of a real communicative situation.

5. A final feature of an analytic strategy is that it pays attention to accuracy and error correction to a degree regarded as appropriate for a given group of learners. There are no absolutes in this, because the demands of correctness depend on the program and the needs or aspirations of the learners.

PROBLEMS OF ANALYTIC TEACHING

The problems that an analytic strategy presents are familiar, because they have brought about the critique as well as the move to experiential teaching as an alternative. Let us briefly remind ourselves what they are:

1. Dealing with language items one by one in isolation and out of context brings with it the danger of fragmentation. The language may not come together as a coherent whole in the mind of the learner. I have previously referred to this phenomenon as the "Humpty Dumpty effect" (Stern 1980, 1983).

2. It has been argued against any systematic ordering of language instruction (for example, by Macnamara 1972) that languages are too complex for the rule system ever to be learned by conscious techniques of study and practice. Moreover, it is impossible to arrange the rule system in any simple logical order. Finally, there are many aspects which are not yet understood. Hence a language as a system can never be fully learned. These arguments merely draw attention to the limitations of an analytic approach, and they suggest that an experiential strategy should complement it, because it deals with a language globally. However, these limitations are no reason why one should not make best use of the order and system that can be managed by the learner and that can be useful to the development of proficiency.

3. A consequence of language complexity is that certain aspects tend to be overstressed or underrepresented. In the past, for example, language educators attributed undue importance to phonetics. As the COLT studies, the immersion observation study, and the experimental study indicate, lexical and functional (including sociolinguistic) features are underrepresented in the classroom today.[7]

4. As Lightbown (1985) has rightly pointed out, practice does not

---

7 I question, however, whether the immersion studies do not make too much of the sociolinguistic competence aspect. As long as the immersion students have problems of the kind listed in the error treatment study, is it not unwise to make too much of the sociolinguistic niceties in distinguishing a formal letter and a note, for example? (Swain's articles have some sound and sobering thoughts on the "new toy" effect).

necessarily make perfect. The uncritical belief of earlier methodologies in massive practice techniques is no longer held. The limitations of conventional practice tasks have led to a critical reassessment of drills, the notion of mechanical training, methods of repetition, and other types of exercises. The kind of careful choice of different tasks, as it occurred in the immersion experimental study, is in line with such a reappraisal.[8]

5. The most severe criticism leveled against the analytic strategy is the common observation that what has been learned in the language class through conventional practice techniques does not automatically transfer to actual language use in real life settings. The need to take care of this transition from specific classroom practice to informal use has led to proposals for meaningful and communicative drills (Paulston 1970), for an increased skill-using emphasis (Rivers 1972), and for a communicative orientation for exercises (Gunterman and Phillips 1981). The kinds of tasks we find in the immersion experimental study are motivated by similar considerations.

What I have tried to do in this characterization of the analytic strategy is to present its main features and its inherent problems. I have not presented it as the old-fashioned or traditional strategy. If we characterize it in such terms, then the analytic strategy becomes simply the ragbag for all undesirable or dated practices, contrasted with another strategy to which we allocate everything that is desirable and novel in language pedagogy, and which we call the communicative or experiential approach.

I think it is important to make a distinction between the principles of analytic teaching and analytic-type teaching as it actually occurs. I do not think this distinction is sufficiently clearly made in some of the treatment studies. For example, Allen et al. (1987) describe under analytic features typical audiolingual teaching as it had developed in the sixties, including features that are today considered pedagogically less sound than those listed under experiential. However, when in the conclusion the suggestion is made that analytic and experiential teaching should complement each other, this surely does not imply that *all* the analytic features should be cultivated. It is therefore important to distinguish what is inherent in the concept of analytic and differentiate it

8 This does not mean that all the tasks in the experimental study are equally appropriate. Some have obviously been more useful than others to bring home the distinction between the two French past tenses. Others obviously misfired: The students enjoyed the task but did not use any past tense as was intended by the designers. The documentation makes it possible, however, to evaluate each of the tasks and to assess its merit as an analytic or experiential activity.

from the accidental practices associated with the analytic strategy because of its historical development.

The experiential strategy

FEATURES OF THE EXPERIENTIAL STRATEGY

What characterizes the experiential strategy? As we have seen above, this has been worked out for us by the COLT studies. The following analysis has benefited from the COLT but deviates somewhat from it:

1. The first and perhaps foremost characteristic of an experiential strategy is that it focuses the activities of the language class on a substantive topic or theme which is not arbitrary or trivial, but motivated by identified educational or personal needs. Ideally the activities that take place in the classroom form part of a syllabus of experiential topics. Immersion classes provide ample examples of focus on content. In the immersion observation study (Swain and Carroll 1987), reference is made to several themes that were talked about in class: for example, the slave trade in a history class, and a discussion on the difference between malnutrition and starvation, presumably in a social studies context. The typical experiential class described by Allen, Carroll, Burtis, and Gaudino (1987) is engaged in a literary endeavor such as reading *Le Petit Prince,* but not from a language point of view: This novel "is read and discussed on many levels – literary, religious, philosophical, etc." (p. 69).[9]

2. As we have seen, the analytic teaching strategy operates through study and practice of the language, with the learner's attention focused on the language itself. Experiential activities are arranged in such a way as to engage the learner in some purposeful enterprise: projects, enquiries, games, problem-solving tasks, scenarios in which the focus of attention is the problem, project or task, planning it, carrying it into effect through different stages, and finally completing it satisfactorily. For example, the high-scoring experiential class in the core French observation study produces twice a year "a class magazine in which the best compositions and poems are published" (Allen, Carroll, Burtis, and Gaudino 1987:69). Any such task involves communication in planning, decision making, and execution. Consequently, language is involved, for example,

---

9 The content category is described in Allen, Fröhlich, and Spada (1987:28). The COLT scheme distinguishes narrow, limited, and broad range of reference. Unfortunately, COLT does not make a clear, specific distinction between the treatment of a topic as analytic or experiential. Presumably, the narrow- and limited-focus topics are to be used for language practice and are therefore analytic, and the broad-range topics are experiential, but in fact this is not always so.

in trying to understand the rules of a game, in deciding on a plan of action, or in jointly or singly carrying out a problem-solving task.

3. Experiential teaching creates conditions for real language use, and above all, true conversation. That is why Part II of COLT rightly focuses on the following characteristics of real talk: use of target language, information gap, sustained speech, reaction to message, incorporation of preceding utterances, discourse initiation, and relatively unrestricted use of linguistic forms. We should perhaps add to this characterization of real talk in experiential teaching the communicative use of all four skills. In an analytic approach these skills are often trained in relative isolation from real-life settings. On the other hand, they can form a natural part of a purposeful set of activities: giving a talk, listening to a recording, participating in a group discussion, reading a literary text, writing a report, a note, or a letter. The more these activities occur in a specified context, are related to clearly identified participants, and have a well-defined purpose, the more they meet the criteria of an experiential strategy. In this way we can distinguish the four skills as communicative or analytic activities.[10]

4. The experiential strategy encourages learners to make sense of written and spoken texts and to get meaning across in language production without worrying too much about absolute correctness. It has counteracted the slow, laborious, and self-conscious approach to the L2 that tries to be perfectly accurate in every respect. Critics of communicative teaching, such as Higgs and Clifford (1982), have accused followers of this strategy of encouraging fluency too early and arresting learners at too low a level of proficiency by not paying sufficient attention to accuracy. It is quite true that the experiential strategy has adopted the developmentally more optimistic belief that errors gradually disappear through rich and varied language experiences.

The evidence for this argument is still open. Provisionally, it seems

10 In the COLT studies the Type A (analytic) and Type E (experiential) classes were in fact distinguished by the following characteristics of the treatment of the four skills (see Allen, Carroll, Burtis, and Gaudino 1987:66–67 and tables): Type A: minimal written text, minimal utterance in spoken interaction, reaction to code rather than message, restricted choice of linguistic item; Type E: extended written text, sustained speech, reaction to message rather than code, topic expansion. One of the immersion studies is especially concerned with the sustained talk criterion in immersion classes. It attributes some of the linguistic weaknesses of immersion students to lack of opportunity for sustained talk in the immersion class. The study concludes that less than 15 percent of student turns are greater than a clause in length (Swain and Carroll 1987:232), and suggests that more opportunities for more sustained talk are needed for adequate proficiency development. It is on this score that the immersion studies find the "comprehensible input" hypothesis inadequate and recommend, as Swain has done repeatedly recently, more attention to output: "At least part of the content lesson needs to be substituted with activities which demand longer, more complex, and coherent language from the learners" (Swain 1988:81).

right to assume that an emphasis on meaning and fluency is beneficial and can be justified, provided it is matched by an equivalent attempt to develop accuracy through the analytic strategy. The specific function of the experiential strategy is to cultivate fluency and meaning and to downplay linguistic error. The problem presented by errors in experiential teaching is, quite justifiably, a serious concern for the treatment studies. It is explicitly discussed by Swain and Carroll (1987) and by Swain (in press). The study on error treatment notes the large number and variety of grammatical errors, not counting errors of pronunciation. The study also notes the absence of corrections or lack of consistency in correction. However, it concludes somewhat inconclusively simply by identifying error in a content-oriented program as a special problem.[11]

5. Social interaction is an important teaching strategy in its own right which is as relevant to the analytic strategy as it is to the communicative-experiential one. If the language class is meant to be a place where learners experiment with communication in the second language, it is particularly important to establish a social climate in which students are not afraid, inhibited, or aggressive. A good many communicative activities can best be done in a language class that operates with a socially flexible arrangement, including individualized work, pair work, and work in small groups. Whole-class, teacher-directed activities are not excluded, but for an experiential strategy to work, interpersonal relations should be more diversified.[12] While it is right to point out that communicative activities require a diversified social interaction, it is not inherent in the analytic strategy to have a different (teacher-whole class) arrangement. Therefore the inclusion of group activity under experiential and of whole-class activity under analytic (Allen, Carroll, Burtis, and

11 "In immersion classes the goal of language learning through content learning is paramount. This brings with it the question of when to correct, what to correct and how to correct.... These are questions of major pedagogical import that the joint teaching of language and content must seriously begin to address" (Swain and Carroll 1987:240). In a similar vein, we read in Swain (1988): "We do not know what error correction strategies might be most effective." What is suggested is that feedback to learners should be consistent, that feedback could come from peers as well as teachers, and that students must be led to understand that in language use there is a stage of revision and editing which is the appropriate time for error correction. It is clear that these suggestions imply a fairly heavy emphasis on analytic procedures, and this is obviously an area for further investigation.

12 This interpersonal aspect is reflected in COLT under the heading of "participant organization," which distinguishes whole class, group work, and individual work (Allen, Fröhlich, and Spada 1987:25–26). Another feature COLT rightly finds important is whether the topic control is in the hands of the teacher, of the students, or shared. In communicative situations, topic control is not exclusively in the hands of the teacher (Allen, Fröhlich, and Spada 1987:28–29). Finally, in the conversational analysis of Part II of COLT, the interpersonal aspect is reflected in the fact that students have the opportunity "to initiate discourse instead of always having the role of respondent" (p. 34).

Gaudino 1987:63) may reflect what is actually found in traditional analytic classes; but the analytic could also benefit from a flexible social organization.[13]

PROBLEMS OF EXPERIENTIAL TEACHING

Like the analytic strategy, the experiential one presents some problems:

1. Experiential activities are often linguistically demanding, sometimes too demanding for the proficiency level of the class. Many of the problems of experiential teaching arise from this fact, and this is therefore obviously an important area for systematic experimentation.

2. An experiential activity is intended to offer, within the time restrictions and physical limits imposed by classroom teaching, the conditions of natural language use. These conditions are not always easy to meet but the literature on communicative language teaching offers ingenious suggestions that meet some of the requirements of real communication in the language class; for example, information gap tasks, information transfer tasks, informal talk tasks, role play, drama techniques, and scenarios.

3. An experiential activity must, as far as possible, be motivating for students and in this way involve them as participants in the activity. It requires a great deal of ingenuity to capture the interest of all the members of a class or to allow for the diversity of interests.

4. The assumption is that the activity contributes to proficiency. It is in the nature of an experiential activity to be linguistically less specific than an analytic task. Therefore the language benefits may also be more indirect and sometimes less tangible.

Summary: experiential and analytic features

On the basis of this discussion we can now present a comparative tabulation of experience and analysis (see Table 7.1). This tabulation contains only criterial features and does not present a mix of desirable and undesirable characteristics. If all criteria are met for either analytic or experiential features, the strategy is fully realized. If only some are met, the strategy is realized to a lesser degree.

Combining analytic and experiential strategies

The main message the treatment studies seem to convey is the one so clearly expressed in the COLT studies; in order to achieve the highest

---

13 For example, in the experimental study, we find an illustration of an analytic activity in which the class operates in groups. One unit, described as a "function-focused grammar lesson," was based on a competitive team arrangement of the class.

TABLE 7.1 EXPERIENTIAL AND ANALYTIC FEATURES

Experiential features	Analytic features
1. Substantive and motivated topic or theme (topics are not arbitrary or trivial).	1. Focus on aspects of L2, including phonology, grammar, functions, discourse, sociolinguistics.
2. Students engage in purposeful activity (tasks or projects), not exercises.	2. Cognitive study of language items (rules and regularities are noted; items are made salient, and related to other items and systems).
3. Language use has characteristics of real talk (conversation) or uses any of the four skills as part of purposeful action.	3. Practice or rehearsal of language items or skill aspects.
4. Priority of meaning transfer and fluency over linguistic error avoidance and accuracy.	4. Attention to accuracy and error avoidance.
5. Diversity of social interaction.	5. Diversity of social interaction desirable.

degree of effectiveness, the two orientations should be considered complementary. This is likely to mean that where languages are taught as a subject, as in the core French program, there should be more emphasis on experiential strategies; for immersion-type programs, more attention should be paid to analytic strategies. This is the point of view implicit in all the DBP classroom treatment studies. The hard evidence that the studies provide, however, is by no means overwhelming. The COLT studies and the immersion experimental study, which have specifically attempted to relate proficiency findings to analytic or experiential treatment or a combination of the two, report somewhat ambiguous results. Suggestions for or against ways of combining or sequencing analytic and experiential procedures are therefore tentative. Several of these have been identified by the treatment studies, but the problems involved have not yet been completely ironed out.

To begin with, we should be clear about what the options are. One option is to place more emphasis on one strategy. It is evident that different programs, by the way they are designed, are more clearly analytic or more clearly experiential. This difference in emphasis is certainly confirmed by the first of the COLT studies, which applied the COLT scheme to French immersion, extended French, ESL classes, and core French. The communicative-experiential emphasis varied from one group of classes to another. It was found that, by COLT criteria, the French immersion classes were the most experiential and the core French classes were the most analytic (Allen, Fröhlich, and Spada 1987).

The second COLT study, which compared eight grade 11 core French classes, was able to distinguish degrees of communicativeness within one type of program, core French. Two classes were more communicative-experiential (Type E), and the other six classes were more analytic (Type A) in their treatment, but as the investigators pointed out: "None of our classrooms correspond to a prototypic Type A program (i.e., one in which only analytic activities are used) or to a prototypic Type E program (one in which only experiential activities are used)" (Allen, Carroll, Burtis, and Gaudino 1987:65).

The immersion observation study assumes that immersion programs are mainly experiential because of their emphasis on substantive content, and imply a strong recommendation that there should be more emphasis on an analytic strategy in immersion teaching. However, it is not merely a question of providing for both strategies side by side. Swain and Carroll (1987:191) observe that there is always some formal grammar teaching in the immersion programs when "formal rules, paradigms and grammatical categories are learned," but that grammar teaching is isolated from the use of grammatical forms in content classes. This leads to the sound observation that, "in immersion classes, where language and content learning are equally important goals, a closer alliance than has been observed between the teaching of structure and meaning deserves our future attention" (Swain and Carroll 1987:192).[14]

In the attempt to combine the two strategies, we can envisage two main ways of establishing links: (1) one in which an analytic strategy is dominant and the experiential in a supporting role, and (2) another in which the experiential is dominant and the analytic is supportive. If the analytic strategy is dominant, we set out from a linguistic syllabus; that is, we identify specific points of grammar, phonology, or discourse on which we base explanations and exercises, and we then devise activities that bring these points of language into action in as natural a way as possible. This was the approach that prompted Paulston's sequence from mechanical to meaningful and communicative drills, Rivers's distinction between skill getting and skill using, Gunterman and Phillips's com-

---

14 In the thinking of the treatment studies on this issue, I believe there is a lack of differentiation between two ideas. Both are important, but I believe they should be separated. One is a criticism of the quality of grammar teaching in immersion programs. It is argued that immersion programs observed as part of the treatment studies are more concerned with the "formal paradigms and categories" than "relating forms to meaning in context" (Harley 1989c). This criticism could be described as inadequacies of analytic teaching, since teaching grammatical forms should pay attention to form, function, and meaning – a criticism that might well apply to nonimmersion treatment of grammar as well. This is a different question from relating analytic teaching to the teaching of content in an immersion program. It is the latter issue, which in general terms, deals with the relationship of experiential to analytic teaching, that is our main concern in this paper, and I believe also of the treatment studies.

municative exercises, and the type of inherently interesting but grammatically motivated activities we find in the immersion experimental study.[15] Alternatively, as we have seen, we can envisage the dominance of the experiential strategy, with the analytic in a supporting role; there are unfortunately no examples of this paradigm in the treatment studies.[16]

A good deal of further experimentation is needed, in core French classes or other analytic language classes, as well as in immersion-type situations where experiential teaching is dominant and analytic teaching supportive. Analytic teaching in these situations is meant mainly to advance the activity or project, but it would be interesting to observe to what extent learners benefit linguistically from language instruction in a situation where analytic strategies are subordinated to the demands of an experiential activity, project, or other task.

Conclusion

In retrospect it is perhaps ironic to note that, in this series of inquiries, the COLT studies looked for experiential teaching in core French programs and found little, whereas the immersion studies looked for analytic teaching in immersion programs and again found little they liked. The limitations suggest important new directions: for core French to extend into experiential teaching, and for immersion programs to add ways of combining experiential teaching with some degree of necessary and helpful analytic support.

15 The materials used in the experimental study are described as designed "to bridge the gap between form-focused grammar exercises and natural communicative subject-matter teaching" (Harley 1989b). The eight-week program of tasks that formed the content of the experimental teaching, involving the use of the two French past tenses, consisted of activities some of which were experiential (for example, reading a legend), and others that were analytic in character – for example, drawing pictures to match captions in which the use of one or the other of the two past tenses was used. The experimental study provides a kind of model for other experiments and further investigations on the pedagogical issues involved in relating analytic and experiential teaching to one another. Not only was the outcome studied, but the study was complemented by workshops with teachers, classroom observations, teachers' (but regrettably not students') reactions to the materials in use, and questionnaires to teachers. What adds to the usefulness of this study is that the concept of transition from analytic to experiential is not merely programmatic, but is experimentally tried and extensively documented.

16 One outstanding example of lack of an analytic teaching component in an experiential situation is offered within the lexical study by the record of an informal immersion class discussion on starvation and malnutrition in which students lacked the vocabulary to talk about this question in French (Swain and Carroll 1987:214–15). It illustrates the need to provide some kind of language support in order to make experiential teaching feasible as well as useful for both the teaching of content and of language.

For future research directions arising from the DBP treatment studies, we would probably look for the following: a revision of the COLT scheme that would document not only experiential but also analytic features of teaching and would at the same time attempt to distinguish appropriate and sound treatment of both strategies from inappropriate and unsound treatment; a further group of studies, along the lines of the immersion experimental study, that might investigate the effect of different mixtures of experiential and analytic approaches in the classroom.

8 Response by DBP project members to the discussion papers of Patsy Lightbown and H. H. (David) Stern

In his discussion paper, David Stern provides a valuable review of the historical development of communicative language teaching. In addition, he clarifies the conceptual distinction between analytic and experiential strategies and discusses the advantages and disadvantages of both. One issue that leads to difficulty is the existence of two distinct approaches to communicative language teaching which are often confused: (1) a functional-analytic approach that emphasizes teaching *about* communication through the study of speech acts, discourse analysis, and sociolinguistics, and (2) an experiential approach that emphasizes teaching *through* communication in a natural manner without any prior selection or arrangement of the language items to be learned. Stern points out that the COLT studies did not always succeed in clearly distinguishing these two concepts. For example, "explicit focus on function/discourse/sociolinguistics" is listed as an experiential feature in the table that served as the basis for rank-ordering the schools in the core French observation study. This was in fact done deliberately in the expectation that talking about discourse coherence and situational appropriateness (in the target language) would constitute a communicatively rich activity. However, with the benefit of hindsight, we agree with Stern that the activities he cites are inherently analytic rather than experiential. This categorization problem did not affect the core French results, since less than 1 percent of observed time was assigned to activities focusing on functional, discourse, or sociolinguistic aspects of language.

We will devote the rest of our allotted space to responding to Patsy Lightbown's comments on the core French observation study. First, however, it will be necessary to provide some additional background. The treatment section of the DBP included a series of three studies based on the COLT observation scheme. The purpose of the first study was to develop an observation instrument that would contain categories to measure features of communication typical of classroom discourse. The aim of the second study was to validate the instrument by using it to collect data from a sample of twelve classes representing four different L2 programs, the purpose being to see whether the COLT was capable of capturing differences in the pedagogic orientation of classrooms in a variety of instructional settings. The next step was to attempt to find out what kind of pedagogic orientation is most beneficial for developing various aspects of second language proficiency. This was the aim of the third study – the core French observation study – which included pre-testing, classroom observation, and posttesting within the context of a single instructional program.

The core French program was chosen as the context for the process/product study because it consists of a relatively homogeneous group of students with respect to amount of previous instruction time and exposure to French outside the classroom. The sample consisted of eight grade 11 core French classes that were selected in a two-part process. Initially, three metropolitan Toronto school boards were asked to suggest the names of a number of teachers who were known to be using either experiential or analytic approaches in their classes and who might be prepared to participate in the study. A preliminary list of 13 teachers was compiled. Subsequently, all the teachers were observed by one of the researchers who had been instrumental in the design of the COLT. A final selection of eight classes was made on the basis of these informal observations.

No analysis of the classes using the COLT was done at this time, but we worked on the assumption that we would eventually be able to divide the classes into two distinct groups, an experiential or functionally oriented group, and an analytic or structurally oriented group. The final classification and ranking of the classes depended on the outcome of the observations conducted throughout the course of the study using the COLT, leaving open the possibility that classes might be more or less experiential or more or less analytic according to a theoretically defined absolute scale.

Patsy Lightbown questions our use of the labels experiential and analytic to describe these two groups of classes. It should be recalled that at the time we began this study, in the early eighties, there was a widespread tendency to assume a simple dichotomy between types of classrooms; a structurally oriented, teacher-directed class could not be simultaneously communicative, and a functionally oriented, student-centered class could not be simultaneously analytic. One of our objectives was to investigate the validity of this viewpoint. In fact, it quickly became apparent that all the classes in our sample were marked by combinations of analytic and experiential features. The COLT analysis revealed that the sample as a whole was intermediate along an absolute scale ranging from prototypically high experiential classes at one extreme to prototypically high analytic classes at the other, and that the sample was closer to the analytic than the experiential end of the scale. Since there were many similarities between the classes, as well as differences, it became clear that we were looking at relative degrees of experiential or

TABLE 8.1 COLT CATEGORIES

Experiential feature	Analytic feature
	COLT Part I
group activity	whole-class activity
classroom management	
function/discourse/sociolinguistic focus	form focus
broad/limited range of reference	narrow range of reference
student or shared control	teacher control
extended text	minimal text
L1/L1 adapted/student-made materials	L2 materials
	COLT Part II
use of French	use of English
giving unpredictable information	giving predictable information
information request	display request
sustained speech	minimal speech
reaction to message	reaction to code
comment, expansion, clarification, elaboration	correction, repetition, paraphrase
initiation by student	
unrestricted form	restricted form

analytic emphasis. These findings were not particularly surprising; we were, after all, observing classrooms in the real world, not the hypothetical, idealized classes that feature so prominently in the communicative language teaching literature.

As previously indicated (Chapter 5), the instructional variables selected for examination in the COLT scheme were motivated by a desire to describe as precisely as possible some of the features of interaction that occur in second language classrooms. Our concept of "pedagogic feature" was derived from current theories of communicative competence, from the literature on communicative language teaching, and from a review of recent research into first and second language acquisition. In order to distinguish between Type E (experiential) and Type A (analytic) classrooms, the COLT categories were grouped in such a way that each experiential feature was matched by a corresponding analytic feature. The result of this grouping was as shown in Table 8.1. All Part II categories were coded for student and teacher speech, apart from *Initiation by student* and *Form restriction,* which were coded for student speech only. Since the target language was generally used for *Classroom management* during the observation periods, this category was counted as an experiential feature. The categories *Individual seat work, Audio/ visual materials,* and *Student modality* were omitted, since it was not possible to determine whether they referred to experiential or analytic activities.

After completion of the observation process, the eight classes in the sample were ranked on an experiential-analytic scale on the basis of the experiential features listed above. In order to arrive at a score that would permit ranking, we took the total percentage of time spent on each of the experiential features in COLT Parts I and II and added the figures together. These calculations yielded the ranking and scores shown in Table 5.1. In order to maximize the differences between the more experiential classes and the more analytic classes, the schools were divided into two groups, using the mean as the dividing point. This gave two schools in the experiential group (Type E) and six schools in the analytic group (Type A), rather than two groups of four schools each.

We then examined the detailed differences between Type A and Type E classes, as revealed by Parts I and II of the COLT observation scheme. The COLT analysis indicated significant differences between Type A and Type E classrooms with regard to: topic control by teacher and student, student extended and minimal written text, teacher and student reaction to message/code, student sustained and minimal speech, form restriction, source/purpose of materials, and student topic expansion. Type A classrooms made significantly more use than type E classrooms of the following features (S = students):

Topic control by teacher
Minimal written text (S)
Minimal utterance in spoken interaction (S)
Reaction to code rather than message (S)
Restricted choice of linguistic item (S)

Type E classrooms made significantly more use than Type A classrooms of the following features (T = teacher, S = students):

Topic control by student
Extended written text (S)
Sustained speech in spoken interaction (S)
Reaction to message rather than code (T, S)
Topic expansion (S)
Use of student-made materials

The COLT findings were supported by teacher questionnaires providing information about classroom activities throughout the year, and by descriptive profiles compiled for each of the classrooms on the basis of field notes made during the observation periods. We disagree, therefore, with Lightbown's statement that the differences between the two types of classroom were "minimal." As a result of examining the observation data, the teacher questionnaires, and the classroom profiles, we concluded that there were major differences between the two types of classroom which could have an effect on learning outcome.

As indicated in Chapter 5, the analysis of the effects of classroom process on second language proficiency proceeded in three stages. First, the eight classrooms were divided into two groups (Type A and Type E) according to the overall COLT score for experiential versus analytic orientation, and the relative improvement of the two groups on the various proficiency measures was examined. At the second stage, the same analysis was repeated using only the two most extreme classrooms from each end of the continuum (Type A* and Type E), in order to maximize the chances for differences to emerge. As Lightbown points out, the most striking thing about the data is the lack of difference between the groups in adjusted posttest scores. These results, though disappointing, are not without interest. It could be that the similarities between the two groups outweighed the differences, or that pedagogic orientation is less important than other factors such as student motivation or the general rapport teachers are able to establish with their classes. Or perhaps, as Lightbown suggests, one hour a day at the end of eight years of core French is not likely to make much difference to proficiency, whatever method of instruction is used. Only further research can clarify these issues.

The third stage of the analysis was based on correlations between individual COLT categories and posttest performance by all classes. As already noted in Chapter 5, the overall pattern suggests that core French students benefited from a generally experiential approach, but at the same time there were positive correlations between various form-focused, teacher-directed activities and adjusted posttest scores. Our analysis was based on a sample of only eight classrooms, and few of the correlations reached significance. Moreover, as might be expected, the correlations were often difficult to interpret. For example, with regard to participant organization, classes in which relatively more time was spent with the teacher addressing the class, or with students working individually on the same activity, showed relatively good improvement on most proficiency measures, whereas classes that spent more time on student/whole class and choral work showed relatively little improvement. This may mean that these activities do not contribute to learning. On the other hand, it may be that student/whole class and choral work are not so much bad in themselves, but rather take time away from the more effective types of organization.

Lightbown notes that focus on form tended to be positively related to improvement, while discussion of general topics with limited or broad range of reference tended to be detrimental. At the same time, there were positive correlations between oral and written measures of proficiency and teacher/student reaction to message. At first sight, these results appear to be contradictory. However, the pattern is explained if we recognize that focus on form does not necessarily exclude attention to meaning, and focus on message does not necessarily lead to communicatively rich interaction in the classroom. We have already indicated that the high-scoring class spent 66 percent of observed time on activities which focused on formal features of language, but that this was usually done in a meaningful context involving the discussion of form-meaning relationships in student compositions. The "quality interaction" that resulted from this activity contrasted with the stereotyped nature of student presentations in our low-scoring class 5. Although the class 5 students were dealing with topics of general interest (coded as "broad range of reference"), the task was too difficult for them and meaningful discussion in French failed to develop. In other words, it cannot be assumed that focus on form and broad range of reference are criterial features in themselves. The quality of instruction – how content is negotiated in the classroom and its appropriateness relative to students' target language knowledge – is clearly important in both analytic and experiential teaching.

There is no doubt that communicative language teaching theory has raised important questions about the relationship between classroom variables and language learning. Any such theory must be subject to empirical investigation if it is to provide us with a better chance of identifying treatment factors that are the most relevant to learning particular aspects of language structure and use. As the next step, we would like to undertake research in classes where more extreme contrasts can be established through the use of the COLT to see if we can find further differences in student proficiency under these more prototypic conditions. In addition, we need to refine our theory of communicative language teaching so that the essential COLT features can be identified and weighted accordingly; we need to investigate the role played by individual learner variables; and we need to pay more attention to the quality, as distinct from the quantity, of classroom interaction. We predict that these issues will provide a major focus for future research.

PART III
SOCIAL AND INDIVIDUAL VARIABLES

9 Social and individual factors in the development of bilingual proficiency

Jim Cummins,
Birgit Harley,
Merrill Swain,
and Patrick Allen

Several studies in the Development of Bilingual Proficiency project were designed to investigate the relationship between individual and social-environmental factors and the development of bilingual proficiency in both majority and minority language learning contexts. In one large-scale study of Portuguese-Canadian students (Cummins, Lopes, and King 1987), the relationship between language use patterns, language attitudes, and bilingual proficiency was investigated by means of correlational and regression analyses. In a small sample of beginning school-age children of Portuguese home background, a detailed study of language interaction at home and at school was carried out with a view to relating interactional variables to later academic achievement (Cummins, Lopes, and Ramos 1987). In another minority context, an ethnographic study focused on students attending a French language elementary school in Toronto (Heller 1983, 1984).

The social context of bilingual development among Portuguese–Canadian children

In the large-scale study of grade 7 Portuguese-Canadian students, bilingual proficiency was investigated in relation to family background variables, students' patterns of language use, and their language attitudes. Theoretical issues examined were: (1) the nature of language proficiency indicated by the pattern of relationships within languages – specifically, the extent to which grammatical, discourse, and sociolinguistic competence could be distinguished in context-embedded and context-reduced situations; (2) the cross-lingual dimensions of language proficiency, indicated by the pattern of relationships across languages

119

– in other words, the extent to which there is evidence for a "common underlying proficiency" that accounts for variance in both the bilingual's two languages; and (3) the extent to which proficiency in English and Portuguese could be predicted by language use and attitude variables.

The study also sought to describe the language use patterns and attitudes toward cultural identity of the students. In designing the language use and attitude questionnaires,[1] we attempted to address issues that derived from a number of theoretical frameworks (e.g., Gardner and Lambert 1972; Bourhis, Giles, and Rosenthal 1981), but we did not attempt to test specific theoretical predictions regarding the interrelationships among use and attitude variables. In other words, the study was essentially exploratory in this regard.

The sample consisted of 191 students enrolled in Portuguese heritage language programs[2] in seven inner-city Toronto schools. More than half these students were of Azorean background. All students completed two questionnaires. One was a language use questionnaire concerning family background (e.g., birthplace, parents' language use, education, occupations), language use patterns (use of Portuguese and English at home, in school, and in the community), and self-ratings of proficiency in English, Portuguese, and French. The other was a language attitude questionnaire that investigated dimensions such as integrative and instrumental orientations toward English and Portuguese, language use preferences in different contexts, the role of English and Portuguese in the students' ethnic identity, perceived attitudes of parents toward students' education and language use, attitudes toward Portuguese dialects and language mixing, cultural assimilation, and attitudes toward French. Tests in English and Portuguese were also administered.

In each school, the students were divided randomly into three groups. One group did multiple-choice grammar tests in English and Portuguese. A second group received a multiple-choice discourse test in each language similar to the one administered in the large-scale proficiency study (see Chapter 1). Students in this group were also given individual oral tests in English and Portuguese, each of which contained tasks to be scored for grammar, discourse, and sociolinguistic proficiency. The sociolinguistic task in each language was adapted from the oral sociolinguistic test administered in the large-scale proficiency study. A third group of students in each school was given sociolinguistic written production tests

---

1 The principal investigators would like to acknowledge the contribution of Dr. Ellen Bouchard Ryan to the design of the questionnaires.
2 The provincially funded heritage language program consists of 2.5 hours per week of instruction in languages other than English and French. For students in the sample, this instruction took place during the regular school day.

in each language, again based on the test designed for the large-scale proficiency study.

Language use and attitudes

The language use questionnaire revealed that the majority of the sample was of rural Azorean background and had been exposed primarily to Portuguese at home before starting school. After the beginning of school, a rapid transition to English appears to have taken place, with the result that with friends, as well as with brothers and sisters, English was the language used almost all the time. For most students, use of Portuguese was restricted to Portuguese classes (in both the provincially funded heritage language program and classes organized by Portuguese community clubs), to attendance at mass, and to some other Portuguese community activities (e.g., festivals, dance groups), as well as to address grandparents and, somewhat less frequently, to communicate with parents. Students also had some exposure to Portuguese on television (on average 2 hours per week), but this was overshadowed by the amount of time spent watching English television (23 hours per week on average). Finally, about half the sample had traveled to Portugal at least once during the past five years.

The patterns of language use are reflected in students' self-ratings of current proficiency in speaking, understanding, reading, and writing Portuguese and English. On all indices English proficiency was rated considerably higher than Portuguese proficiency. The high level of confidence that students have in their use of English is indicated by their mean self-ratings of 4.6 (out of 5) for English oral and 4.4 for English written, compared to 3.8 and 3.1 for the equivalent Portuguese self-ratings. More specifically, only 28 percent felt they could speak and understand Portuguese "extremely easily," compared to 70 percent for English. On written language measures, 17 percent felt they could read and write Portuguese "extremely easily," compared to 62 percent for English.

With respect to language attitudes, students expressed a preference for using English when talking about their feelings or about things that happened in school, but generally preferred to use Portuguese in communicating with their families. The majority of the sample considered themselves to be speakers of English and Portuguese; they showed a desire to become, in the future, speakers of Portuguese, English, and French; to marry Portuguese/English speakers; and to have their children be fluent in both Portuguese and English. Respondents showed similarly positive attitudes toward both Portuguese and Canadian history and achievements; the majority considered that Portuguese should be kept

TABLE 9.1 PRINCIPAL COMPONENTS FACTOR ANALYSIS OF SELECTED MEASURES
OF PORTUGUESE PROFICIENCY, USING THE SAMPLE EXCLUDING OUTLIERS AND
STUDENTS WITH LESS THAN THREE YEARS' RESIDENCE

	Factor 1	Factor 2	Commonality
Oral grammar	.61639	.44529	.57822
Oral phonology	.61794	.02532	.38249
Oral vocabulary	.72321	.25852	.58986
Oral discourse	.73298	.27231	.61141
Multiple-choice discourse	.48803	.47314	.46203
Oral sociolinguistic	.78819	− 0.10468	.63219
Self-rated oral competence	.13839	.80470	.66669
Self-rated written competence	.00941	.91955	.84566
Percent variance	.338	.258	

alive in Toronto, but were realistic about the higher status of English both in Toronto and in the world generally.

In summary, most students appeared to be comfortable with their dual identity as Portuguese-Canadians. Although they viewed English as considerably more important for activities outside the Portuguese community and for future educational and job-related success, the importance of Portuguese within this community was recognized and valued by the students themselves. There was little evidence of rejection of their Portuguese identity in favor of an English-Canadian identity.

Relationships among proficiency variables within and across languages

A considerable degree of interrelationship was found among Portuguese self-ratings of proficiency, multiple-choice discourse scores in Portuguese, and the various oral measures of Portuguese proficiency. A principal components analysis (Table 9.1) suggested a global Portuguese proficiency dimension, supplemented by academically related aspects of proficiency. There was little evidence that grammatical, discourse, and sociolinguistic components of proficiency had become differentiated.

There were considerably fewer significant intercorrelations among the English variables than among the Portuguese variables that assessed similar proficiency traits. Only two correlations involving test (i.e., non-self-rating) variables attained statistical significance. A major reason for the lack of relationships among the English oral proficiency measures appears to be that virtually all students had attained a high degree of ease in expressing themselves in context-embedded situations. Thus, the variation that did exist was unrelated to broader dimensions of proficiency in English.

Across languages, self-ratings of proficiency in English, Portuguese, and French tended to be significantly related to each other. Further, relatively strong r = .5, p < .01 cross-lingual relationships were observed for each set of written measures: between multiple-choice grammar scores in English and Portuguese, between multiple-choice discourse scores in each language, and between written sociolinguistic scores in each language. A principal components analysis (varimax rotation) showed the English discourse multiple-choice measure loading on the first factor that also had strong loadings from the bulk of Portuguese proficiency variables (Table 9.2). The correlations and factor analysis also revealed some weaker cross-lingual relationships for oral discourse and sociolinguistic variables. One finding of interest to emerge from the factor analysis was the fact that Portuguese vocabulary spread its loading across three factors, suggesting that vocabulary knowledge is involved in most aspects of proficiency.

These data reinforce the conclusion that the relationships among components of language proficiency cannot be considered outside of particular language acquisition contexts. The considerably greater degree of intercorrelation among the Portuguese as compared to the English measures is likely to be related both to reduced variability for English oral skills and the related fact that the interaction/acquisition contexts differ considerably for English and Portuguese for these students. English is the language of peer interaction, television/radio, and school, whereas the home and the Portuguese heritage language classes are the major contexts for use of Portuguese. Thus, the knowledge that students require for appropriate use of English in context-embedded situations is probably further developed and less variable between individuals than is the case for their knowledge of Portuguese.

In conclusion, the results do not support any absolute distinction between grammatical, discourse, and sociolinguistic competence apart from contexts of acquisition; however, there is strong evidence of interdependence of academic skills across languages, and some evidence that weaker cross-lingual relationships may also obtain for aspects of context-embedded proficiency.

Predictors of bilingual proficiency development

On the basis of both conceptual and empirical considerations, a subset of use and attitude variables was created to use as predictor variables in the regression analyses. The primary criterion for grouping variables together was conceptual – namely, the extent to which the clustering was theoretically interpretable with respect to potential influences on bilingual proficiency development. Empirical considerations were taken into account insofar as individual variables with low correlations with

TABLE 9.2 PRINCIPAL COMPONENTS FACTOR ANALYSIS OF SELECTED MEASURES OF PORTUGUESE AND ENGLISH PROFICIENCY FOR THE SAMPLE EXCLUDING RECENT ARRIVALS AND OUTLIERS ON PORTUGUESE VARIABLES

	Factor 1	Factor 2	Factor 3	Factor 4	Commonality
Portuguese oral grammar	.65670	.35767	.20667	− 0.23449	.65688
Portuguese oral phonology	.63787	.08047	.06481	− 0.28381	.49811
Portuguese oral vocabulary	.43639	.37614	.49260	− 0.08244	.58137
Portuguese oral discourse	.56473	.18588	.51335	.08116	.62360
Portuguese multiple-choice discourse	.68076	.19454	.17005	.33281	.64096
Portuguese oral sociolinguistic	.34848	.02113	.69636	− 0.09729	.61626
Portuguese self-rated oral competence	.09766	.86359	.10972	.06701	.77186
Portuguese self-rated written competence	.15739	.84216	− 0.05834	.26265	.80639
English oral discourse	.16034	.14499	.55089	.03611	.35151
English multiple-choice discourse	.71921	− 0.21745	.07392	.51369	.83389
English oral sociolinguistic	− 0.20632	− 0.29725	.71125	.13591	.65526
English self-rated oral competence	− 0.03975	.03749	.04851	.81634	.67174
English self-rated written competence	− 0.00426	.26723	− 0.00943	.76294	.65359
Percent variance	.196	.156	.146	.144	

ere generally excluded from composite vari-
mmins, and Swain 1987, for further details).
yses revealed that a considerable amount of
ngs of Portuguese proficiency could be related
e use variables such as students' acceptance
vledge and pride in Portuguese culture and
Portuguese media, exposure to Portuguese in
ptance of and liking for French. Thirty-four
accounted for by such variables in Portuguese
rcent in written self-rating.
glish self-ratings appeared to be at least partly
at relatively little variance was accounted for
lf-rating measures (21 percent was accounted
15 percent in written self-rating). For oral self-
rating, the most strongly related variable was students' liking for English,
followed by the extent to which English was used in talking with siblings
and students' acceptance of French. The latter variable was the only one
to enter the equation for English written self-rating.

With respect to the formal measures of Portuguese proficiency, amount
of exposure, both formal exposure in heritage language classes and the
informal exposure involved in visits to Portugal, amount of Portuguese
television watched, use made of other forms of Portuguese media (e.g.,
radio, reading books, writing letters), and going to mass in Portuguese,
appeared to play a major role in predicting different aspects of proficiency, particularly oral grammatical proficiency. The importance of
exposure to the language is a typical finding in the case of minority
languages to which students tend to be minimally exposed outside the
home.

Attitudes also appeared important, although to a considerably lesser
extent. Knowledge of and pride in Portuguese culture and achievements
tended to show consistent positive relationships with the dependent
variables, although this variable did not enter the regression equations
because the program excluded it as a result of co-linearity with other
variables. A number of attitude and use variables that might have been
expected to relate positively to Portuguese proficiency failed to do so.
For example, family use of Portuguese did not predict proficiency, nor,
in general, did students' perceptions of parental and societal attitudes
toward Portuguese.

In contrast to Portuguese proficiency, few strong trends emerged for
prediction of English proficiency. Father's job classification (an index of
socioeconomic status) was related to the English discourse multiple-
choice measure. However, indices of exposure and use tended to relate
in the opposite direction to what might have been expected. For example,
language used with siblings and language of mass both related negatively

to the oral and written English discourse measures, indicating that use of Portuguese in talking with siblings and attendance at Portuguese mass were *positively* related to English proficiency. This trend suggests that students are exposed to English to such an extent that further increments make little difference; in fact, it may be that students who are developing more of an additive bilingualism (as indicated by some continued use of Portuguese in certain contexts) experience benefits for some aspects of their English proficiency.

Comparison of students' Portuguese proficiency with Azorean native speakers

To further investigate the extent to which the social and educational context influenced the development of bilingual proficiency, data were collected from 69 grade 6 native Portuguese students in San Miguel Island in the Azores. There were significant differences between the Toronto and Azorean students on most measures of Portuguese proficiency. Differences were extremely large on the written grammar measure and less apparent on the written sociolinguistic measures, with discourse measures occupying an intermediate position. Major differences do appear on the written discourse multiple-choice measure, but they are less obvious on the oral discourse measures.

These results parallel to some extent the differences found in the comparison (reported in Chapter 1) between French immersion and native francophone students where differences in grammar were most salient with less major differences in sociolinguistic proficiency and least in discourse proficiency. The data are also consistent with the findings of the regression analyses which indicated that indices reflecting exposure to and use of Portuguese were more clearly related to grammatical proficiency in Portuguese (at least oral grammar) than they were to discourse and sociolinguistic proficiencies.

In conclusion, the large differences between the Canadian and Azorean students show how formidable is the task of maintaining first language proficiency in a minority context. Despite the fact that the Toronto sample also consists of native speakers of Portuguese and that many are quite fluent in oral Portuguese in context-embedded situations, their explicit knowledge of the formal structure of the language appears relatively limited in comparison to the Azorean native speakers. We should not forget, of course, that the Toronto students appear to have developed nativelike competence in oral English and thus are not in any sense linguistically disadvantaged. The strong relationship between attendance at Portuguese language classes and the performance of the Toronto students suggests that more intensive exposure to Portuguese in an academic context could have a significant impact on bridging the gap between their Portuguese proficiency and that of native Portuguese-educated students.

This study has pointed to the importance of the transition from home to school as a potentially important phase in the extent to which minority students will maintain their first language. This transition is the focus of an ongoing study again involving students of Portuguese background.

The transition from home to school: an ongoing longitudinal study

The major purpose of this ongoing study is to investigate the development of proficiency in both Portuguese and English in the transition from home to school. Twenty children from Portuguese backgrounds are being followed from the junior kindergarten year through grade 1 with respect to patterns of language interaction in the home, performance on a variety of language proficiency and literacy awareness measures, and (in grade 1) reading performance. Patterns of interaction in the home and knowledge of Portuguese and English will be used as predictors of English reading performance in grade 1. The study thus addresses theoretical issues such as the interdependence of L1 and L2, as well as practical issues related to the interaction between home and school variables in affecting the extent to which minority students are successful academically. The study will also provide a corpus of longitudinal data for an analysis of students' developing proficiency in their two languages.

The main sample consists of 20 Toronto students receiving the following battery of tests: the Draw-a-Person Test (Harris 1963), the Record of Oral Language (sentence repetition, English and Portuguese) (Clay et al. 1976), Letter Identification (English and Portuguese), Concepts about Print (English and Portuguese) and, in Year 3 (spring 1987), Test of Writing Vocabulary (English and Portuguese) (all derived from Clay 1981), and the Gates-McGinitie Reading Test (comprehension subtest). In addition, children were taped in their homes for 1.5 hours each year of the study.

Twenty-six grade 1 students (average age seven) in the Azores were also administered the Concepts about Print test, an oral interview, and Test of Writing Vocabulary (Clay 1981) in Portuguese for comparison purposes with the grade 1 Toronto data. In addition, 6 five-year-old students in the Azores were taped for 1.5 hours in their homes. Data were also collected in mainland Portugal from 10 five-year-old children in a village situated a hundred kilometers northwest of Lisbon. A Portuguese version of the Record of Oral Language was constructed and administered to the children. Six of the 10 were randomly chosen to be taped in the home. All the data for this study have been collected, and analysis was being completed as the present volume went to press.

Ethnographic study of a Toronto French-language school

The final study of social factors investigated the social pressures within schools that influence students' language use and identity choices. In this ethnographic, sociolinguistic case study of a French-language elementary school in Toronto (Heller 1983, 1984), patterns of language choice and language use were investigated in relation both to the micro level interactional context and to the macro level context of school and community. The study examined the role that the use of French and English played in the development of students' social identities.

Micro level data were collected in the school by means of participant observation over a six-month period, mainly in a grade 7/8 class, and through tape recordings of 8 students who each wore a tape recorder for two entire school days. Four of the students were selected as ethnolinguistically representative of the school, and the other 4 were randomly selected. Macro level data were collected through a schoolwide parent questionnaire and in interviews with school administrators, staff, members of the parent-teacher association, and an ethnolinguistically representative subsample of parents.

Just over half the parents returned their questionnaires, which indicated considerable heterogeneity of family origin, linguistic background, and goals with respect to bilingualism and the maintenance of French. For example, over 40 percent of the families were of linguistically mixed marriages (usually with a francophone mother); 30 percent were francophone, 11 percent anglophone, and the remainder from a great variety of linguistic backgrounds. Very few parents and under half the children were Toronto born. Family homes were widely dispersed over half of the city, making it hard for students to maintain friendships outside school. In-school observations revealed three distinct groups of students: English dominant, bilingual, and French dominant. The first two preferred to speak English among themselves, and the third – a minority – preferred French. Access to the different peer networks depended on appropriate language choice. Each group experienced its own tensions: French-dominant students reported pressure from peers to speak English outside class, while for English-dominant students, performance in French in class could be stressful. Bilingual students were observed to take part in occasional bilingual word-play and code switching, which was seen as their way of resolving the social tensions they experienced from their intermediate position and suggested that, for them, French and English were separate domains.

The heterogeneity of the school population and the varied linguistic experiences of the students were seen to militate against the formation of a monolithic French identity. Instead, observed patterns of language use indicated a close connection for the students between language choice and their evolving social identities.

The age factor

In addition to the studies that investigated social factors, a number of studies undertaken within the DBP project investigated issues concerning learners' age in relation to the development of bilingual proficiency. This individual factor was selected as one that was clearly of educational significance. In this section, we consider four studies in which age-related issues were involved. The findings can be described in relation to the following four issues:

1. Is there a means of assessing the conceptual skills of minority children at different ages that does not penalize them for lack of proficiency in the majority language?
2. How does age of arrival for immigrant children in the host country affect proficiency in the first and second language?
3. How does starting age for an immersion type of school-based second language program affect second language proficiency in majority students?
4. How do environmental and maturational considerations interact in determining the age-related effects that are found?

1. Measuring conceptual skills

The first issue is one that arose in a study of metaphor comprehension in bilingual children (Johnson 1987). This study compared the development of metaphor comprehension in Spanish-English bilingual children and monolingual English-speaking children in order to test the hypothesis that metaphoric processing in bilinguals, as well as in monolinguals, is constrained more by age and mental-attentional capacity than it is by language proficiency. Subjects were 20 Hispanic and 20 monolingual English-speaking children in each of three age groups: 7–8, 9–10, and 11–12 years, selected on the basis of a Figural Intersections Test as being of normal mental capacity.

An oral language proficiency test and a metaphor comprehension task in English were individually administered to each child. Hispanic children were also tested for oral proficiency in Spanish, and a subsample was tested for metaphor comprehension in Spanish. The language proficiency tests were similar to verbal IQ tests, while the metaphor comprehension task involved the oral interpretation of ambiguous metaphors, such as "My sister was a rock." The relative complexity of the children's metaphoric interpretations was coded with reference to the degree of semantic transformation involved in mapping an aspect of the vehicle (predicate) onto the topic (subject).

The findings indicated that for bilingual as well as for monolingual children, measured language proficiency was less predictive of metaphor performance than were age and nonverbal mental capacity scores. On a standardized test of English proficiency, the Hispanic children scored significantly lower than the English-speaking children. But on the metaphor task, the Hispanic children scored almost as well as the English-speaking monolinguals. These findings suggest that the metaphor comprehension task could be a more appropriate measure of conceptual skills in a second language than an academically oriented proficiency test. This study points us in an interesting new direction vis-à-vis the testing of minority children of limited L2 proficiency, too many of whom, as Cummins (1984) has pointed out, may be wrongly assigned to special education classes, when what would be more appropriate is help with the second language.

2. Age of arrival for immigrant children

A large-scale study of Japanese immigrant children of relatively high socioeconomic background (Cummins and Nakajima 1987) involved 273 children between grades 2 and 8 attending a Japanese school in Toronto. The focus of this study was on reading and writing skills in English and in Japanese.

In the area of English, this study found a strong advantage in *English* reading for older-arriving students, once the effect of length of residence was removed. In other words, the older the students were on arrival in Canada, the more likely they were to have strong second language reading skills. The measure used was the Gates-McGinitie Reading Test. A similar, but somewhat weaker, effect was also observed on a number of aspects of English writing skills, as demonstrated on a letter-writing task. These findings suggest, in line with the interdependence hypothesis (Cummins 1979), that the older-arriving children have benefited from prior literacy experience in Japanese.

In the area of Japanese reading, it was found that length of residence was a stronger predictor of performance than age. The longer students had been in Canada, the weaker their reading skills in Japanese. However, when length of residence was controlled for, there remained a small but significant effect of age, indicating a tendency for older-arriving students to maintain academic skills in their first language better than younger-arriving students, who would have had less experience of reading in the first language. There were relatively few students in the higher age brackets in this study. It is possible that a stronger relationship between age and first language skills would have been found had there been more older students.

Another small-scale study of 22 Japanese immigrant students in grade 2/3 and 5/6 (Hulstijn 1983) had findings with respect to second language skills that complement those of the large-scale study. In the small-scale study (see Chapter 1), the tests used included school-type academic measures, the narration of a picture story, and some interactional tasks, including a face-to-face interview and role-playing on the telephone.

Among the results of this study was that length of residence was strongly predictive, and age moderately predictive, of performance on a general proficiency factor composed mainly of academic types of tasks and the story narrative. Age was not predictive of vocabulary knowledge, however, which was related to length of residence, and neither age nor length of residence affected performance on communicative style variables such as amount of spontaneous turn taking and continuation of turns by students. The study thus suggests an advantage for older immigrant children on largely academic types of second language tasks, but no such advantage on vocabulary knowledge or on communicative style, the latter being interpreted as reflecting personality rather than linguistic proficiency.

In sum, these two studies found advantages for older immigrant children in academic types of second language skills, particularly in reading. In addition, there appeared to be some advantage for the older Japanese immigrant children in maintaining first language reading skills.

3. Starting age for classroom L2 learning

The third issue concerned starting age for an immersion type of second language program designed for majority students. In this study (Harley 1987), the oral second language proficiency in French of three groups of English-speaking classroom learners was compared. One group had begun an early French immersion program in kindergarten, while the other two groups had started intensive exposure to French several years later, in grade 7. One of these groups consisted of late immersion students, and the other of extended French students who had received somewhat less time in French than the late immersion students. At the time of oral testing, all three groups were in grade 10, and close to sixteen years old. There were 11 or 12 students per group and a similar-sized group of native French speakers, also in grade 10. IQ scores for the learner groups were relatively high and not significantly different from each other.

The purpose of the study was to determine whether there are specific long-term advantages in oral second language proficiency that can be associated with an early start in a total immersion classroom setting. It was thought that by examining aspects of proficiency in greater detail than is normally possible in the context of program evaluations, further insights might be obtained on the linguistic aspects of beginning such classroom programs at an earlier or later stage.

The guided individual oral interviews were of a relatively context-embedded nature. They were designed in the first place to provide students with communicative contexts for the use of a range of verbs and verb forms, but they were also suitable for examining fluency in the second language (seen as an aspect of oral discourse proficiency). At the close of the face-to-face interviews, the oral sociolinguistic test from the large-scale proficiency study (see Chapter 1) was administered in a slightly adapted form to permit between-group comparisons of socio-linguistic proficiency. With respect to verbs, scoring of the interviews focused on the use of target verb forms in the context of specific questions. For fluency, the groups' relatively long responses to three questions were compared on the nature and frequency of markers of disfluency, and the linguistic contexts in which they occurred.

Results with respect to verbs indicated that the early immersion students were closer to the native speakers on a number of features, such as use of the imperfect and the conditional, and the placement of object pronouns in clitic position before the verb. On other verb features, however, such as time distinctions, number and person agreement rules, and vocabulary range, they were no further ahead than the late-entry groups. In the area of fluency, some advantages were found for the early immersion students over the other learner groups, although as might be expected, none of the learner groups was as fluent as the native speakers. The early immersion group produced fewer disfluencies of certain kinds than the late-entry groups, and they were less likely to use hesitations ("um," "uh," etc.) in within-phrase locations where they could be considered more disruptive to discourse coherence. On the sociolinguistic test, there was no overall advantage for any of the learner groups: The early immersion students produced more attenuating conditionals, but the late immersion and extended French students did better on the appropriate use of *vous* and *tu*.

In sum, this comparison of starting ages for an immersion-type of second language program showed some advantages for the early start, but these advantages were not evident across the board.

4. The interaction of maturational and environmental considerations

Whether we are examining minority or majority students' age in its relationship to language proficiency, we are left with an important question, which is in need of considerable further research effort: that is, how maturational and environmental factors interact in the results that are found. In interpreting the Japanese findings, for example, a parsimonious interpretation is that the cognitive maturity of older learners (at least up to teenage levels) may be providing them with an advantage in academic skills across both their languages. In the case of starting age for majority learners in a classroom setting, cognitive maturity may indeed be an important factor too. Yet we need to explain why it is that the early start which provides so much more time for L2 acquisition is not providing more substantial differences from the late-entry groups on the kinds of oral production tasks administered.

One explanation, depending partly on motivational factors, is that there have been benefits for the late-entry students in having access to written forms of the second language at an early stage in their program. These students may also have benefited from an early focus on the code in L2 texts. Characteristically, such texts emphasize formal features such as verb agreement rules, and here the late-entry students were performing as well as, if not better than, the early immersion students. Motivational factors may also have played a role in both the Japanese immigrant and French classroom studies. Snow and Hoefnagel-Höhle (1978), for example, commenting on the faster rate of L2 acquisition by adolescent L2 learners compared with younger children in an empirical study conducted in The Netherlands, suggest that the adolescents, who were learning academic subject matter via their L2, were confronted with a much more demanding task than were young children, and that this may have prompted more effort on their part.

Other environmentally oriented explanations also arise in connection with the early French immersion setting, where it has been observed (see Chapter 5) that individual students have relatively little opportunity to produce the L2 and that some forms are infrequent or not salient in the natural talk of the teachers. Although the experimental study described in Chapter 5 did not produce a lasting effect, the results suggest that more research of this nature, involving a variety of age groups, would be well worth carrying out. At the same time, there is a need for new kinds of age studies that look in depth at how learners of different ages process the L2.

10 Social and individual factors in language acquisition: some models of bilingual proficiency

Richard Y. Bourhis

My comments are focused on the social and individual variables aspect of the Development of Bilingual Proficiency project, specifically the research presented in the final DBP report entitled "The language use patterns, language attitudes, and bilingual proficiency of Portuguese-Canadian children in Toronto" (Cummins, Lopes, and King 1987).

Overview of the Portuguese–Canadian study

The Cummins et al. (1987) study is particularly interesting, since unlike other second language learning studies conducted in Canada (Gardner 1985), it focused on the bilingual proficiency of nonofficial language group speakers, in this case Portuguese-Canadian pupils. As pointed out by Cummins et al. (1987), Portuguese-Canadians are members of a low status group whose job mobility is relatively limited and whose socio-economic standing remains working class within the social structure.

While research by Reitz (1980) has shown that Portuguese-Canadians have experienced job segregation since their arrival in Canada, research by Balakrishnan and Kralt (1987) has also shown that Portuguese-Canadians are highly concentrated residentially within cities such as Toronto, Montreal, and Vancouver. Indeed, Balakrishnan and Kralt (1987) have found that recent immigrant groups such as Portuguese-Canadians are more segregated residentially than black-Caribbean and Indo-Pakistani minority groups in major cities across Canada. Prejudice and discrimination against newly arrived immigrant groups (Berry, Kalin, and Taylor 1977) are not the only reason for the high rate of residential segregation found among Portuguese-Canadians. Balakrishnan and Kralt (1987) suggest that lack of fluency in English among first-generation Portuguese-Canadians helps to account for the residential segregation as well. Given their concentration in specific sectors of urban settings such as Toronto, first-generation Portuguese-Canadians can better communicate with each other in their own language as they struggle to adapt to their new circumstances. Thus, even though Portuguese-

I wish to thank Bob Gardner for his valuable comments on an earlier version of this chapter.

Canadians account for only 3 percent of the total metropolitan Toronto population (1.4 million as of the 1981 census), Cummins et al. (1987) were able to recruit Portuguese-Canadian pupils who came from schools where the proportion of Portuguese-Canadians ranged from 60 to 90 percent of the school population.

We briefly review the major results of the study in order to provide a context for discussion of their significance. The language attitude questionnaire results reflected the diglossic situation many immigrant groups find themselves in when they arrive in anglophone or francophone majority regions of Canada (O'Bryan, Reitz, and Kuplowska 1976). Self-reports of language use showed that whereas Portuguese was used mostly in the home with parents and relatives, English was used mostly for higher-status functions associated with school- and work-related activities outside the home. Furthermore, whereas Portuguese was viewed as more important for ingroup activities related to the home, English was viewed as the language of economic and social advancement in the dominant outgroup world. However, as is often the case with other heritage language group speakers in Canada, much value was attributed by students to bilingual proficiency (O'Bryan et al. 1976; Bourhis 1987).

Unfortunately for one of the important conceptual premises of the study, the results did not yield evidence for a differentiation between grammar, discourse, and sociolinguistic proficiency in either Portuguese or English. The pupils scored very strongly on the English language proficiency measures, and these scores matched well with self-ratings of English proficiency. Self-ratings of English proficiency were higher than self-ratings of Portuguese proficiency. There was evidence for cross-lingual relationships between Portuguese and English, especially in context-reduced academic aspects of proficiency, thus reflecting the effect of learning context. These results further support Cummins's (1984) linguistic interdependence hypothesis, which suggests that a common underlying proficiency characterizes bilingual proficiency, especially as regards academic/cognitive aptitude.

Regression analyses showed that measures of self-rated Portuguese proficiency were positively related to the following language attitude measures: (1) acceptance and liking of the Portuguese language, (2) knowledge and pride in Portuguese culture and achievement, (3) use of Portuguese language media and amount of exposure to Portuguese at home. Though not comprising the usual items used to assess integrative motive, the attitude items listed in 1 and 2 above could be construed as reflecting the integrative orientation documented by Gardner (1985) and his colleagues. As regards measured proficiency in Portuguese, the regression analyses showed that the following attitude items had positive regression coefficients in the prediction of oral/written Portuguese proficiency scores: (1) formal study of Portuguese in the classroom, (2) number of visits to Portugal, (3) use of Portuguese language media, (4) attendance at Portuguese language masses, (5) knowledge of and pride in Portuguese culture and achievement. While item 1 may be taken to refer to the formal language training experienced by the pupils in their heritage language classes, item 2, 3 and 4 predictors can be taken to represent the informal language experience of the speakers in their native Portuguese. As for the self-rating predictors, attitudes in item 5 again suggest the presence of an integrative orientation for Portuguese proficiency.

Regression analyses also showed that measures of self-rated English proficiency (oral/written) were predicted by only a few language attitude measures: (1) acceptance and liking of the English language, (2) amount of English use with siblings. The language use and language attitude items that were related with measures of English language proficiency were puzzling conceptually and empirically. Indeed, it is difficult to understand why use of Portuguese in talking with siblings and attendance at Portuguese language masses should be positively related to English proficiency. In commenting on these results, Cummins et al. (1987) pointed out that "positive attitudes towards Portuguese language maintenance and actual use of Portuguese in the community are in no way detrimental to students' English proficiency." In an intergroup setting where English is the undisputed dominant language, proficiency in a minority language can emerge as an additive form of bilingualism, especially if the desire to master both the dominant and minority language is consensually valued as a desired goal (see Lambert 1974; Clément 1986).

Cummins et al. (1987) rightfully attributed the lack of clear-cut attitudinal predictors of English proficiency to the fact that very little variability emerged in the English proficiency scores. Other reasons for the dearth of attitudinal predictors found in this study could be due to methodological problems already discussed at length by Gardner (1985:74–83). Gardner questions the accuracy of null findings obtained in some language attitude/language proficiency studies by noting the following types of flaws, which are often found in such studies.

First, Gardner (1985) warns against forming unitary groups from heterogeneous sources. Students who may differ in language experiences and training should not be treated as a homogeneous sample. A difficulty arises when students are sampled from qualitatively different classes, or different levels of language instruction, or different schools, *if* these groups *differ* on one or both measures (language proficiency and/or language attitudes). Gardner's (1985) demonstration shows that significant relationships between attitude and proficiency measures can be lost when such scores are combined across groups. The present study may have erred in this direction, since analyses were conducted using a single collapsed group made up of students from different classes originating from seven different schools across downtown Toronto. Gardner (1985:78–80) proposes that standardizing the data *within* groups (in this case within each of the seven groups) can help eliminate possible confounds due to the different groups used within the unitary group analyses.

Second, Gardner (1985:74–78) demonstrated that indices of attitudes and motivations (e.g., integrative/instrumental orientation) should not be based on single-item scores, but on multiple-item scales developed to assess specific attitude constructs and orientations. Single-item predictors of language proficiency can be quite unreliable and may lack validity. In the present study, most language proficiency scores were based on multiple-item scores. However, in the case of language attitude scores, the number of items varied, with some scores being based on as few as two items. Thus the present study may be vulnerable to some of the shortcomings documented in Gardner's analysis.

Third, Gardner (1985:80–82) illustrated the dangers inherent in using multiple regression as an interpretive tool for predicting language proficiency measures from language attitude scores. Gardner's concerns are focused on the problems inherent in trying to interpret regression coefficients derived from multiple correlation analysis. He suggests that it may be more meaningful to focus attention directly on the correlations of each variable with the criterion. Since the present study did use multiple regression as an interpretive tool, conclusions drawn from such analyses should be viewed with caution.

These methodological issues should be taken into consideration when revising the results obtained in the present study. A reanalysis of some of the results may reveal predictors of language proficiency that are more conceptually coherent and valid than those obtained on the basis of the present set of analyses.

The Portuguese–Canadian study and Cummins's model of language proficiency

Notwithstanding the methodological issues discussed above, the results of the Cummins et al. (1987) study have implications for current models of bilingual proficiency. The most relevant such model is that formulated by Cummins (1984), which proposes that though the surface features of a bilingual's L1 and L2 languages may be different, linguistic interdependence at a deeper level of processing can be shared within a "common underlying proficiency." Results obtained with the Portuguese bilinguals did show interdependence of academic skills across languages and provided support for Cummins's hypothesis.

The DBP study also hypothesized a distinction between grammatical, discourse, and sociolinguistic components of language proficiency. However, despite the conceptual value of the distinction between these three components of language proficiency, little evidence for differentiation in either Portuguese or English emerged in the Portuguese-Canadian study. The distinction between linguistic (grammar and discourse competence) and nonlinguistic/communicative competence (sociolinguistic) has been made elsewhere in the second language learning literature (e.g., Gardner 1985). The Cummins et al. (1987) study was important, since it specifically sought to test the empirical status of these distinctions in the field. Further research may yet uncover the circumstances under which these different aspects of language proficiency become manifest.

The Portuguese–Canadian study and other models of bilingual proficiency

In their study, Cummins et al. (1987) did not articulate a conceptual framework that could help structure the relationship between language attitudes and various measures of language proficiency. However, a number of such models do exist in the literature, and it may be worthwhile to enumerate some of them for the sake of better assessing the unique contribution of the Portuguese-Canadian study within the existing literature.

We will mention six bilingual proficiency models dealing with links between language attitudes and language proficiency to illustrate the prodigious conceptual activity currently going on in the area of second language acquisition. Space limitations do not permit an adequate description or explanation of the functioning of each of these models. However, five of them have already been discussed and compared conceptually and empirically as social process models in Gardner's (1985) recent book entitled *Social Psychology and Second Language Learning*. It is to this volume that researchers should turn for a more adequate presentation of the models enumerated here.

According to Gardner (1985), "social process models" are conceptual formulations concerned less with the linguistic details of language proficiency than with the social factors that motivate individuals to learn languages or prevent them from doing so. These models are social, since learning a language involves both contact with the linguistic features of the target language and some contact with the cultural products of that language, including interpersonal relations with speakers of the target language group. Thus, these models have in common not only a concern with individual factors such as linguistic and academic aptitude, but also a focus on predictors of language proficiency such as attitudes and orientations toward the target language and its speakers, motivational processes for learning and using the target language, formal/informal language learning context, and outcome variables such as linguistic and nonlinguistic/communicative proficiency.

Six models can be included within Gardner's (1985) social process models:

1. Lambert's (1974) social psychology model
2. Schumann's (1978) acculturation model
3. Clément's (1980) social context model
4. Giles and Byrne's (1982) intergroup model
5. Hamers and Blanc's (1982) bilingual development model
6. Gardner's (1983) socio-educational model

A major point of Gardner's analysis is that each model contributes in its own way to a better understanding of bilingual proficiency processes. Gardner points out that at this early stage of empirical verification, it would be premature to embark on a task whose goal would be the articulation of a single supermodel designed to account for all that is known about bilingual proficiency. The aim in this last section is to introduce each model as a way of initiating some discussion of how the Cummins et al. (1987) research can be integrated within the existing literature on bilingual development. With this goal in mind, let us look at the six models.

1. Lambert's model

Lambert's (1974) social psychology model of second language acquisition remains the precursor and basis of all the other models and is depicted in Figure 10.1. The basic point of Lambert's model is that the development of proficiency in a second language has important implications for an individual's self-identity. This is the case since language often emerges as the most important aspect of group members' self-identity (Giles, Bourhis, and Taylor 1977).

Lambert (1974) distinguishes *attitudes,* which refer to attitudinal reactions concerning the ingroup and/or outgroup language and community, from *orientation,* which refers to reasons for learning the language that may be instrumental or integrative (Lambert 1974). Attitudes and orientation together influence the individual's level of *motivation* to learn the target language. *Aptitudes* refer to any class of cognitive abilities, including intelligence and language aptitudes. Aptitudes, motivations, and attitudes are each hypothesized to have a direct impact on language *proficiency.* Once bilingual proficiency develops to a high level, it is shown to have an influence on *self-identity,* which,

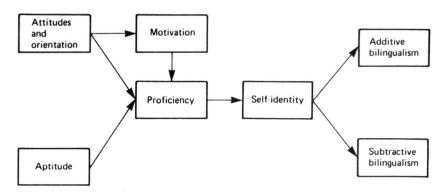

Figure 10.1   Lambert's (1974) social psychology model of bilingual proficiency (from R. C. Gardner, Social psychological aspects of second language learning. London: Edward Arnold. Reprinted with permission)

depending on the dynamics of the intergroup context, will result in *additive* or *subtractive* bilingualism.

When language proficiency in the second language fosters no need to replace or reduce the importance of the first language, additive bilingualism results and changes in self-identity are positive. When proficiency in the second language entails a threat to the first language, subtractive bilingualism results and may lead to loss of cultural identity and social alienation. Subtractive bilingualism is often experienced by linguistic minorities who are encouraged to learn a national language as a way of promoting cultural assimilation to the dominant host culture (Bourhis 1987).

Cummins et al. (1987) did find evidence for the linguistic interdependence hypothesis that could be related conceptually to the language aptitude factor found in most models of bilingual proficiency, including Lambert's (1974). Indirect evidence for Lambert's integrative orientation was found for both Portuguese and English proficiency in the Cummins et al. (1987) study.

2. Schumann's model

Schumann's (1978) acculturation model is concerned mainly with second language acquisition in "natural," noninstructional settings such as the street and the playground. Schumann's (1978) model proposes that second language acquisition is only one aspect of acculturation, and the degree to which learners acculturate to the target language group will control the degree to which they acquire the second language. Gardner

(1985) points out that the Schumann model could be adapted to second language learning situations that are both informal and formal such as classroom learning. The Schumann model alerts us to the importance of a broad range of social, affective, personality, cognitive, and biological factors that could influence bilingual proficiency.

3. Clément's model

Clément's (1980) social context model places great emphasis not only on the motivations of speakers to learn a language, but also on the cultural milieu and relative group vitalities of the speakers involved in becoming bilingual. Like the Lambert (1974) model, this model also focuses on self-identity changes that occur as a result of learning a second language.

Clément's (1980) model was designed to apply in cultural settings where one of the two language communities has a low level of ethnolinguistic vitality relative to the other. Since the notion of ethnolinguistic vitality is incorporated in three of the other bilingual proficiency models presented in this chapter, it is worthwhile to present the group vitality concept here. *Ethnolinguistic vitality* has been described as that which makes a group likely to behave as a distinctive and active collective entity in intergroup situations (Giles, Bourhis, and Taylor 1977). The more vitality an ethnolinguistic group has, the more likely it will be to survive as a distinctive linguistic collectivity in multilingual settings. Conversely, it was proposed that ethnolinguistic groups with little or no group vitality would eventually assimilate linguistically or cease to exist as distinctive groups (Bourhis and Sachdev 1984). The societal variables making up the vitality of ethnolinguistic groups were conceptualized under three main headings: demography, status, and institutional support. A group's strengths and weaknesses in each of these domains must be considered to arrive at an overall assessment of its ethnolinguistic vitality. This structural analysis of the relative strength of language communities within specific intergroup settings has been found to be useful not only in the elaboration of bilingual proficiency models (Clément 1980; Hamers and Blanc 1982; Giles and Byrne 1982; Gardner 1983), but also in other fields of research such as cross-cultural communication and intergroup relations (Bourhis 1979, 1987; Giles and Johnson 1981).

Within Clément's (1980) social context model, a unicultural context is defined as a setting where one language community is clearly in the majority. Primary motivational process is defined as the net result of two opposing forces, integrativeness minus fear of assimilation. *Integrativeness* refers to the desire to become an accepted member of the outgroup culture; *fear of assimilation* refers to the fear that belonging to this "other" culture might result in the loss of the first language and culture. When the difference between these two forces is positive, the primary process reflects integrativeness and a high motivation to learn the outgroup language results. When the difference is negative, the primary process reflects fear of assimilation, and motivation to learn the other language is relatively low. Assuming equivalent linguistic aptitudes, these contrasting motivational states are expected to have a differential impact on communicative competence (bilingual proficiency). In multicultural contexts where the ethnolinguistic vitalities of the language communities are more equal and relatively high, Clément proposes that factors such as self-confidence with the second language become more important, such that both primary and secondary motivational processes are involved in determining levels of bilingual proficiency.

For the Cummins et al. (1987) research, the importance of the Clément (1980) model lies in the fact that this model does take into consideration the relative structural position of the linguistic communities involved in the bilingual proficiency process. Conceptually, the Clément model could differentiate between Portuguese-Canadians who feel threatened by the learning of English in school from those who feel that their ethnic and linguistic identity is not threatened by attendance in English schools. Different rates of bilingual proficiency could be expected, depending on the learner's wish to integrate and fear of assimilation systems. By virtue of their respective ethnolinguistic vitality position, different heritage language groups may also vary in their beliefs concerning the desirability of gaining proficiency in the dominant language of the outgroup majority.

Another important feature of the Clément model is that it can be tested through empirical studies. In the last few years Clément and his colleagues have tested many aspects of the model using a broad range of methodological tools, including LISREL causal modeling (Clément 1986; Clément and Kruidenier 1985). However, none of these tests has been conducted with heritage language groups, and a study such as that of Cummins et al. (1987) could help verify the applicability of the Clément model to heritage language groups.

4. Giles and Byrne model

The Giles and Byrne (1982) intergroup model of bilingual proficiency focuses specifically on the second language acquisition of linguistic minority groups and as such is directly relevant to the Cummins et al. (1987) studies. The major construct in this framework is the self-concept, and the major motivating force is one of developing and maintaining a positive social identity (Giles et al. 1977). Giles and Byrne (1982) propose that *motivation* is central to second language acquisition and that the *integrative motive* is the strongest form of motivation. Along with Lambert (1974) and Gardner (1983), the intergroup model proposes that the acquisition of a second language requires some form of identification with the target language community. The Giles and Byrne (1982) model incorporates the notion that how minority group members perceive their own ethnolinguistic vitality can be as important as their actual group vitality (Bourhis, Giles, and Rosenthal 1981; Johnson, Giles, and Bourhis 1983).

Giles and Byrne (1982:25) propose that people will see themselves in ethnolinguistic terms and strive for positive psycholinguistic differentiation from outgroups when they:

1. See themselves strongly as members of a group with language as an important dimension of its identity
2. Regard their group's relative status as changeable
3. Perceive their ingroup's ethnolinguistic vitality as high
4. Perceive intergroup boundaries as hard
5. Identify with few other social groups, and ones that offer unfavorable social comparisons

Those for whom these five propositions hold true are identified as subgroup A. Those for whom they are false are referred to as subgroup B. Giles and Byrne propose that members of subgroup A will demonstrate a fear of assimilation and will tend to be relatively unsuccessful at learning the second language (Clément 1980). Such minority-group speakers will tend to avoid informal learning contexts and develop proficiency only on those skills specifically learned in the formal classroom context. In contrast, members of subgroup B would be integratively motivated, would seek informal learning contexts, and would be relatively successful in acquiring the language of the majority group.

Though the Giles and Byrne (1982) model has begun to receive some empirical attention (Hall and Gudykunst 1986), it is still in the process of being developed (Giles, Garrett, and Coupland 1987) as new data emerge on how minorities can maintain their cultural identity while acquiring the language of the dominant majority (Pak, Dion, and Dion 1986). The Cummins et al. (1987) study with Portuguese-Canadians is particularly relevant to this model and should contribute to reformulations of some of its features.

5. The Hamers and Blanc model

Hamers and Blanc (1982) have put forward a model known as the bilingual development model. An important feature of this model is that it analyzes the acquisition of bilingual proficiency from a social-developmental framework, and focuses on bilingual acquisition in the child. Important elements within the model include the *relative value system* and *social networks* of language learners. The model also in-

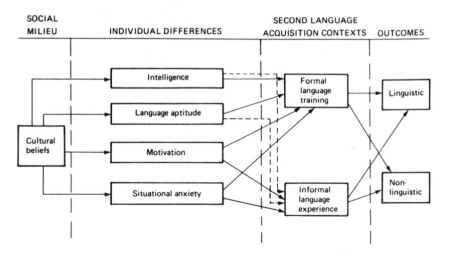

Figure 10.2   Gardner's (1983) socioeducational model of bilingual proficiency (from R. C. Gardner, Social psychological aspects of second language learning. *London: Edward Arnold. Reprinted with permission)*

corporates the notion of *perceived ethnolinguistic vitality,* the *valorization* of functional and formal aspects of L1 and L2, and the *motivational* process for learning and using L1 and L2 for different language functions. As in the previous models, these sociostructural, social, and motivational factors interact to affect the development of linguistic and communicative competence in the L1 and L2. The Hamers and Blanc (1982) model has not received a great deal of empirical attention despite its focus on the development of bilingual proficiency in the child. In line with the Cummins, Lopes, and Ramos (1987) study, it would be interesting to test some of the basic notions of the Hamers and Blanc model by examining the development of bilingual proficiency of heritage language children during their transition from home to school.

6. The Gardner model

As can be seen in Figure 10.2, the Gardner (1983) socio-educational model incorporates many of the features included in the other models. As the model is extensively discussed in Gardner's (1985) recent volume, it need not be discussed in much detail here. The major features of the model include the *social milieu, individual differences, second language acquisition contexts,* and linguistic and nonlinguistic *outcomes* of the learning process.

Gardner proposes that four different types of individual differences will directly influence bilingual proficiency: *intelligence, language aptitudes, motivation,* and *situational anxiety.* Depending on whether the learner has experienced formal language learning and/or informal language experience, each of these individual factors has an impact on the development of bilingual proficiency in linguistic and nonlinguistic domains. Gardner's model is receiving a good deal of support from empirical studies testing the validity of the model with mostly anglophone majority group speakers learning French as a second language in Canada (Gardner 1985; Gardner and Lalonde 1983). The Cummins et al. (1987) research with heritage language groups such as Portuguese-Canadians would provide an ideal opportunity to test the validity of the Gardner model with language minorities who have little choice in deciding whether or not to learn the language of the dominant majority (Bourhis 1987).

Concluding note

This overview of bilingual proficiency models is meant to illustrate the rapidly developing literature on first and second language acquisition. Empirical studies investigating bilingual proficiency phenomena must take into account the numerous conceptual developments that already exist in the literature. It is by subjecting theoretical models to the rough-and-tumble reality of empirical research that we give valid and enduring models of bilingual proficiency the best chance to emerge in the years to come.

11 The role of context and age in the development of bilingual proficiency

Alison d'Anglejan

This chapter focuses on the set of DBP studies relating to the issue of the role of context and age in the development of bilingual proficiency. As I approached the task, it was my hope to use the two themes as a point of departure and to see how they were dealt with empirically in the various papers. However, because the papers are so disparate, they will be discussed sequentially and then synthesized.

Language attitudes and bilingual proficiency of Portuguese–Canadian children in Toronto

Perhaps the most exciting aspect of this study by Cummins, Lopes, and King (1987) is the focus on assessing the mother-tongue development of these minority group children. It is paradoxical that whereas the assessment of mother-tongue proficiency has been at center stage of the immersion evaluations, the mother-tongue development of Greek, Portuguese, Italian, or Arab children in Canada being schooled in English is so easily overlooked, or viewed as irrelevant or not amenable to systematic investigation by mainstream investigators. It has taken a long time for Lambert's (1974) writings on additive bilingualism and Cummins's (1981a) interdependence theory to give rise to research in which a lesser-status minority language mother tongue is granted equal resources in terms of testing and data analysis. While I think this study will stimulate other researchers (including myself) by showing us that such research can be successfully carried out in the context of the public school system, I believe it may have an even greater impact on minority group students, their parents, and anglophone educators, for it removes Portuguese, at least symbolically, from a marginal status and enhances its legitimacy in the school.

Language use and attitude questionnaires

The descriptive results of the language use and attitude questionnaires provided a valuable backdrop for the proficiency data. The patterns of

146

use for the two languages are quite predictable. They show the typical pattern of Portuguese being used in the home, but with a sharp decline in use with the different generations: Portuguese is spoken with the grandparents, less with the parents, and scarcely at all with contemporaries. One wonders whether this pattern leads inevitably to language attrition and assimilation, or whether the formal study of the language in heritage language classes or elsewhere will make it more possible for the language to be passed on to the next generation. Some indices, such as the amount of reading done in Portuguese, do not augur well for the future. However, responses to some questions indicate a strong identification with a bilingual or trilingual identity for students themselves (now and in the future), and for possible marriage partners and future children. They consistently massively reject a unilingual identity, be it English or Portuguese. Note that my reading of these results differs somewhat from that of the authors, who state (Cummins et al. 1987:40) that there is little evidence the children reject their Portuguese identity in favor of an English one. They appear to be opting for additive bilingualism, which may be a form of identity quite different from that of the Portuguese or the Anglo unilingual. In other words, it is not simply the sum of two unilingual identities; it is probably qualitatively different (this interpretation is reinforced by Heller's ethnographic study, discussed below).

The authors remind us that these attitudinal data reflect only one point in a developmental process and that at earlier stages students may have had more negative feelings toward Portuguese, a possibility that might have influenced their relative skills in each language. This is an important point, and the authors might have tried to relate the findings to the existing literature on the developmental aspects of ethnic identity, some of which is cited by Heller (1983). An alternative conjecture concerning the relationship between students' attitudes and lesser proficiency might be that the students perceive quite accurately that their use of Portuguese with the older generation, coupled with small daily doses of Portuguese in class, does not add up to the same thing as their experiences with English. One wishes the authors had provided some information about the heritage language classes. It would be important to find out if they are stimulating children to read for pleasure in the home language. We might expect that such experience would be critical for sustaining the continued development of Portuguese vocabulary, syntactic complexity, and metalinguistic awareness – in other words, academic language proficiency. Without such experiences in the school, the language background in the home, where parents' level of schooling is low, is not likely to be adequate to sustain more than a highly context-embedded dialect form of the language. Studies of minority francophone communities in Canada suggest that this situation is likely to lead to language shift, even when some schooling via the minority language is provided.

Portuguese and English language proficiency

According to the authors, the extensive set of proficiency measures was developed in order to gain additional empirical evidence to test the Canale-Swain model of language proficiency, to examine relationships between the various aspects of language development and contextual and attitudinal variables, and to test the interdependence model. I hoped that as a spinoff from these theoretical goals, I might also learn something about the students' ability to handle the language demands of the school situation.

With respect to the Canale-Swain model, I was left with the impression that the statistical exercise had not contributed much to the quest for construct validity. Furthermore, this quest gave rise to the use of such an extensive array of language proficiency variables that in the end it seemed difficult to see the forest for the trees. The persistent problem in validating the model seems to center on the difficulty of demonstrating empirically the specificity of the discourse and sociolinguistic constructs. Halliday's writings on language as social semiotic (1978) would certainly suggest such strong interrelationships and overlapping among the hypothesized components of communicative competence that it might be unreasonable to expect them to emerge as orthogonal factors in psychometric studies. Likewise, Gumperz in his discourse strategies (1982) discusses aspects of language knowledge that would, according to the Canale-Swain model, be subsumed under sociolinguistic competence. It may be that whereas the model provides a useful conceptual framework for thinking about language and language teaching, hypothetical constructs such as sociolinguistic competence and discourse competence, which are in fact aspects of language variation – and highly complex ones at that – cannot be operationalized, other than trivially, in ways that make them amenable to empirical validation. In fact, Hudson (1980) argues convincingly that while many current conceptualizations of variation may be a reasonable reflection of common-sense knowledge, they actually misrepresent sociolinguistic processes.

One additional question that emerges is the extent to which these conceptualizations of language provide a parsimonious set of criteria in relation to which the development of bilingual proficiency can usefully be described. Do they tell us anything about the criteria that should be met for a child to be deemed communicatively competent at a given stage in his or her development? What I don't know and didn't learn from the paper is which variables are the critical ones for understanding the development of Portuguese-English bilingual proficiency in the context of Toronto schools. The comparison of the Toronto students with their Azorean native speaker peers is interesting. It is a pity some similar data for English native speakers were not gathered, for in the absence of such a comparison group or of some other external yardstick, few inferences can be drawn from this rich set of data as to where these students stand with respect to English proficiency.

The self-evaluation ratings indicate that the vast majority find reading, writing, understanding, and speaking English quite easy to extremely easy. Should these ratings be taken to mean that the students have near native speaker competence? And if so, can we infer that they are firmly on the road to literacy and academic success, with only the specter of assimilation to worry about? As an educational researcher, I would like to have known the relationship between the two sets of language scores and students' marks in language arts or some other school-based measures of academic language proficiency. This would have provided a benchmark that has credibility for schools, and helped to establish external, concurrent evidence of construct validity.

The development of bilingual proficiency in the transition from home to school

Kindergarten-age Portuguese children in Toronto and their native speaker peers in the Azores are the target of this longitudinal study, which will follow their development through grade 1 (Cummins, Lopes, and Ramos 1987). By examining the spontaneous use of language in the home, as well as performance on various elicitation tasks, the researchers propose to examine the concurrent development of English and Portuguese as the children undergo early schooling and initial exposure to literacy training. One of the study's five stated objectives is to determine to what extent the language and literacy measures are sensitive to potential learning problems children from minority language backgrounds may encounter. According to the authors, such problems are often difficult to identify at an early age because the language difference masks the learning problem.

The study places greater emphasis on literacy than did the grade 7 one and in my opinion involves a more interesting and tightly focused set of language indices. The home background is brought into the study through a parents' questionnaire and the yearly taping of the 1.5 hours of spontaneous interaction between parents and children in the home. The questionnaire (administered in June 1985, when the first year's testing was carried out) was based on that used in the grade 7 study, but included more information about the child's exposure to printed material, the extent to which he or she knew how to read or write before going to school, and whether the parents read or told the children stories, all indices of literacy in the home.

In examining the proposed scoring scheme for the analysis of the home interactions, we may note that the focus is entirely on the child's production on such criteria as C-units, grammar, word order, and lexicon. It appears that the study will not examine the nature of the interactions between the child and the parent. Wells's work (1981) suggests that this might be of considerable interest.

As in the previous study, Portuguese native speaker peers are included, but no English native speaker comparison group is involved. Should we infer that this element has been systematically excluded, possibly to avoid invidious comparisons, or to enhance the symbolic status of Portuguese? Or do the authors feel that no additional information regarding English is required other than that provided by comparisons with the Portuguese results? This issue warrants clarification, particularly since the language of instruction is primarily English and the research is based in education. Should learning problems be found, will it be possible to exclude proficiency in English as a factor on the basis of these scores alone?

This leads to an additional observation regarding the two Portuguese studies, namely, the students' apparent relative success in acquiring the two language systems. The sociocultural background profile – minority group parents with low levels of schooling, probably low support for literacy in the home, a home-school language switch, a fairly encapsulated low-status ethnic group, and so on – would lead us to predict possible language-related problems in schooling. Yet all appears to be well at the end of kindergarten and at the grade 7 level. Are our theories wrong? If so, so much the better. On the other hand, if the Quebec experience is any indication, we find in some English secondary schools and colleges disproportionate numbers of students from backgrounds similar to those in the Portuguese studies who cannot handle the language and literacy requirements of their programs. Could it be that the research should be looking more closely at what goes on at the secondary level as the literacy requirements of schooling become more demanding? Perhaps it is there that the lack of comparison data for English native speakers might be apparent, particularly if we want to be able to tease apart the language factor from social class effects.

One interesting question the study could not address is the extent to which the Portuguese children's native language proficiency is the result of the heritage language program and how enduring any such effect might be.

Age of arrival, length of residence, and interdependence of literacy skills among Japanese immigrant children

I read this study by Cummins and Nakajima (1987) with particular interest, given the great difference between Japanese and English at the surface level. At stake were the critical period or optimal age hypothesis (Scovel 1988) and the interdependence hypothesis (Cummins 1981a). The students are of a higher social class than those in the Portuguese study, belong to a very achievement-oriented culture, and intend to return to Japan, factors that could be expected to enhance the development and maintenance of bilingual proficiency. I was pleased to see the selection of literacy measures as the criterion variables, given their relevance for school learning. The finding that the older students are when they come to Canada, the better the prospect for a strong, continued development of Japanese literacy, is not surprising, since they are no doubt better readers to begin with and can bring more powerful metacognitive skills to the task.

The negative correlation the analysis revealed between Japanese reading and length of residence seems to indicate that the literacy classes held on weekends are not adequate to sustain reading proficiency. This finding corroborates the findings from the Portuguese study. However, before concluding that more instruction in Japanese is the required solution, one might question whether the children are doing enough leisure reading in their native language. The motivation to do so might be rather low, but amenable to improvement. The characteristics of the children's home background suggest that it might not be unreasonable to expect the parents to play some role in this area. What is clear, however, is the importance of reading in the home language during the initial period when the child has little knowledge of the second language and has not yet developed literacy skills in that language. Once again, this is a reminder of how vital the role of the school would be at this critical time in providing support for reading for children from less literate homes.

With respect to the development of English literacy, the power of the length of residence variable can be interpreted as reflecting both exposure to the language itself and the impact of schooling, with the emphasis placed at the early primary level on the enhancement of literacy. The fact that those arriving at age 6–7 made more rapid progress in English reading than the others would seem to reflect the benefit derived from the systematic teaching of reading that is initiated at that level. The implications of this finding for the interdependence hypothesis are not too clear. The theory would predict that the absence of full L1 literacy would make the acquisition of literacy in the new school language particularly difficult. Can the success of this group be attributed to the simultaneous teaching of L1 literacy in the Japanese weekend classes, notwithstanding the decline in Japanese reading proficiency associated with length of residence?

Whereas the availability of grade level norms does provide some information about the relative ability of the Japanese children on the reading measure, such scores do not tell us anything about the actual ability of these children to handle grade-level reading material. The literacy demands at the upper grade levels would be particularly challenging, and one might hypothesize that any discrepancy between the school performance of the non-native speaker and the majority group child might be particularly apparent at the high school levels. I am puzzled as to why the researchers have focused all their attention on the primary level, and I would like to know more about the role of social class and ethnicity in the development of bilingual proficiency.

It is interesting that the findings of this study do not corroborate those reported by Collier (1987) in her study of the relationship between age and acquisition of cognitive-academic language proficiency involving 10,531 students. In this study, children who arrived in the United States at the ages 5, 6, and 7 did not achieve at a rate equal to children at other grade levels. Furthermore, the data clearly showed a dramatic difference in school demands for academic skills in the upper grades: Even with a strong academic background in the native language, students who arrived in grade 7 at age 12 and were tested five years later in grade 12 were substantially behind national norms in achievement in all subject areas except mathematics.

The relationship between starting age and oral second language proficiency in three groups of classroom learners

The theme of age is once again the focus of attention in this paper by Harley (1987), which examines the relation between starting age and oral second language proficiency in three groups of classroom learners. The study addresses the question of the relative advantages of early total immersion, late extended French, and late immersion. The issue is of practical interest to administrators, concerned as they are with rationalizing programs by means of cost benefit analyses. It also has implications for parents who want to make informed choices for their children's schooling, and of course it can provide an additional test of the optimal age hypothesis.

The discovery a few years ago that the early immersion children's head start in French did not seem to result in the systematic advantages that might have been predicted came as a surprise to many of us. Wilder Penfield's writing on the advantages of early bilingualism were particularly well known to Canadians and we were, both as individuals and researchers, predisposed toward an uncritical acceptance of his views. The present study confirms once again the lack of any systematic advantage ascribable to an early start. Indeed, it suggests that some good things and some bad may result from all three types of program.

It seems, however, that this study cannot address the age factor per se, since that variable overlaps with the program factor. In addition to an early start, early immersion entails an initial period of unstructured exposure, followed by a focus on form, whereas other program variants involve, in addition to immersion at a later age, a more analytic introduction to the language. As the author points out in her very thorough discussion and interpretation of the data, content-focused classroom talk does not necessarily provide learners with a great deal of exposure to some problematic L2 forms, nor does it necessarily encourage the productive use of such forms by students. In the absence of form-focused teaching and reliable error correction, the students develop non-native patterns of use strongly influenced by their mother tongue, and these become established as a mutually comprehensible interlanguage. A number of questions come to mind with respect to this issue.

The social dialect that appears to develop in an immersion classroom, according to visitors and researchers, may reflect, in addition to the lack of a francophone peer group, the absence of any consensus transmitted by the school regarding the importance of a standard norm. In his discussion of pidgin and Creole language varieties, Hudson (1980) argues convincingly that the force behind the development and maintenance of inflectional irregularity in speech is pressure on the individual to conform. Similar pressure from society prevents the disappearance of inflectional morphology and prevents it from being eliminated, as happens when the sole criterion is efficiency and ease of communication. In comparing the learning of English in foreign language and second language settings, Richards (1972) notes that in the former context, the target language is not involved in any societal functions, and there is always an attempt to teach the standard form of the language and to present facts about the target culture. Any deviation from the standard is an error. In second language situations, local varieties may come to be accepted as standards, and there tends to be less reference to a standard norm. The immersion classes would seem to be somewhere between these two examples in that the language does not really fulfill any societal function, yet is taught as though that were the case.

In the case of French in immersion classes, we are dealing with a language that has undergone considerable standardization (the Académie française was established in the seventeenth century), and that has a morphology very much more inflected than that of English (Hudson, 1980). Considerable effort must be invested in the teaching of the written form, since many inflections which are homophones in the spoken language are distinct in the written form. Thus, whereas the teaching of spelling is appropriate for English, the explicit teaching of grammar coupled with some form of dictée has traditionally been used to teach francophone children, even at a young age, the grammatical distinctions that underlie the written language. Although some of these practices were abandoned during recent years in favor of more communicative approaches, they are being reinstated within communicative programs for native speakers as it becomes apparent that they are necessary for the teaching of the written form.

The norm is a very salient concept among educated francophones. Indeed, Paul Daoust, a doctoral student in the Faculty of Education at the University of Montreal, is now working on a dissertation focusing on pronouncements on the norm in pedagogical publications in Quebec between 1957 and 1985. The corpus is proving to be very much more vast than expected, involving thousands of texts. The question that arises with respect to the fossilized forms noted in the immersion students is, To what extent are they attributable solely to insufficient exposure to standard forms, or to the fact that the school may not be transmitting any awareness of the importance of standard speech or any motivation to conform? The question is prompted by my own perception of the extent to which the norm is a salient, explicit cultural value in francophone communities, including Quebec.

It seems to me that, in the absence of an adequate cultural consensus or explicit common will transmitted by the school regarding the role of the standard language, a concern that is so much a core value of francophone culture, we may be deluding ourselves by expecting linguists to produce the required remedies. Some of the errors made by the children appear to concern forms they would inevitably have encountered in their reading (if they are doing any in French) and some of the aspectual distinctions which differ in French and English, while complex indeed, are surely learnable through such analytic activities as reading and dictée.

In addition to observing immersion classrooms, perhaps we should be looking at cultural settings where the norm is transmitted more explicitly to see what we can learn from them; in particular, how this value is translated into pedagogy. Richard Duran's (1985) work on the sociolinguistic cultural schemata that underlie learning might also provide valuable insights. As the situation stands, I suspect that the prevailing cultural norm in immersion schools with respect to the importance of standard language is that which underlies North American

English, rather than French. In summary, I believe that the potential of the immersion setting has not really been put to the test. It would be particularly interesting to know whether the non-native fossilized forms are truly dead, or whether they might undergo metamorphosis and emerge in glory under sociocultural conditions where the students would be more motivated to conform. The question is whether such conditions can be generated in a minority language situation.

Language and ethnic identity in a Toronto French-language school

This paper (Heller 1983, 1984) is a fine-grained ethnographic study of the forces that shape ethnic identity in a Toronto French school (not to be confused with the immersion schools). The study is a compelling one; it reveals once again the pervasive influence of English and the pressure it exerts on the language and ethnic identity of francophone minority group children. The dynamics of the social interactions that shape the definition of the children's ethnic identity reflect not only the micro-sociolinguistic forces at work within that particular school, but at the macrosociolinguistic level, the tension between French and English in Canada. The study makes clear, in a way no others were able to, the meaning of context in the development of bilingualism. The efforts of the francophone teachers to affirm the culture of this French school are poignant. One gains a new appreciation of the formidable task that confronts immersion teachers.

In both situations, by virtue of a collective will, education is taking place in French, whereas the natural ecology of the situation would have it take place in English. One senses that the culturally transmitted motivation of the francophones to try to preserve their language and identity through schooling is so different from the goals that explain the presence of the anglophone children that cohabitation scarcely seems a desirable common goal. Yet in the absence of cohabitation, as in the case of immersion, the learning and using of French by English-speaking children seems to lack an adequate underpinning of values. The meaning of the collective will that gave rise to the immersion programs perhaps needs to be made more explicit to the students.

Synthesis

Having examined the individual elements in this set of studies, I will now attempt to synthesize.

My reading of the grade 7 Portuguese study left me with the impression (possibly unjust) that the researchers were more interested in the psychometric properties of the data and the opportunity they afforded to test their theoretical models than in the language proficiency of the Portuguese students. In this study, and to a certain extent in the Japanese one, the statistical findings could have been interpreted or discussed in greater depth; certainly little attempt was made to link them to existing research, other than to the authors' own work.

The studies reveal that for most of these bilingual students, gains in English have been accompanied by declines in aspects of their L1 proficiency (the Japanese students) or by a lower level of development than in the case of native speaker peers (the Portuguese grade 7 students). The absence of English native speaker reference groups, or of an attempt to relate the myriad first and second language measures to any external school-based criterion (in the Portuguese study particularly) leave the reader wondering what all these data have to say about bilingual language proficiency and schooling. As a result, the rationale for the longitudinal study is not entirely clear. Furthermore, since all the children in the study were enrolled in heritage language classes, the impact of that support for mother tongue maintenance could not be singled out.

Future resources might be used to carry out more ethnographic work in the schools attended by the Portuguese children. Indeed, both the Portuguese sociolinguistic questionnaire and Heller's ethnographic study have served to remind us of the preponderant role played by ethnicity and culture in the development of bilingual proficiency. We need to know more about the cultural climate in heritage language classes and the extent to which adequate attention is paid to the development of literacy. We have learned from these studies that reading, like piano playing and athletics, benefits from coaching and practice. If the interdependence model predicts a positive transfer of academic language skills between languages, why do the native language skills seem so vulnerable? Does the answer lie in the sociocultural status of the languages, in the amount of exercise they get, or in the quantity and quality of teaching? On the topic of teaching, the researchers might have provided more information on the content and focus of the L2 programs to which the students were exposed. The ethnographic study whetted my appetite to see more work of this type in conjunction with quantitative approaches.

Finally, we are beginning to realize that the worldwide spread of English has endowed it with a status that tends to make it prevail over other languages in contact situations. For that reason, we need to know more about the development of bilingual proficiency in French schools in Montreal. What is the fate of the Arabic, Portuguese, Greek, or Italian spoken by students being educated in French? According to popular belief and some research evidence (e.g., Bredimas-Assimopoulos 1975), they suffer a kinder fate than when they are in competition with English.

Is the development of the analytic skills necessary for the acquisition of written French and awareness of standard French norms being adequately addressed in teaching practices, or is the assumption being made that approaches appropriate for teaching English can simply be transferred to French? The importance of the teaching of vocabulary emerged clearly from the research.

With respect to the culture of the school, or of the classroom, it is clear that teachers in immersion programs and in francophone schools in minority settings have difficulty in transmitting some of the values which underlie francophone culture. The ethnographic study makes us sensitive to the reasons that prompt francophone educators to seek control over French schooling and to be wary of cohabitation.

This set of studies has deepened and enriched our perspective on the development of bilingual proficiency during the elementary school years. Collier's study should provide a new impetus for the researchers to look more closely at the secondary level.

12 The relationship between first and second languages: language proficiency and language aptitude

Barry McLaughlin

The focus in the social context and age section of the DBP report (Volume III of Harley, Allen, Cummins, and Swain 1987), is on the relationship between individual and social-environmental factors and the development of bilingual proficiency. The report is rich and stimulating. The findings are of considerable interest to researchers, and even the questions raised by the report move the field forward. There is a great deal to discuss, but I would like to restrict my remarks to the topics of language proficiency and language aptitude. Language aptitude receives little explicit attention in the report, but I will argue that it is a factor of considerable importance in understanding the relationship between first and second language proficiency.

Individual differences in language learning

I would like to begin by making some comments on current theory and individual differences in language learning. Then I will turn to some research on individual differences, before addressing the question of language aptitude generally.

Current theory and individual differences

UNIVERSAL GRAMMAR THEORY

As I read the *Zeitgeist* in first and second language research, there seems to be a resurgence of interest in the Chomskyan notion of an independent language-learning faculty. Advocates of a Universal Grammar approach to language learning (e.g., White 1985b, 1987a) maintain that, in addition to relatively close-to-surface levels of syntactic representation, there are more abstract levels of representation which children learning a first language cannot induce simply from the data presented to them in adult speech. This is the "poverty of the stimulus" argument – that input to children is meager and degenerate and therefore cannot provide an adequate basis for setting the parameters of the language. To solve this projection problem – to work out a complex grammar on the basis of insufficient data – the theory contends that children acquire first language so effortlessly because the crucial abstract principles of Universal Grammar are available to them innately. Children can learn their first language readily because Universal Grammar constrains the hypotheses they make about input.

There are problems with the poverty of stimulus argument, however. A great deal of research indicates that parents and caregivers tailor their speech to young children in a way that makes the input more understandable (McLaughlin 1984, chap. 2). In attempting to communicate with the child, caregivers provide:

1. Conversational lessons when they help the child to sustain a conversation by means of attention-getters and attention-holders, prompting questions, and expansions.
2. Mapping lessons when they provide utterances that can be decoded by use of context.
3. Segmentation lessons when they give clues as to how utterances are divided into words, phrases, or clauses (Clark and Clark 1977).

Language to young children is more simple, slower, related to events and objects in the here-and-now, and contains a more limited vocabulary than speech directed at older children or adults. The effect of these features of the input language on children's language acquisition is debated among language researchers, but there is general agreement that the input is more suited to the child's needs than Chomsky saw it to be. At least in the early stages, environmental influences may be important in language acquisition.

Furthermore, another argument for the need for an innate mechanism has been criticized. This is the notion that children do not receive enough negative input to explain how they form correct hypotheses about the language. Schachter (1984) has pointed out that phenomena such as confirmation checks, clarification requests, and failures to understand qualify as negative input. Consider these conversations:

CHILD: Read to me a book.
ADULT: What?
CHILD: Read a book to me.

NON-NATIVE SPEAKER: Um in Harvard, what you study?
NATIVE SPEAKER: What?
NON-NATIVE SPEAKER: What you es study?
NATIVE SPEAKER: What am I studying?
NON-NATIVE SPEAKER: Yeah.

Such examples suggest that language learners can be led to appropriate speech in other ways than through explicit corrections. Once one accepts a broader reading for negative input, the learning problem becomes less intractable than Universal Grammar theory supposes. This does not mean that the problem is solved; it is not entirely clear whether negative feedback leads to the kind of corrections that are called for. Nonetheless, environmental factors may play more of a role than is allowed by the poverty of the stimulus argument.

There is another bothersome fact for an approach which supposes that a wired-in universal mechanism automatically generates a rule-governed language system. This is the evidence for individual differences in the _rate_ of first language acquisition. UG theory emphasizes sameness – the way all individuals learn languages regardless of external characteristics and internal abilities. The theory has no way of accounting for variation, either in first or in second language acquisition (Skehan 1986). But people do vary in language acquisition – especially in second language acquisition. How is the theory to account for this? Are some people able to access the Universal Grammar more efficiently? Is the UG more efficiently organized in some people, more automated? These are questions the theory has yet to address.

THE MONITOR MODEL

The other major theory in the field – at least in the eyes of practitioners in the United States – is Krashen's Monitor theory, which also fails to account for individual differences. Krashen, as you know, employs the ephemeral distinction between "learning" and "acquisition," and relegates individual differences to the learning component. Individuals differ in their use of the Monitor, which controls conscious learning. Acquisition, on the other hand, is unconscious and the product of the Language Acquisition Device, which is universally available to language acquirers.

In Krashen's theory, differences in performance show up because of different reactions to teaching, differences in the ability to induce rules, and differences in other types of conscious performance that occur during monitored learning (Krashen 1981). In contrast, acquisition is thought to be the product of innate, natural processes that are universal.

The problem is that learning is relevant only to special circumstances of language performance. In fact, these circumstances are so rarefied that they are of little practical importance (McLaughlin 1987). Empirical attempts to demonstrate conditions of Monitor use have led Krashen to change and redefine those conditions. Indeed, Krashen's repeated failures to demonstrate the operation of the Monitor have led him essentially to abandon the concept in his latest writings on input (Krashen 1985). As Seliger (1979) concluded, the Monitor is limited to such specific output modalities and requires such carefully confined conditions for its operation that it cannot be thought to be representative of the learner's internal, conscious knowledge of the grammar.

Without the Monitor, however, the theory has no way of accounting for individual differences. In fact, Krashen (1981) rules out language aptitude as a predictor of second language success in children (and, presumably, in adults). What individual differences are observed are thought to be the result of attitudinal factors that influence the "affective filter" – another murky theoretical concept that lacks empirical justification (McLaughlin 1987).

To summarize, current theory – at least the two most popular formulations – has little room for individual differences in language-learning ability. First and second languages are thought to be acquired via the Language Acquisition Device, which relies on universal, wired-in principles. What differences are observed in language performance are assumed to be the result of attitudinal differences. Little attention is given to the possibility of differences in language-learning ability.

Some research on individual differences

My interest in the topic of language-learning ability or aptitude was stimulated by a comment of G. L. MacNab in a critical review of studies of the cognitive consequences of bilingualism. In discussing research from immersion programs, MacNab made the point that there is a possibility of a selection bias in such studies:

Consider two families living side by side in similar houses with fathers going off to very similar nine-to-five jobs. Both families have a five-year-old whose birthday is in August. The girls are matched for sex, age, and SES (measured by residence and father's occupation). One family sends their daughter to an immersion program. The other chooses the regular program. This choice probably means some basic difference between families or the children. For example, the family choosing immersion may be more open to people of different cultural backgrounds, more willing to try new experiences. Or the child in the other family may have been slower than "average" in learning to talk. (1979:242).

Elsewhere, MacNab noted that research on the cognitive consequences of bilingualism is typically done on children who

...tend to come from homes where there is an open cognitive ambiance and where there is encouragement of learning in general and language learning in particular. In this environment the brighter, more able child picks up the second language and becomes bilingual, the less able child is less apt to become fully (or balanced) bilingual, in part because he has other options open and does not have to spend energies becoming fluently bilingual if that is difficult for him. (1979:251)

MacNab's point is that, lacking fully random selection, it is impossible to say whether bilingual experiences lead to positive cognitive consequences or whether differences in initial aptitude lead to bilingual experiences.

RESEARCH ON INTELLIGENCE

To the lay person, it seems obvious that intelligence is an important factor determining an individual's success in learning a second language. Yet research with this variable has not shown intelligence to be a necessary component of aptitude in second language learning. This appears to depend, however, on the way the language is taught. As John B. Carroll noted:

Apparently, verbal intelligence is more extensively required in the more formal, literature-oriented courses taught in high school, college, and university courses than it is in more audio-lingually and practically oriented courses ... I have also speculated that the extent to which verbal intelligence is required in foreign language courses depends upon the degree to which the mode of instruction puts a premium on a student's verbal intelligence in order to understand the content of instruction. (1981:106)

If Carroll's surmise is correct, one would expect verbal intelligence to play a greater role in second language learning when the material is taught in a formal manner, with great emphasis on reasoning analytically about verbal material.

This may be one reason why intelligence has been found to correlate less strongly with second language learning in younger than in older learners (Genesee and Hamayan 1980). Children who learn the second language in an immersion setting or in a bilingual classroom do not approach the language as analytically as do students in traditional high school or college classes. In general, there seems to be little relationship between measures of intelligence and oral language proficiency in young children, although, as Genesee (1976) observed, there may be some relationship between intelligence and literacy skills in a second language.

RESEARCH ON THE RELATIONSHIP BETWEEN
FIRST AND SECOND LANGUAGE DEVELOPMENT

In the search for individual difference variables other than intelligence that might affect second language learning, researchers have looked at such factors as empathy, field independence, and other cognitive styles – with mixed success (McLaughlin 1985). Some recent work points in the direction of a general language aptitude factor. I am referring here to work coming out of the Bristol Language Project (Wells 1981, 1985), specifically research reported by Peter Skehan (1986). The Bristol project showed, among other things, that the variation Roger Brown (1973) observed in the rate of language acquisition in Adam, Eve, and Sarah was a general phenomenon. With a much larger sample, Gordon Wells and his associates demonstrated that there is tremendous variation in the speed at which children acquire their first language. Some children reach a given point of language development well in advance of others.

Skehan decided to conduct a follow-up study with children in the original Bristol project, who are now of secondary (high) school age, to determine whether the rate of acquisition demonstrated by individual children in first language learning had any relationship to second language learning. Some 100 of the original sample of 125 children were studied as teenagers learning a second language in a classroom setting. The basic research question was whether children who were more rapid first language learners showed higher aptitude and performance in second language learning.

Skehan's study focused on language analytic aspects of aptitude (grammatical sensitivity and inductive language learning ability), which were used as dependent measures in a series of regression analyses. The results indicated that second language learning, when measured at the age of thirteen to sixteen, related to two factors. First, there was evidence that children who developed more quickly in their first language, as indicated by such measures as mean length of utterance (MLU) and sentence structure complexity, performed better in learning a second language. Similarly, a test of vocabulary given early in life correlated consistently with subsequent aptitude. That is, there appears to be a general language-processing capacity that affects language learning ability in first and subsequent languages.

A strong relationship was also found with a set of measures relating to family background, parental education, and parental literacy. Skehan noted that Gordon Wells and others (Tizard and Hughes 1984) have found evidence that middle-class families are more likely to use language in a way that communicates to the child that words stand for things and are manipulated with an internal logic of their own, removed from immediate context. This use of decontextualized language in the home is highly predictive of educational success. Skehan's research thus suggested that aptitude in learning a second language in school relates both to a general language-processing capacity and to family influences that inculcate in the child the ability to use language in a decontextualized manner.

Aptitude and language learning

I would like to turn now to a consideration of the issue of aptitude and language learning. Again, I am indebted to Peter Skehan, who in a recent paper (1986) made the important point that the role of language aptitude has been neglected in much recent research on second language learning. Specifically, Skehan noted that the model of aptitude developed by John B. Carroll (1967, 1981) is one of the best worked out in applied linguistics and foreshadows a number of developments in contemporary cognitive psychology. I think it is worth looking at Carroll's ideas briefly and at their relationship to information-processing theory. Then I would like to turn to some current research on expert-novice systems that bears on second language learning and conclude with some general comments on the DBP studies of individual and social-environmental factors in second language learning.

Carroll's model and information-processing theory

THE COMPONENTS OF FOREIGN LANGUAGE APTITUDE

Carroll proposed a model of language aptitude that attempted to account for the variance in foreign language learning (which may account for its neglect in current treatments of second language acquisition). Many second language researchers have focused on naturalistic and "untutored" learning and theorists have speculated, as we have seen, on natural processing mechanisms common to first and second language acquisition. A model directed at the sources of individual variation in classroom learning does not fit well with this *Zeitgeist*.

Moreover, current popular methods of language teaching, such as the Natural Approach (Krashen and Terrell 1983), assume that learners simply need to be exposed to "comprehensible input" – the rest happens naturally. But any teacher is aware that whatever happens, happens more naturally for some children than for others. Carroll's model provides some suggestions as to why there are such marked individual differences in second language learning. The model postulates several relatively independent subcomponents:

1. Phonetic coding ability – an ability to identify distinct sounds, to form associations between those sounds and symbols representing them, and to retain these associations.
2. Grammatical sensitivity – the ability to recognize the grammatical functions of words (or other linguistic entities) in sentence structures.
3. Rote learning ability for foreign language materials – the ability to learn associations between sounds and meanings rapidly and efficiently, and to retain these associations; and
4. Inductive language learning ability – the ability to infer or induce the rules governing a set of language materials, given samples of language materials that permit such inferences (Carroll 1981:105).

These components were arrived at by statistical analyses of correlational data involving Carroll's Modern Language Aptitude Test (MLAT) and other tests of language aptitude and classroom language performance.

One can argue that these components of language aptitude apply to all language-learning situations. Both tutored and untutored learners need to distinguish the sounds of the new language, to develop sensitivity to how sentences are put together, to associate sounds and meanings, and to infer and induce rules. These aptitudes are even more important in a natural situation, because without instruction the learner is thrown on his or her own devices and has to impose structure on complex input without the help of a teacher (Skehan 1986).

APTITUDE AND INFORMATION PROCESSING

Carroll (1981) pointed out that the tasks contained in aptitude tests are similar to the performances described in information-processing accounts of cognitive functioning. He proposed an analysis of the four components of language aptitude in information-processing terms (Table 12.1).

In this analysis cognitive operations are seen to consist of storing information in sensory buffers (visual or auditory), retrieving information from such buffers, storing and retrieving information in different kinds of memory stores (short-term memory [STM], intermediate-term memory [ITM], and long-term memory [LTM]), and manipulating information in the executive working memory. Strategies are seen to represent possible variations among subjects in their manner of approaching the task, or special cognitive operations that make processing more (or sometimes less) efficient than otherwise.

The object of the analysis is to focus on where in these operations and strategies individual differences are most likely to exhibit themselves. Thus individuals are likely to vary in their ability to recognize grammatical functions and to match functions in different sentence structures. Such variation is thought to reflect differences in the ability to operate in working memory and to store and retrieve information from short-term memory.

Note that differences in aptitude can be quite complex. Individual differences in phonetic coding ability can appear in the capacity to encode auditory phonetic stimuli and in the temporal parameters of this process, as well as in the capacity to store and retrieve images of these auditory stimuli in short-term or intermediate-term memory. Furthermore, individuals differ in the contents of long-term memory stores of relevant phonetic-orthographic information.

Carroll has always stressed the interaction of variables. Time available thus has an effect on the success of learners: Some students will be able

TABLE 12.1 POSTULATED INDIVIDUAL DIFFERENCES IN COGNITIVE PROCESSES AND MEMORY STORES ASSOCIATED WITH POSTULATED FOREIGN LANGUAGE APTITUDE FACTORS*

Factor	Principal memory involved	Cognitive processes			Strategies
		Addressing sensory buffers	Operations	Manipulations in executive and STM	
			Addressing ITM or STM		
Phonetic coding	ITM (phonetic images)	Encode auditory phonetic stimuli, and if necessary, orthographic symbols (C,T)	Store and retrieve phonetic images and associations in ITM (C) Retrieve relevant phonetic-orthographic information from LTM	Store phonetic images in STM (T,C) Match phonetic images with orthographic symbols (T,C)	Find mediators in LTM (P)
Grammatical sensitivity	LTM (grammatical concepts)		Retrieve grammatical concepts from LTM (C)	Recognize grammatical functions Match functions in different sentence structures	

Rote-learning ability (associative memory)	ITM (associations between linguistic forms and meanings)	(1) Store in ITM (T,C) (2) Retrieve from ITM (T,C)	Find mediators in LTM (P,C,T) Rehearse associations (P)
Inductive language learning ability	ITM (novel linguistic rules)	Search LTM for types of hypotheses concerning possible linguistic rules (C,T)	

*Individual differences in: (C) contents or capacity of memory store involved; (T) temporal parameters of the process; (P) probability of a strategy.

Source: From Carroll (1981, p. 110) in *Individual differences and universals in language learning aptitudes*, edited by K. C. Diller. Reprinted by permission of Harper & Row, Publishers, Inc. Copyright © 1979 by Justin Lieber.

to cope with material in less time than others. Some learners will not be able to acquire a language skill in a short time or to show what they are capable of under time pressure. Other variables that mediate the effect of aptitude include intelligence, manner of presentation, and motivation.

Carroll emphasized that his analysis was intended to serve as a heuristic device to guide further thinking and research. His focus on the cognitive abilities of the language learner antedates recent work on expert systems that is quite consistent with this framework. I would like to turn now to some of this work.

Current research on expert-novice systems

Research in a number of domains suggests that experts use different information-processing strategies and techniques than do novice learners. For example, Chase and Simon (1973) replicated de Groot's (1965) finding that master chess players reconstructed with greater than 90 percent accuracy midgame boards they had seen for only 5 seconds. They observed that master players recalled clusters that formed attack or defense configurations, whereas beginners lacked the skill to form such abstract representations. McKeithen, Reitman, Rueter, and Hirtle (1981) found that intermediate programmers clustered the words of a programming language by concept, whereas novices clustered the same words alphabetically. Strategy differences were also reported by Adelson (1981, 1984), who found that expert programmers used abstract, conceptually based representations when attempting to recall programming material, whereas novices used more concrete representations.

Differences between experts and novices have also been found in research on learning mechanisms in physics (Chi, Glaser, and Rees 1981), arithmetic (Brown and Burton 1978), algebra (Lewis 1981), and geometry (Anderson, Greeno, Kline, and Neves 1981). For the most part these studies show that experts restructure the elements of a learning task into abstract schemata that are not available to novices, who focus principally on the surface elements. Thus experts replace complex subelements with single schemata that allow more abstract processing.

EXPERT-NOVICE DIFFERENCES

In the realm of language learning, experts can be operationally defined as individuals who have learned a number of languages. There is considerable anecdotal evidence that once a person has learned a few languages, subsequent language learning is greatly facilitated. Presumably, some positive transfer results from the process of language learning and carries over to the learning of a new language. The expert has learned and routinized complex skills that have become automatic through experience with languages.

Nation and McLaughlin (1986) carried out an experiment in which they compared information processing in multilingual, bilingual, and monolingual subjects learning a miniature linguistic system. Subjects were exposed to a limited subset of permissible strings from a finite-state Markov grammar. We were interested in whether they could apply generalizations derived from the learned subset to novel strings and if so, what the nature of these generalizations was. Subjects viewed a miniature linguistic system under conditions in which they were exposed to it without instructions to learn (implicit learning) or under conditions in which they were told that the system was rule-based and they should learn the rules (explicit learning). Multilingual subjects were found to learn the grammar significantly better than bilingual or monolingual groups when the instructions called for implicit learning, but not when the instructions called for explicit learning. Nation and McLaughlin argued on the basis of their data that the superior performance of the multilingual subjects on the implicit-learning task was the result of better automated letter- and pattern-recognition skills.

In general, it may be that individuals with more language learning experience build up certain basic skills that transfer to new situations. I would argue that these skills include the components of language aptitude in Carroll's model – phonetic coding ability, grammatical sensitivity, rote learning ability, and inductive language learning ability. In the Nation and McLaughlin study, where pattern recognition skills had become relatively automatic in multilingual subjects, attention is freed to be devoted to the recognition of rule-governed regularities.

In another experiment from our laboratory (Nayak, Hansen, Krueger, and McLaughlin 1987), monolingual and multilingual subjects were exposed to a linguistic system that involved a phrase structure grammar in which constituents were defined by dependencies between words, as well as by regularities of substitution and equivalence (Morgan and Newport 1981). We found no differences between multilingual and monolingual subjects in vocabulary or rule learning. The experts were not better than the novices on these tasks, but there were differences in how the two groups went about the tasks. In this experiment, half of the multilingual and the monolingual subjects were told to memorize the material they were exposed to and half were told to look for underlying rules. All subjects were asked at three points during the learning phase to verbalize for another potential subject exactly what they were doing and what strategies they were using.

We coded the verbalizations of all subjects into four categories. The first two referred to strategies that involved the use of mnemonic devices, either *visual* – for example:

First, I was trying to look at the abstract form above the word and just try and remember what they looked like, see if there's some type of correlation... CAV looked like a cave.... I tried to associate the words with the symbols.

or *verbal* – for example:

...I tried looking at the words themselves and seeing if I could eliminate certain letters like the first letter of each thing, if I could form a word out of that or I kept just trying different combinations to see if by reading it backwards and forwards and all these different ways, if it would make some sense.

Two other categories reflected the use of linguistic strategies, either *structural:*

This time it seems like I'm inclined to finding places more than... I uh, it seems like I'm splitting them up into nouns and verbs and objects, and if one goes into a place where, say if an object goes into a place where I think a verb should be, I think it shouldn't be there...

or referring specifically to *word order:*

I still feel like the rectangular one goes at the beginning, and then either the straight line or the zigzag lines comes in second place, and then the CAV or DUP usually are at the end. When they come into the middle, I feel like the sentence isn't in its proper order.

We found that multilingual subjects were more likely to use mnemonic devices than linguistic strategies in the memory condition, but that in the rule-discovery condition, both groups of subjects preferred linguistic strategies to mnemonic devices, although the difference was statistically significant only for the multilingual subjects.

In addition, we found that multilingual subjects used a wider variety of different strategies in the rule-discovery than in the memory condition, and that no such difference existed for the monolingual subjects. This suggests that more experienced language learners are more able to switch strategies when the task calls for such flexibility. This is consistent with the research of Nation and McLaughlin (1986), who found that multilingual subjects were able to avoid perseveration errors more than were other subjects in their experiment. Similarly, Ramsey (1980) reported that multilingual subjects demonstrated greater flexibility in "restructuring mental frameworks" than monolingual subjects.

So there is evidence to suggest that more expert language learners show greater plasticity in restructuring their internal representations of the rules governing linguistic input. This ability to exert flexible control over linguistic representations and to shift strategies may result from "learning to learn," in the sense that experience with a number of languages may make the individual more aware of structural similarities and differences between languages and less constrained by specific learning strategies. More experienced learners may more quickly step up to the metaprocedural level and weigh the strategies and tactics they are using.

In the Nayak et al. study we found that expert learners did not surpass novice learners in overall performance, presumably because of limited amount of time and exposure to the linguistic system. In the longer run, we would expect multilingual subjects to perform better on vocabulary and rule learning, precisely because of their superior ability to shift strategies and restructure their internal representations of the linguistic system.

EXPERT STRATEGIES

Just as in other domains, expert language learners use more systematic and useful problem-solving and comprehension strategies than do novices (Naiman, Fröhlich, and Todesco 1975; Rubin 1975, 1981; Wenden 1985). Recently, Rebecca Oxford (1986) has reviewed the methodological problems associated with research on expert strategies in language learning and has presented a taxonomy of strategies she regards as empirically supported by valid research.

An obvious methodological problem is that expert language learners are often not aware of how they are going about learning a new language. Retrospective and introspective reports may yield only incomplete information. However, studies using strategy lists, observations, interviews, note-taking, diaries, structured self-report surveys, factor analysis, and strategy training have begun to yield a picture of what the expert does that the novice cannot do.

Oxford's taxonomy was based on a thorough review of the literature, followed by extensive field testing and revision. Teachers, students, and researchers gave comments and contributed to the final product. This is not the last word on strategies of good language learners, but it is certainly one of the most extensive (Appendix). Note that this is only the simplified taxonomy.

The taxonomy contains two main groups of strategies: primary and support. The distinction is based on whether or not a strategy is thought to operate directly on the language itself, as is true of primary strategies. Support strategies are thought to enhance or support learning indirectly by creating a good attitude in the learner, establishing learning goals, and reducing the learner's frustration, tension, fatigue, or anxiety. Support strategies are also conscious and include what some researchers refer to as "metacognitive" strategies. This distinction, however, is not hard and fast, since such conscious metacognitive strategies as asking questions, getting organized, and focusing attention are included as primary strategies because they directly involve use of the language.

I mention Oxford's taxonomy because it is recent, extensive, and based on a thorough review of relevant research. Also I believe that it is in the use of such strategies that experts excel over novices. Oxford makes the point that such a taxonomy is helpful to teachers because the strategies it lists are teachable. Obviously native ability is not changed by teaching; nonetheless, I believe that aptitude has a teachable component – that novices can become experts by learning appropriate strategies.

Conclusion

What I have tried to do thus far is argue for considering learner aptitude in any discussion of the relationship between individual and social-environmental factors and the development of bilingual proficiency. I suggest that even when the social environment is the same, two children can differ in their acquisition of bilingual proficiency because of native ability. Skehan's finding of a relationship between the rate of first language acquisition and second language learning in middle-class families suggests that there is a general language-processing capacity that affects language-learning ability, both in first and in subsequent languages.

Skehan also found a strong relationship between second language learning in a school situation and a set of measures relating to family background, parental education, and parental literacy. Thus, in addition to native ability in processing language, family influences inculcate in the child the ability to deal with language in a formal, decontextualized context. I believe that family variables influence the child's ability to use the kinds of strategies that Oxford lists. For example, children from some homes learn how to ask questions and keep a conversation going, how to practice and develop routines, how to use memory aids, and how to plan and set goals.

By emphasizing aptitude, as reflected in native ability and acquired strategies, I do not mean to denigrate the importance of attitudes and motivation in language learning. It is clear from the study on language use, attitudes, and bilingual proficiency of Portuguese-Canadian children (Cummins, Lopes, and King 1987) that attitudes toward the native culture play an important role in predicting bilingual proficiency. In Carroll's model, attitude, like intelligence, manner of presentation, and motivation, is a moderator variable that interacts with aptitude to predict performance in a second language.

I would like to note in this context that in the study of Portuguese-Canadian children, factor analysis of the cross-lingual relationships (Cummins, Lopes, and King 1987, Table 21) showed both context-reduced and context-embedded proficiency relationships. That is, there is evidence for the interdependence of academic skills across languages, *and also* for the interdependence of context-embedded skills. This supports the notion that a general language-processing ability plays a role in bilingual proficiency. Another way of thinking about the interdependence hypothesis, then, is to say that as expertise develops in one language, it develops in another. This applies equally well to the kinds of skills Carroll spoke of and to the higher-order strategies involved in context-reduced language tasks.

The study of the development of bilingual proficiency in the transition from home to school (Cummins, Lopes, and Ramos 1987) is especially important for the insight it may give us into how the family environment develops in children strategies that enable them to do well in school. Much of this research focuses on such linguistic factors as code switching, vocabulary knowledge, and mastery of grammatical forms such as the verb tenses, conditional, and subjunctive. However, data from the parental questionnaire concerning amount of exposure to printed material, parental attitudes and expectations, and language learning experiences may shed light on how differences in the family environment affect language learning in the school context (year 3 data).

Finally, the study titled "Age on Arrival, Length of Residence, and Interdependency of Literacy Skills among Japanese Immigrant Students" (Cummins and Nakajima 1987) provides evidence, once again, for a strong relationship between first and second language skills in reading (the relationship in writing was not as strong). At least part of this correlation, I would argue, relates to general language aptitude. But aptitude should not be viewed as a static personality trait; novices can become experts with experience. I believe there is an interdependence between first and second languages in the cognitive/academic domain because experience with one language gives the learner strategies and metacognitive skills that generalize to subsequent languages. Teachers, in my view, need to do more than provide "comprehensible input." They need to make these strategies and metacognitive skills available to learners.

Appendix[1]

Taxonomy of Strategies in Second Language Learning

Primary Strategies
Getting organized
  Previewing, focusing attention
Getting the meaning
Showing you understand
  Taking notes, outlining, summarizing, highlighting, recognizing and using contexts

1 Adapted from Oxford (1986).

Communicating
Asking questions, keeping the conversation going
Practicing
Recombining, practicing the real thing, talking to yourself, playing games, developing routines, imitating
Learning the rules
Rule strategies
Rule search/application, rule generation/revision, rule overgeneralization, rule exercise
Reasoning strategies
Deductive reasoning, analysis of word parts, contrastive analysis across languages
Learning outside the classroom
Memory building
Elaboration, listing, locating new material in places, situations, and contexts, using sounds, using images, using actions, other memory techniques

Support Strategies
Setting the stage
Scheduling, organization, environment
Dealing with attitudes and motivation
Self-encouragement, anxiety reduction, perseverance
Planning and goal setting
Long-term goal setting, short-term goal setting, functional planning
Self-management
Self-monitoring, self-assessment, self-evaluation, self-estimation, self-diagnosis and prescription, self-reinforcement
Social cooperation
Creating practice opportunities
Cultural orientation

13 *Response by DBP project members to the discussion papers of Richard Bourhis and Alison d'Anglejan*

Richard Bourhis questions the extent to which the results of the large-scale Portuguese study might have been affected by methodological problems that commonly occur in this type of study. Following Gardner (1985), he suggests that the study might be vulnerable to: (1) forming unitary groups from heterogeneous sources, (2) constructing indices of language attitudes from insufficient items, and (3) using multiple regression analyses inappropriately to interpret the relationships in the data.

The sample for the study was drawn from seven schools that shared a variety of common characteristics. All had a high proportion of students of Portuguese background and an integrated Portuguese heritage language program. No major differences among the schools or the students in the sample from the different schools were apparent to the researchers who collected the data. In short, we are confident that the students who formed the sample are representative of the Portuguese-background population in metropolitan Toronto. As Bourhis suggests, however, standardization of the data within school groups would have been an appropriate cautionary measure to ensure that the trends in the data were not obscured by possible heterogeneity in the groups that formed the sample.

With respect to indices of language attitudes, a large majority were based on multiple items. It is interesting to note that one of the indices that related most consistently to the dependent measures (knowledge and pride in Portuguese language and achievements) was one of the few based only on two items.

Gardner's point regarding the pitfalls inherent in interpreting multiple regression coefficients is well taken. The variables that form the final regression equation are a function not only of their individual relationships with the criterion variable, but also of their collective interrelationships. Thus, variables that may have strong and consistent correlations with the criterion may not appear in the regression equation and their influence may be overlooked. In an attempt to guard against this problem, we reported all significant partial correlations between predictor and criterion variables after the initial predictor (age of arrival in Canada) had been entered into the equation. Thus, we are confident that important trends in the data have not been overlooked or misinterpreted.

Bourhis also suggests that it would have been useful to have located the study directly within one of the theoretical models of the social context of bilingual proficiency development that he reviews. This would have allowed the testing of specific hypotheses regarding the influence of particular variables. We agree that there would have been advantages to this strategy. However, at the time the study was conceptualized, we were very conscious of its exploratory nature; no other study, to our knowledge, had examined the relationships between use, attitudes and a variety of bilingual proficiency measures for this type of minority group. Thus, we wanted to include a wide variety of indices of use and attitudes, rather than constrain the selection by locating the study within a particular theoretical framework. The variables investigated were motivated by theoretical considerations and were designed to tap particular constructs. These constructs, however, were derived from a variety of theoretical conceptualizations.

Alison d'Anglejan raises the issue of to what extent heritage language classes stimulate children adequately to read for pleasure in the home language. We have no data regarding the specific heritage language classes that students in the sample attended, but our general impression from discussing this question with many heritage language teachers and parents is that most classes are not successful in stimulating self-motivated literacy activities outside the class itself. This is due to the relative lack of suitable reading materials in various heritage languages (although many public libraries have responded vigorously to this need), the lack of awareness among many parents that literacy activities are important for maintenance of the language, the fact that the heritage language is often taught with a focus on form rather than communication, and the relative status of the heritage language vis-à-vis English in the environment which reduces children's motivation to use the language in both spoken and literate modes. For the Japanese students, the situation may be more favorable than is the case for the Portuguese students, both as a result of social class factors and the fact that they will be returning to Japan.

D'Anglejan also suggests that constructs such as sociolinguistic and discourse competence may not be able to be operationalized, other than trivially, in ways that make them amenable to empirical validation. This is certainly one possible explanation for the lack of clear-cut validation in our data of the proposed distinctions between grammatical, discourse, and sociolinguistic competencies. Despite considerable effort (and expense), we experienced difficulty in developing measures of the three traits that had both construct validity from a linguistic perspective and adequate psychometric properties. This is clearly an issue that should be further investigated.

In neither the large-scale nor longitudinal Portuguese studies was a comparison group of English native speakers included in the design. The decision not to include a native English-speaking comparison group was made for a number of reasons. First, in the inner-city schools from which we sampled, native English speakers are virtually an extinct species. Finding a suitable comparison group would have been difficult and would have introduced a number of confounding variables (social class differences, school differences). Second, had a native English-speaking comparison group been included, it would have meant reducing the scope of the studies in other respects (sample size, detail of linguistic scoring). Finally, we considered that although a comparison group would certainly have added to the questions that could be addressed, it was not necessary to answer the questions to which the studies were addressed.

With respect to the Japanese study, d'Anglejan questions the implications of the fact that those arriving at ages 6–7 made more rapid progress in English than those arriving at older ages. She also points out that these findings seem to diverge from those reported by Collier (1987), who found that immigrant children who arrived at ages 5, 6, and 7 did not achieve at a rate equal to those who arrived between ages 8 and 12. Two qualifications need to be made regarding the interpretation of the age data. First, it is necessary to distinguish between English T-scores and English grade equivalents, the former representing students' scores standardized according to age and the latter representing the absolute level of English attained by students. The students who arrived at age 6–7 years are doing relatively well in relation to their English-speaking peers (T-score = 40.85, length of residence 0–35 months; T-score = 48.80, length of residence 36–48 months), but are making somewhat less progress in absolute terms than students who arrive at age 8–9 and 10–11. In the category 0–35 months length of residence, few differences are apparent between the three age of arrival (AOA) groups, but differences do emerge between the groups between 36 and 48 months length of residence. The respective grade equivalent scores for the three groups are 4.5 for AOA 6–7, and 5.7 for both AOA 8–9 and 10–11. These trends for students who arrive at older ages to make more rapid progress (in absolute terms) than those who arrive at younger ages are consistent with the interdependence hypothesis. The findings are probably less clear than they might be because of the considerable variation that may exist within the 0–35 months length of residence category.

With respect to the relationship between the Japanese findings and those reported by Collier (1987), the relatively good performance (in relation to grade norms) by Japanese students arriving at age 6–7 in comparison to those arriving at older ages is consistent with other data from Toronto (Cummins 1981b). These data do appear to be at variance with those reported by Collier and other researchers in different contexts (see Cummins 1984 for a review). Factors associated with the particular groups involved or the language learning environment probably account for these differences, and further research is clearly required to pinpoint the reasons for the different trends. However, certain consistencies are also apparent across the different studies. Both Collier and the present study found that a period of at least four years is required even for socially advantaged students to attain grade norms in English academic skills, and length of residence was a strong predictor of attainment in both studies.

PART IV:
PRACTICAL AND POLICY
IMPLICATIONS

14 The complementary roles of researchers and practitioners in second language education

Jean Handscombe

This chapter provides an administrator's evaluation of the DBP classroom treatment studies (see Chapter 5), designed to examine the relationship between instructional practices and the development of L2 proficiency. In summary, they comprise the following:

1. The development and validation of the COLT observation instrument across a variety of FSL and ESL settings
2. The core French observation study which used the COLT instrument to describe instructional practices, then analyzed these differences in relation to L2 proficiency outcomes
3. The French immersion observation study which focused on vocabulary instruction, *vous/tu* input, student talk in teacher-fronted activities and error treatment
4. Functional grammar instruction in French immersion which investigated the effect on L2 proficiency of providing focused input around the use of the imparfait and passé composé, as well as increased opportunities for student use of the target tenses.

Significance of the studies for practitioners

Development and validation of COLT observation scheme

Providing an accurate description of what actually takes place in a classroom is, in my view, a most worthwhile endeavor. Much of the conflicting data concerning the relative effectiveness of various approaches to second language education in North America have resulted from a lack of specificity as to what exactly is going on in the various programs (Enright 1984). In this regard, the development of the COLT observation scheme (Allen, Fröhlich, and Spada 1987) is a welcome one. The categories used in the scheme provide an excellent starting point for helping teachers monitor their, and their students', behavior in the classroom. Program coordinators might well wish to review the categories with teachers, invite discussion of their appropriateness for particular settings,

181

and encourage teachers to modify and then use their version of the scheme in analyzing video or audio recordings of classes.

Teachers would probably find COLT's reminder of the wide range of classroom activities and communicative features helpful in lesson and unit planning. Some might also accept the invitation to experiment with aspects of the scheme that were missing from their established repertoire. For example, if their normal sequence was presentation of material to be learned followed by practice, they might consider providing practice first, followed by a class discussion to identify the main language points being practiced. If class tests were usually given individually and competitively, they might want to see the results achieved by different types of collaborative group effort. As Fanselow (1987) points out, the purpose of such experimentation is not to persuade teachers that one approach works and another does not, or even that one approach is substantially more effective than another. Instead, the intent is to increase their confidence in their ability to make decisions as to what strategy to use on what occasion.

Core French observation study

The results of this study (Allen, Carroll, Burtis, and Gaudino 1987) provide a clear warning to practitioners that, despite the usefulness of the COLT scheme in the areas mentioned above, it would be premature to use COLT for the purpose of comparing the effectiveness of approaches. Since the categories are not sufficiently sensitive to capture important differences in the quality of interactions, any tallying would produce misleading results. The discussion of the more detailed discourse analysis required to document the way in which meaning is negotiated in the classroom, while interesting, is too sketchy to provide practitioners with additional tools of investigation.

Immersion French observation study

The results of all four substudies indicate that students learn to understand language to which they are exposed and to produce language which they are encouraged to use. While these findings come as no surprise, they do encourage practitioners to examine carefully every L2 curriculum and its delivery to ensure that classroom tasks match expected outcomes. The studies provided sobering examples of settings in which the match was anything but good.

I was particularly interested in the suggestions made within this study for a much heavier emphasis on teaching the sociolinguistic rules of use. A regular focusing of student attention on who uses what language forms and under what circumstances seems to me to be a highly desirable component of quality L2 instruction. The area of sociolinguistic variation, and its extension to the development of a metalinguistic awareness, is one in which we might do well to build on work already underway in the teaching of the L1. Raleigh (1981:ii), for example, introduces a text designed for L1 learners as follows:

This book is about language and how people use it. It's about: different languages and dialects, learning to speak, what languages share, playing about with words, how English has changed, special ways of talking, who says what to who, writing and reading, how people learn to read, different kinds of writing, what other people think about the way you speak and what you think. But everyone who reads this knows much more about language than can be put in a book. Everyone has managed the amazing job of learning at least one language – and, when you think about it, you use even *one* language in so many different ways that even *one* is a lot.

Students are then asked to look at a number of statements about language, and to discuss them with someone else. The students have to decide which statements they agree with, and which they are not sure about. Here are some typical statements:

1. People who can't speak and write can get by all right.
2. Girls talk differently from boys.
3. Babies don't start talking sense until they are about five years old.
4. Life would be much easier if everyone in the world spoke the same language.
5. There's nothing wrong with slang: it's just lively language.

I suspect that teachers who communicate their fascination with such topics, and who use every opportunity to engage their students in discussions of language appropriateness, would in the process be doing much to help their students see the need for accuracy, fluency, and range as they develop proficiency in L2.

Functional grammar in French immersion

The conclusion reached in this study (Harley 1989b) was that though the teaching approach with the experimental group had succeeded in developing control of the target tenses in the short term, the advantage was not maintained over time. It was noted that the results were probably affected by the fact that the control group also appeared to have worked on the tenses. Since it was not known exactly how, no comparison of the approaches was possible. The solutions suggested were revisions to the materials, together with more specific guidelines to teachers about the provision of corrective feedback. A further possible explanation put forward for the failure of the treatment to achieve the expected results was the short period of time spent on the materials. This seems to me to be a very plausible explanation. It is clear that neither the teachers nor the students were familiar with the approach being tried. If time to learn how to teach – and just as important, how to learn – using a particular approach is a crucial factor, then it points to the unsatisfactory nature of the kind of research design that attempts to measure instructional effectiveness after short-term intervention. To my mind, the case for functional grammar teaching in L2 classes is neither supported nor discredited by this study.

Theoretical constructs applied to the L2 classroom

Not all theoretical constructs are equally usefully applied to the L2 classroom. As Brumfit (1984) pointed out, oppositions such as competence/performance, competence/communicative competence, acquisition/learning, elaborated/restricted, accommodation/assimilation were each developed as part of an argument aimed at a particular group of workers within a particular field, and each of them, for better or for worse, has been taken over by teachers and teacher educators. He argues that risks are involved in this largely because these oppositions were designed to solve theoretical problems, not teaching ones. The researchers are not all to blame, however, for trying to foist their categories on teachers. Common distinctions made by teachers, such as those between listening/speaking/reading/writing and controlled/guided/free writing in his judgment lack any kind of respectable theoretical justification, but turn up quite frequently in research studies. He suggests that we need a negotiation between researchers and teachers as to what categories will be mutually satisfying.

I have some concerns about one such opposition mentioned across several of the studies in the classroom treatment studies, namely the one, particularly usefully fleshed out in Stern's paper (Chapter 7), between experiential and analytic. Experiential teaching is characterized as focusing on a substantive topic or theme, with many tasks and activities going on in the classroom in an effort to provide opportunities for "real" communication. Analytic teaching, on the other hand, is seen as focusing on code, with opportunities for practice mostly taking the form of exercises that result in "non-real" communication. Although the parallels are not consistently maintained throughout the studies, there are indications that experiential = content teaching and that analytic = language teaching. The researchers make the valid point (Swain 1988b) that not all content teaching is necessarily good language teaching. I would argue, however, with support from such sources as Moffett (1968), Britton (1970), Rosen and Rosen (1973), Martin et al. (1976),

Torbe and Medway (1981), Cazden (1986), Mohan (1986), and Enright and McCloskey (1988) that the best content teaching is also the best language teaching. Detailed accounts of exemplary practice can be found, for example, in Levine (1981) and Wigginton (1985).

I would describe the teacher's role in such teaching as follows:

1. Selecting content of interest to students
2. Structuring activities to explore that content in ways in which students will want to participate actively in the lesson, attending to the teacher and each other
3. Ensuring interaction among students at different levels of proficiency in the target language
4. Monitoring student comprehension and adjusting input accordingly
5. Finding ways of linking with the students' previous experiences, both conceptual and linguistic
6. Drawing attention to important and interesting language forms, including their sociolinguistic dimension
7. Upping the ante to build on what students have learned

Lessons conducted in this way could not be characterized as either experiential or analytic. They are clearly both. In this integrated approach, no content is taught without reference to the language through which that content is expressed, and no language is taught without being contextualized within a thematic and human environment. The classroom treatment researchers do insist that the oppositional categories should be regarded as complementary, with the relative emphasis on each as yet not being a decided quantity. There is, however, no guidance for practitioners as to how to put this into practice. In the absence of a clear statement on this issue, we might well see the development of a curriculum containing units of experiential work followed by units of analytic work or a scheme of program evaluation listing activities under these two headings. Such uses of the two concepts could well be damaging pedagogically.

Researchers and practitioners as collaborators

Though I have naturally focused on what was included in the classroom treatment studies, many areas of crucial interest to practitioners were not addressed – questions such as how language instruction can accommodate a wide range of conceptual development within a class, what instructional strategies involving L1 are helpful in developing L2, what aspects of the target language are best presented and practiced within the language classroom and what aspects elsewhere. In addition, since ongoing staff development is a constant concern of program administrators, I would have expected a much greater emphasis on finding out what kind of input is most effective in helping teachers improve their teaching.

Predictably, different practitioners would have different priorities. It could be reasonably argued that, in a project of limited duration and funding, only some of these priorities could be attended to. But in the documentation provided, I did not find any evidence of consultation with practitioners to select which areas were considered most important. I would suggest that setting the agenda for research in a collaborative way would be an excellent place to start in improving communication between researchers and practitioners.

With a mutually agreed-on agenda in place, I would then want to go a step further and involve practitioners in conducting the research itself. Researchers have a great deal to offer teachers, including keen insights into what is involved in teaching and learning a second language and an array of research tools, many of which could be very helpful to teachers in monitoring their classrooms. Teachers, on the other hand, could make accessible to their research colleagues the best of their teaching practices and provide reminders of the many decisions they make in planning, delivering, and evaluating every minute of instruction. I would like to see far more joint projects designed to enable researchers and practitioners to get together in order to plan the details of what will be investigated, to collect data, to examine and discuss the information gathered, and to draw conclusions and make plans for further activity that is relevant and useful to both parties. Such collaboration, carried out on a much larger scale than at present, would provide the opportunity for many more researchers and practitioners to learn to value each other's skills and knowledge and would, in my view, make a significant contribution to the improvement of second language teaching.

15 Educational language policies in Utopia

Christina Bratt Paulston

This chapter explores the range of policies and their implications for language teaching (developing bilingual proficiency) that reasonably seem to follow from the data, findings, and discussions in all the DBP reports, including the second-year report (Allen et al. 1983) and the three-volume final report: Volume I, *The Nature of Language Proficiency;* Volume II, *Classroom Treatment;* and Volume III, *Social Context and Age* (Harley et al. 1987).

In what follows, two of the major factors in considering research on bilingual education are ignored. The first concerns the theoretical perspective on which the research is based. In an earlier discussion of the immersion programs research, I concluded (with a conflict theory bias) that "unless we try in some way to account for the socio-historical, cultural, and economic-political factors which lead to certain forms of bilingual education, we will never understand the consequences of that education" (Paulston 1980:33). Here I have chosen to ignore all these factors and have indeed considered instruction and school programs as the independent variables in trying to understand the consequences of the various programs. A caveat in passing, however: We have to be extremely cautious in drawing generalizations based on a sample of middle-class children with IQs around 115–117 (Harley et al. 1987, Vol. III:223) who are in voluntary programs. Although we would not expect any reputable scholar to recommend it, we should be concerned about those who advocate importing the immersion program model for minority bilingual education in the United States.

This brings me to the second factor. I referred above to policies that seem to follow from the research. It is naive to think that educational language policies, especially status planning, are based on criteria that reasonably follow from research on developing bilingual proficiency; decisions are made primarily on political and economic grounds and reflect the values of those who have the power to make them. This factor also will be ignored; instead I will consider the DBP project's implications for policy in a perfect world where schol-

TABLE 15.1 THE DISTINCTION BETWEEN CORPUS AND STATUS PLANNING

Criteria	Corpus planning	Status planning
Determination		
Who makes the decision?	Language specialists, i.e., linguists, philologists, language teachers, native informants	Government officials, agencies, ministries
Development		
Factors in evaluating results?	Primarily linguistic or pseudolinguistic	Primarily nonlinguistic, such as economic, political, ideological
Implementation		
Factors in evaluating results?	Passive acceptance	Strong attitudes, negative or positive*

*See Paulston (1983) for a discussion of these issues.

arship and common sense are the major factors in making decisions – in short, Utopia.

Concepts of language planning

The setting of educational policies vis-à-vis language falls within the field of language planning. Although no generally accepted theory of language planning exists, several basic concepts are typically recognized and used in the literature. The basic dichotomy is between language policy and language cultivation (Neustupny 1970), or between status planning and corpus planning (Kloss 1969). The latter terms are gaining general acceptance, and I will use them here. I take corpus planning to refer to technical linguistic decisions about language, such as language standardization. Status planning deals with policy formulations such as choice of official language, and choice of medium of instruction. Table 15.1, adapted from my earlier work, may help clarify this distinction.

Under both status planning and corpus planning we can identify stages or subsets of steps of (1) determination, (2) development, (3) implementation, and (4) evaluation. *Determination* refers to the initial decisions about goals, means, and outcomes. Bill 22 in Quebec concerning languages of education was a status planning determination step, while the parents' insistence on carrying through the St. Lambert experiment in French immersion (see Lambert and Tucker 1972) was a corpus planning determination step. This decision led to further *development*, in Rubin's terms (1973), the working out of means and strategies to achieve the outcomes such as the preparation of texts and curricula. Teacher training also deserves to be mentioned here, although it is typically ignored as an aspect of language planning. *Implementation* refers to actual attempts to reach the desired goals. The St. Lambert pilot class of the home-school language switch experiment was the first implementation of the immersion programs, and in retrospect one may question how much of a development stage had actually preceded it. From various DBP studies dealing with French immersion we can see that the basic assumption of the St. Lambert experiment – namely, that the anglophone children be taught just like francophone children – was too simplistic. The DBP findings point to the need for more emphasis on the development stage of immersion programs. Finally, there is *evaluation*, which is often missing from language planning efforts, especially in status planning. The Canadian immersion programs are unique in their constant and careful evaluation efforts, which were originally undertaken to assure parents and administrators that the programs were working. Certainly most of the present studies can be considered as essentially evaluation research.

We can, then, organize a discussion of the implications the DBP project has for educational language policies according to this framework. First, there are implications for status planning in the form of national and regional (provincial) policies, which in this situation will typically concern choice of program rather than the more common choice of code. Second, there are implications for corpus planning in the form of educational policies regarding (1) classroom methods, procedures, and techniques of language teaching; (2) curricula, texts, and materials; and (3) teacher training.

Status planning: implications for national and regional policies

Research

My reading of the four volumes of the DBP project leads me to the conclusion that the strongest implication for national policy is the importance and need for further research. This is not to say that the present findings are not very informative, but rather that the study advances our knowledge and ability to ask better questions. The notion of bilingual proficiency as a dynamic process rather than a quantifiable state is one that particularly merits further exploration.

The model of proficiency that emerges is one that reflects the nature of the language contact situation, here mostly majority children in a friendly school setting. It is not surprising that the proficiency studies (see Chapter 1) fail to confirm the hypothesized sociolinguistic trait in French, since there have been no attempts to teach the immersion students culturally appropriate behavior in French, and they are not exposed to francophones outside school. They behave in and with French as they do in and with English. One direction for further research is to study the attitudes of educated francophones toward the faulty fluency of the immersion students. I once visited an immersion program with such a person, and it was precisely his criticism of the poor quality of the French and of the "un-French" quality of the children's language behavior that showed me another interpretation of the programs as one of the lack of respect for the glorious heritage which is French. Later I encountered the same attitudes about the Spanish immersion program in Culver City (which, impressionistically, seems considerably worse in quality of language).

Any minister of education who decreed that the objectives of the immersion programs should be francophone student behavior would be in an unenviable position. It would be interesting to know if such objectives are even feasible in the real world at anything but a surface level of correct and appropriate language use, and it is certainly far from immediately apparent that objectives of any kind of bicultural proficiency are even desirable in the Canadian situation. Lest the reader be inclined to dismiss this entire issue, it should be pointed out that we certainly expect the schools to be the major socializing institution in making blacks and Chicanos and other minorities behave and think like mainstream children – that is, in internalizing the values of mainstream society. In Utopia we would want as our teaching objectives linguistically correct and culturally appropriate language behavior.[1]

Another research issue that emerges is the law of the hammer. Give a small boy a hammer, and everything he encounters needs hammering. In the DBP model validation studies the hammer was factor analysis, and I found it interesting how very little elucidation resulted from the analyses. Any study that can have three mutually exclusive "solutions" (Chapter 1) leaves me confused. "An inherent difficulty in validating models of L2 proficiency is that measures faithfully reflecting a particular construct may not have adequate psychometric properties, while other

---

1 In parenthesis, for it is really not an implication except perhaps for future research, it should be noted that the multiple-choice test purporting to tap sociolinguistic competence is rather suspect and underscores the difficulty in using paper and pencil tests in exploring sociolinguistic knowledge. And while discussing the model of proficiency in parenthesis, let me add that I am convinced of the claim that "the immersion students' strong performance in discourse may have been due to positive transfer from prior experience in their mother tongue" (Harley et al. 1987, Vol. I:4). Most certainly the tripartite (quadripartite if the lexical component is included) model of proficiency (Chapter 1) merits further exploration.

psychometrically acceptable measures may fall short of representing the construct" (p. 24). The implication is quite clear that we need qualitative and quantitative approaches to understanding language acquisition; and that any reliance on quantification and psychometrics, however rigorous, is not sufficient.

One aspect not covered by the DBP project is the matter of individual differences in school language acquisition among students of the same age. We know that people learn differently, whether it has to do with field dependence/independence, right/left brain specialization, communicative strategies, basic interpersonal communication skills (BICS)/ cognitive academic language proficiency (CALP), or other learner characteristics. Two implications follow. The first is that one needs to be very careful about making categorical statements because what is helpful to one child may not be so to another. The second implication is that if children learn differently, there should be enough variety of activities in the classroom to help all types of learners. The core French observation study (Allen, Carroll, Burtis, and Gaudino 1987) mentions a class where the teacher always follows the same rather dull routine, with poor results for the students; one feasible explanation, besides the boredom, is the lack of variety of language experience. An additional implication is, of course, that funding is needed for future research in this area.

Another finding from the DBP classroom treatment studies (Chapter 5) that has implications at the national and regional levels for budget allocations, program planning, and the like is the importance of instructional quality for developing bilingual proficiency. The last decade has seen a steady emphasis on student learning rather than on teaching. "Humanistic methods" have been much in vogue, and the emphasis is on an anxiety-free sharing of knowledge rather than on any teaching behavior per se. The classroom treatment studies document, as did the Significant Bilingual Instructional Features Study (SBIFS) (Paulston 1984), the importance of effective instruction. Students learn more from good teachers, and it is simply not accurate to claim that all that is necessary for developing bilingual proficiency is comprehensible input.

Choice of program

The burning question at the national level of status planning has typically been choice of national language. For example, to this day the majority of African nations still have an ex-colonial language as the official national language precisely because of the politically sensitive nature of the problem. Canada has seen its share of legislative status planning concerning the rights and official status of French and English, and the popularity of the immersion programs is at least partially attributable to this legislation. This educational success illustrates the point that closely tied to choice of national language is the choice of medium of instruction.

Medium of instruction seems at first glance a much less volatile subject than choice of national language, but that is not necessarily so. It is worth noting that the Soweto riots in South Africa started over an unwelcome choice of medium of instruction, namely, a partial change from English to Afrikaans for black youth, who fought to the death in refusal. In this case it was of course not the language that they were opposed to, but the speakers of Afrikaans and all that the language symbolized of hatred, oppression, and apartheid.

The impression the DBP project gives of the Canadian scene, in anglophone Ontario, is not of a symbolic use of language,[2] but rather a pragmatic, instrumental, and tolerant approach to language diversity. Such an approach leaves open a choice of medium of instruction by parents and students, and the findings of the DBP project have implications for making such an informed choice.

Canada is counted as one of the world's major immigration countries, and what we typically find with immigrants is a shift to the dominant majority language. When there are two official languages with a "tacit division of political and economic powers" (McConnell et al. 1979:5), there is possibility for conflict. The Canadian immigrants have chosen overwhelmingly to shift to English, and this "anglicization of immigrants is seen as a major source... of the weakening of the French-speaking group" (Daoust-Blais 1983:209). The shift helped precipitate the spate of language legislation that followed. This is the background against which we need to interpret the DBP project findings.

The project studied several ethnic minorities (see Chapter 9), including the Portuguese and the Japanese, and there is evidence in the data to predict language shift to English for each of these populations, although they are likely to vary in rate of shift. The Portuguese are probably shifting at a pace slower than the general immigrant population (perhaps a four-generation shift rather than a three-generation one), and their lower social mobility (Allen et al. 1983:102) is part of this syndrome. Ethnicity alone will not maintain a language if the dominant group allows assimilation and if incentive and opportunity of access to the L2 are present. The schools clearly and effectively provide access to the L2, but incentive – which is mainly economic for immigrant groups – is lower, and hence the shift is slower.

The Metropolitan Separate School Board in the City of Toronto provides Portuguese heritage language classes, which offer a 30-minute daily program of Portuguese language and culture. It is not clear what percentage of the school population of Portuguese background is enrolled

2 The Parti Québécois certainly used French as a national symbol.

in these programs, but what is clear is the very positive attitude expressed toward Portuguese *and* English. Even so, it is obvious that 30 minutes a day is nowhere near sufficient to maintain "first language proficiency in a minority context" (Cummins, Lopes, and King 1987:50). It is also clear that the students do well in and "are extremely comfortable in English" (Cummins et al. 1987:50).

The Japanese students (Chapter 9) show similar trends and reach grade norms on English academic tasks (after four years), whereas those who arrived in Canada before formal schooling cannot continue development of the L1 to a high level like that of students in the home country, even with weekend classes in the mother tongue in the Toronto Japanese school. And this in spite of middle-class status, a very strong cultural work ethic, and the expectation that they will return to Japan.

These findings corroborate those in my report to the Swedish National Board of Education. If minority students are to maintain their home language at a level of proficiency as close as possible to national norms, but at a cost to proficiency in the majority language of the host country, then the choice is home language classes. If majority language proficiency is desired, but probably with an increasing loss in home language proficiency, the choice is the ordinary majority language classes (with auxiliary teaching in the majority language). Finally, if bilingual students are the goal, the choice is combined classes. There are really no contradictory data to these conclusions. It should be mentioned, however, that the term "bilingual" covers a multitude of degrees of proficiency and that a perfect, balanced, active bilingualism probably does not exist (Paulston 1982: 50–51).

What we see, then, is the considerable influence that medium of instruction has on maintaining and developing L1 skills and/or in influencing shift to the L2. For the Japanese students who will return to Japan, their mother tongue is of obvious importance and concern, but one can question the value of heritage language classes for a group like the Portuguese, who are at present undergoing shift. What does Portuguese as a medium of instruction achieve?

The following points are actually value judgments, and each individual member of the Portuguese community may well have different attitudes about their relative virtues and importance. To my mind, the most important aspect of heritage language classes is that they render the children literate in their mother tongue. The classes provide basic language skills of reading and writing in a standard form of the language, which will make possible a future choice for those individual students who are interested to continue to learn and develop their language proficiency. The DBP project also documents the psychological reality that writing and print hold for speakers of a language; print somehow reifies the language.

The existence of classes in Portuguese language and culture in the public schools also recognizes the legitimacy and value of the students' ethnic background in the eyes of the dominant majority. They help contribute to the positive attitudes students display toward *both* their cultures. It is easy to speculate that in groups undergoing a slow rate of language shift and assimilation, such positive reactions are especially important for a sense of self and a feeling of belonging in the new culture, rather than a sense of being uprooted. Simply by bringing all the children together, the classes contribute to a sense of community cohesion. There are also those who will claim that mother tongue literacy helps promote academic skills in the L2, but I leave that argument to Jim Cummins. An obvious criticism is that 30 minutes is not sufficient class time. In Utopia the length of heritage language classes would be extended, and all students of Portuguese background would be enrolled in them.

The other choice of medium of instruction involves immersion, and early or late or maybe extended French. This choice seems to involve another value judgment, as there is surprisingly little difference among these programs in terms of linguistic achievement in French (see Chapter 9). Early immersion students show definite evidence of fossilized errors and calques, with a well-developed strategic competence "in the use of high coverage verbs (which) appears to enable them to 'get by' " (Harley 1987:218). These are all well-established habits that are difficult to eradicate. (Whatever present fashions in thinking about L2 learning, many aspects of such learning still involve habit formation.) They do show better command of the functional[3] verb rules and a nonsignificant tendency to produce fewer disfluencies.

Pronunciation was not tested as an aspect of bilingual proficiency, but my impressionistic recollection is that the early immersion students have a better pronunciation than the broad accents of the late immersion students I have heard. Their listening comprehension is better too. The late immersion and extended French students are more correct on some formal aspects; on matters like co-occurrence rules of grammatical forms, they show a near-significant tendency to produce more varied verb forms (a richer lexicon) and do as well overall on the sociolinguistic score. So what are the implications parents should consider for the choice of medium of instruction?

We know from experience, if not from research, that the most difficult student to teach is one who is fluent but incorrect (Higgs and Clifford 1982). If parents wish their child to grow up to use French fluently, accurately, and appropriately, then enrollment in a late immersion or ex-

---

3 This is not intended to mean functional as in notional-functional, but rather the knowledge of when, and in what context, it is appropriate to use a certain form. Most grammar rules involve dual formal-functional aspects, and the functional aspect tends to be more difficult.

tended French program followed upon graduation by a year in Quebec or France appears to be a viable option. It is doubtful whether anything else will achieve such a goal – it did take the Japanese students *four* years in an anglophone environment to reach grade level (Cummins and Nakajima 1987).

On the other hand, for those with less linguistically elevated goals who instead have integrative motives and want their children to be full-fledged Canadians with a foot in both language camps, or for those with instrumental motives who want their children to be able to qualify for federal positions with specific language requirements, early immersion programs seem to do well (although it is only now that immersion students are beginning to graduate from college, since the first program only began in 1965). My guess is that intelligent students are less bored in such programs than in the regular English classes, but we need to ask *them* such questions and we need to know what they feel about early versus late and extended programs. No one can deny that the early immersion students are charming as they negotiate in French, but it is questionable whether charm is an adequate criterion for academic decisions.

A third implication of the DBP findings regarding choice of program is that something needs to be done with regard to teaching methodology and curriculum. It is difficult to believe that the early immersion students would not outperform the late immersion students if they were taught differently.

Corpus planning: educational policies

The DBP findings are especially rich in implications for the classroom. The following discussion centers on classroom methods and procedures, but it should be obvious that curricula, materials, and texts should be designed to reflect optimum procedures and that teachers should be trained to use them intelligently.

It is understandable that people who write methods texts on language teaching and who train language teachers find methods[4] to be important in the language classroom. Most nonexperimental language teaching is, in fact, discussed in terms of methods. So the results of the core French observation study (Chapter 5), which investigated how instructional differences affected learning by relating methods to proficiency measures, may come as somewhat of a surprise. The study compares an experiential approach with an analytic one (or in old-fashioned parlance a com-

---

4 In Anthony's terms, as an "overall plan for the orderly presentation of language material, no part of which contradicts, and all of which is based upon the selected approach (theory)." (1972:5)

municative language teaching method with a traditional grammar-focused one) and finds essentially no difference: "The most striking thing about these data is the lack of difference between Groups E and A" (Allen, Carroll, Burtis, and Gaudino 1987:79). Similarly Harley (1987) found little difference between early immersion, a sort of direct method, and late immersion and extended French, where there is more emphasis on formal language teaching from the outset. The SPIFS similarly did not find methods to be significant. Does this mean we can ignore teacher training?

Quite predictably, I think not. Teacher training is important, but not so much so, except for intellectual curiosity, at the level of methods. The lack of significant results in the core French observation study can be explained in two ways. First, teachers tend to be eclectic and do not teach according to "pure" methods, and second the COLT observation scheme does not capture the nature of the interactions and activities. It is counterintuitive that genuine information requesting and sustained student speech should be negatively correlated with improvement, but understandable if this happens only when confused or weak students ask for clarification. We cannot tell from the data. It is surprising that choral work shows any correlation with improvement because it is likely to be audiolingual mechanical drilling, and we may well ask who would want to do that with a class that has studied French for eight years. Maybe they were singing French songs, but we do not know. In other words, we need to stress how important the nature of the classroom interaction is in interpreting the results, what the authors call "quality of instruction." It is exactly the quality of procedures and techniques that makes a difference in teaching, rather than method.

Nevertheless, I think we can accept at face value the classroom treatment findings (see Chapter 5) that indicate a need for the inclusion of form-focused activities in the language classroom. Comprehensible input is not a sufficient condition. One should also keep in mind when interpreting the core French findings that the data come from students who have studied French for eight years. They should need much fewer form-focused activities and interactions than a beginning class, so the findings are even more significant. We should also remember that the core French class that made the highest proficiency gains was the well-taught experiential class where the teacher did focus on form and negative feedback, and used language for genuine and interesting communication. My guess is that the students enjoyed the class. Studies like those of the DBP project tend to obscure the fact that efficient language learning is very hard work, and that an aspect of good teaching is the ability to keep the students working on task with a will.

Conclusions

The conclusion to be drawn from the core French study is clearly what the authors state: "The analytic focus and the experiential focus may be complementary, and they may provide essential support for one another in the L2 classroom" (p. 77). The implications for curriculum and materials development are straightforward; the language learning situation should include these aspects:

1. Comprehensible input with the focus on form
2. Activities for learning (memorizing, internalizing) these forms accurately (I doubt that the activity – choral drills, fill-in-the-blanks, controlled composition, diary writing – is as important as that this stage is present)
3. Functional guidelines for appropriate use of forms, such as the difference between the passé composé and the imparfait (students should not have to figure out such rules by themselves)
4. Genuine communicative use of linguistic forms: in Swain's (1985) terms, comprehensible output

Another major methodological implication that surfaces from the DBP project is the importance of vocabulary in second language learning. One strength of the grammar-translation method was its insistence on vocabulary and word study (basically morphology of affixes), but in North America at least the audiolingual hegemony put a stop to that, and we have since virtually ignored the whole issue, both in research and materials writing. I am not at all convinced by the discussion on vocabulary teaching and learning in the immersion observation study (Swain and Carroll 1987) that linguists' analyses of lexis have much to do with how sixth graders learn words in French, but I am convinced of the importance of finding out.

Two other matters deserve further attention: Is classroom use of the L1 by teachers helpful or detrimental to developing bilingual proficiency? Could it be that *mention* rather than *use* is helpful (glossing only lexical items)? Is there a difference in L1 use at different levels of proficiency? Second, we need to know more about error correction (see Chaudron 1988 for a review of existing research on this topic). Does correcting errors help efface them? Does a more form-focused, vocabulary-insistent early stage result in a lower error rate? Which form of error correction is most efficient, teacher correction or self-correction? How does the teacher signal error? Further research is needed to throw light on all these questions.

PART V:
THIRTY-FIVE YEARS OF
RESEARCH ON BILINGUALISM

16 *Persistent issues in bilingualism*

Wallace E. Lambert

One of my purposes here is to explain to outsiders (those who are not in the research field itself) as well as to insiders (those of us who have the luxury of contemplating, researching, and theorizing about the topic) why and how some of us have focused on the topic of bilingualism over a number of years. This topic, in fact, has grown into a recognized and respected research specialty during the past thirty-five years. It has also become a vibrant, exciting new specialty of study. Consequently, a second purpose I have in mind is to provide a small sample of what it is that makes it exciting. My third purpose is to demonstrate as well as I can that the study of bilingualism is a serious, real-world matter, much more than an academic exercise. The tie-in with the real world means that we insiders have had to extend ourselves through self-education in current political and sociological ways of thinking. This is so because bilingualism is inextricably linked with such basic concepts as personal identity, culture and ethnicity, biculturalism and, on a national level, multiculturalism.

Most outsiders know a good deal about bilingualism because so many people in North America are bilingual to some extent, and because most are cognizant of the juggling act immigrants have to perfect in order not to lose one or the other of their precious linguistic and cultural heritages. But outsiders are preoccupied with their own lives and careers and haven't had the opportunity to specialize on the topic as we have. Consequently, I think insiders congregated at the DBP symposium will have some new ideas for everyone (insiders or outsiders), or at least some new slants on things that may already be known or suspected, but only at a deep personal level.

My plan is to present a sample of some of the questions we at McGill have asked ourselves about bilingualism. We started with concerns about the measurement of proficiency in two languages, but because our research group comprised mainly wildly divergent thinkers, we continually drifted off the proficiency issue to what we saw as inextricably related matters, usually social-psychology ones. In any case, this question-and-answer process creates the specialty and makes it so much fun.

What surprises me is that the issues persist, even though the research approaches evolve and more and more information is accumulated.

The measurement issue

In the early 1950s, when I started on the study of bilingualism, the *Zeitgeist* demanded that we be systematic and clear in our definition of the term *bilingual*. We tried our best to dodge the philosophical or the literary aspects of the concept and to deal with those features of bilingual behavior that can be measured reliably and that describe the whole gamut of bilingual experiences, from perfectly equivalent skills in two languages to marked dominance of one language over another. It became clear to us that bilinguals could be dominant in a home language but weak in the major language of the community, and that their clumsy control of that language and their difficulties in getting their own special ideas across were real features of the bilingual world they found themselves in. Thus, although far from being perfect or balanced bilinguals, they were outstanding examples of people trying to cope in a bilingual world.

The early research literature on this issue used the term "automatic" to differentiate the linguistic behavior of native speakers from those less skilled in a second or foreign language (Warshaw 1934; Dunkel 1948). "Automaticity" was also the term used by neurologists to describe normal speech and various aphasic deviations from normal (Head 1926). Since automatic behavior is characterized mainly by its speed and by its thoughtlessness, one researcher as far back as 1877 (Cattell 1877) measured the time required to translate words from English to German and noted marked differences in automaticity for English speakers with varying degrees of experience with German.

Because of this preoccupation with automaticity in the research background, I started by focusing on relative automaticity among bilingual subjects and noting in milliseconds the time taken to comply with simple directions (Lambert 1955). For example, French-English bilinguals were asked to place their fingers on a bank of eight keys, like those of a typewriter; each key had a stem painted in a different color. They were measured for the time taken to push one key after another, following a series of directions such as "left hand, red key," truncated to *left, red; droite, jaune; right, green; gauche, rouge*. This simple little test became interesting because (a) it was very reliable; (b) it nicely split subgroups who had different amounts of experience with a second language (for example, groups of undergraduate majors in French, graduate students in French, and French natives who had been in the United States for five years or more); (c) it turned up groups who were markedly dominant in one language or the other, as well as others who were "balanced," meaning they were equally fast in both languages; and (d) it revealed some fascinating cases of dominance in the unexpected direction. For example, one American graduate student was significantly dominant in French over English, while two francophones studying in the United States were dominant in English over French. After much delicate follow-up detective work, it turned out that the American was gay but not out of the closet. As I got to know him a little, he explained that he thought France would be a more comfortable place for him to live. The two French people, I learned through interviews, had gone "American" and never wanted to look back to their homeland.

From that starting point, a host of questions came to mind. For instance, would this apparently superficial measure of automaticity correlate with other aspects of a bilingual's language performance? To our surprise, it did (Lambert, Havelka, and Gardner 1959). The relative automaticity on the finger-keys test correlated strongly with a whole set of linguistic performances, including speed of recognizing words in each of the two languages when single words are thrown on a screen for very brief durations; speed of completing words in French and English that had only two starting letters; speed of detecting little French and English words embedded in a nonsense string such as DANSONODEND; and speed of reading words aloud. However, the finger-key test did not relate to relative speed of translating from English to French or from French to English.

Our follow-up detective work in this case indicated that in this Quebec-based study, bilinguals who were studying at universities through their second language (anglophones studying at a French university or vice versa) were usually training themselves to be prepared in advance in the weaker language; they looked up words in the new language to prepare themselves to get their messages across in a second language. Thus, we argued, there was no simple relationship between relative automaticity and translation speed. But other than this interesting exception, it became clear to us that automaticity permeated numerous aspects of a bilingual person's language skill. A balanced bilingual would be balanced in many domains, and a dominant bilingual would experience a lack of linguistic balance of skills in many domains.

The issue of types of bilingualism

From the 1950s on, our research group has been interested in the fact that balanced bilinguals have the capacity to use each of their two languages with great efficiency, and show little interlingual interference. When one thinks for a moment about the psychology and neurophysiology of this capacity, its intriguing nature becomes clear. How is it that the bilingual is able to "gate out" or set aside a whole integrated linguistic system while functioning with a second one, and a moment later, if the situation calls for it, switch the process, activating the previously inactive system and setting aside the previously active one? Both linguists and psychologists have been attracted to this phenomenon because an understanding of it would shed light on various aspects of bilingual behavior – linguistic, psychological, and neurological. In fact, Uriel Weinreich (1953) suggested that any comprehensive or useful theory of bilingualism must account for this "effectively separated use of the two languages," as well as for the interference that takes place between two languages. We have attempted to contribute to the psychology of such a theory by analyzing different features of the bilingual person's skills.

In 1954, Susan Ervin and Charles Osgood (1954) suggested that language-acquisition contexts might contribute to the independence or the interdependence of the bilingual's two languages. Ervin and Osgood believed that bilinguals could develop either a "compound" or a "coordinate" relation between their languages, depending on how the two were acquired. The compound relation would be engendered through experiences in mixed acquisition contexts; for instance, in settings where the same interlocutors used two languages interchangeably to refer to the same environmental events, as often happens in infant bilingualism when two languages are learned starting in infancy. A coordinate relation would be developed through experience in two distinctive linguistic settings where interlocutors rarely switched languages, as happens when a second language is started after infancy and in a context quite different from the home. One implication of this contrast for Ervin and Osgood was that translation equivalents would have more similar meanings and would be more likely to have a common neurological representation for compound bilinguals than they would for coordinate bilinguals who, presumably because of the distinctiveness of their language-acquisition contexts, would be more likely to develop two functionally separated systems of meanings, one attached to each of their languages. In our research on this interesting idea, we used the terms "fused" and "separated" instead of "compound" and "coordinate" to draw attention to the possible independence/interdependence of the underlying neuro-systems of bilinguals with different acquisition histories.

In our first studies (Lambert, Havelka, and Crosby 1958), we argued that if there were anything of importance in this compound/coordinate notion, then extended experience in separated language acquisition contexts should enhance the functional separation of the bilingual's two languages, while experience in mixed language acquisition contexts should reduce the functional separation of the two language systems. We sought out contrasting subsets of bilinguals with different acquisition histories and tested them, anticipating that those with experience in separated contexts would show comparatively greater semantic differences between words in one language and their translation equivalents; in addition, translation equivalents should function more independently for those with coordinate backgrounds.

The research confirmed these predictions. For instance, semantic differences of translation equivalents, measured with semantic rating scales, were greater for coordinate than for compound bilinguals. That is, words like *house* and *maison* or *friend* and *ami* had more distinctive semantic profiles for coordinate/separated bilinguals than for compound/fused bilinguals. When asked to memorize a list of words in language A, compound bilinguals profited more from rehearsing in advance with language B translation equivalents of these words than did coordinate bilinguals. These results supported the basic theory about differences in degrees of connectedness between the two language systems of bilinguals, and these differences were traceable to language acquisition histories.

These findings prompted further questions. We had been reading about aphasia among bilinguals and noted that some bilinguals apparently lose the functioning of only one of their languages following a cerebral insult or accident, while others lose complete or partial facility with both languages. Since coordinate bilinguals were presumed to have more functionally separated neural structures underlying their two languages than compound bilinguals, we predicted that brain damage leading to aphasia would be more likely to affect both languages of compound bilinguals and would produce a more selective disturbance in one or the other of the languages of coordinate bilinguals. With help from the Montreal Neurological Institute, we were able to test a number of bilingual aphasics in the Montreal area and compare their postaphasic linguistic abilities and handicaps with those described in the published medical reports of bilingual aphasics from other parts of the world (Lambert and Fillenbaum 1959).

The results of this exploratory study were very encouraging in that they supported the theoretical contrast between compound and coordinate forms of bilingualism, although it became very apparent that much more research on the topic was called for before alternate interpretations of the results could be ruled out. It was found that patients whose histories suggested that their languages were essentially in a compound relationship showed a generalized aphasic disorder in the sense that both languages were affected by the neurological disturbance. In contrast, patients whose histories fit the coordinate pattern typically showed a more specific language disorder following injury, one language being more affected than the other. The trouble here is that we did not have sufficient information about such factors as pre-aphasia verbal abilities, extent of brain damage involved, type of language retraining given during the recovery period (which might have favored one language), or the details of actual language loss suffered at the time of the aphasia. Nonetheless, pieces of the puzzle were falling into place.

At about the same time, we were investigating the interesting phenomenon of verbal or semantic "satiation," the effects of continuous repetition of a word on its meaning (Lambert and Jakobovits 1960; Jakobovits and Lambert 1961). We developed a means of measuring these effects based on the rating scales of the semantic differential, and found that the continuous repetition of a word would lead to a reliable decrease in the intensity of its connotative meaning. What would happen, we wondered, if a French-English bilingual were asked to continuously repeat *house* and was then examined for the effect of house-repetition on the translation equivalent, *maison?* Would there be more cross-language satiation for compounds than for coordinates, as one would expect?

The results were in the predicted direction, in fact a little too much so: The compound bilinguals showed cross-language satiation of meaning, as expected, while the coordinates went to an unanticipated extreme in that the other language equivalents (*maison*) showed an increase in connotative meaning. The point is, however, that the groups differed as predicted, even though certain mysterious cross-language effects turned up with the coordinate/separated bilinguals.

These crazy things were beginning to make some sense for us: The aphasia study and the satiation study suggested that coordinate bilinguals might have a different or more effective means of shutting down one linguistic system when the other language is in operation. This jibed nicely with the ideas of Penfield and Roberts (1959) who, as neurosurgeons, had the hunch that bilinguals might have some sort of switching mechanism in the brain that shuts one language off when the other is in function. Likewise, Hebb (1958) and P. Milner (1957) were beginning to speculate at that time about possible neural mechanisms that might "gate out" potentially antagonistic or competing systems.

We had noted another phenomenon in several other studies under way at the same time (Olton 1960; Lambert, Ignatow, and Krauthamer 1968). When given mixed-language lists of words to memorize (*glove, printemps, maison, boy*), bilinguals rarely made translation errors; that is, they hardly ever incorrectly recalled that *springtime* or *house* had been in the original list. To us, this meant that bilinguals could apparently store a word and remember not only the concept involved, but also the language it came in, and they could do this as effectively with two languages as monolinguals (who don't have to keep track of the language involved) could with one language. This amazing capacity is still not adequately explained, and although it is more pronounced among coordinate bilinguals (Lambert et al. 1968), it is not exclusively a coordinate/compound matter. Rather, it seems to be a bilingual versus monolingual matter: Bilinguals do not pay a price for "double coding" (remembering the particular concept *and* its language) because bilinguals remember just as many of the words of a 40-item mixed-language list as monolinguals do of a 40-item single-language list. And the bilinguals make hardly any translation errors in recall.

However, if subsets of the words in a 40-item list fall into semantic clusters (that is, 10 of the 40 items are names of fruit), and if the fruit subset is made bilingual (*apple, citron, pear, pamplemousse*), then, as we would expect – and as we found – the coordinate bilinguals have more difficulty remembering the full subset than do the compound bilinguals. What gives the coordinates an advantage over the compounds is to have one set presented in one language (*pomme, citron, poire, pamplemousse*) and a different semantic set in the other language, such as the names of trees: *oak, maple, willow, spruce* (Lambert 1969).

In another related study, we found that compounds can put together a whole set of bilingual clues and arrive at a hidden "core concept" better than coordinates can (Lambert and Rawlings 1969). Let me explain. Statistical norms are available in many languages for free associations made to stimulus words. If I were to ask you to think of the concept *table* and to give your first associate to that word, chances are high that you would home in on the norms: *table*-chair; *table*-wood; *table*-legs. In French, the probabilities are high that *la table* leads to *manger* (not so in the English norms), as well as to *chaise, bois*. Knowing these norms, we worked them backward. We asked subjects to listen to a string of associates and to try and find the underlying core concept: Given *manger, chair, wood, bois*, could they come up with *table* or *la table*? It turns out that compound bilinguals can tease out the hidden core concept better with clues from both languages than can coordinates, who do better with single-language clues.

What these studies indicated, then, is that language acquisition histories make a difference, and that the language histories of compound bilinguals (when they are balanced in their skills) promote a more fused, interdependent bilingual linguistic system, and that the compound case contrasts in fascinating ways with the more separated, independent bilingual linguistic system of coordinate bilinguals. And for sure there are both cognitive and neurophysiological accompaniments to this contrast.

Other findings suggest that being bilingual, whether compound or coordinate, makes the big difference, that the bilingual-monolingual contrast is often basic. In fact, Allan Paivio and I (Paivio and Lambert 1981; Paivio, Clark, and Lambert 1988) are of the opinion that bilinguals have two verbal coding systems that give them cognitive advantages over monolinguals. The idea is that we humans have an important imagery coding system quite distinct from, but in contact with, a separate verbal coding system. As a consequence, we can remember and store visual information with great precision, and actually with much more ease than we can remember or store verbal information. For instance, we can all recall large numbers of concepts represented by pictures (sketches of a firefighter's hat, a baseball bat, a snowflake), but in a long list, we can keep in mind only a small number of words referring to such concepts. However, the more imagery laden the verbal concepts are (as when the words are concrete rather than abstract), the more the verbal hooks catch into our memories.

In experiments, subjects remember only x amount of the verbal inputs if they are presented in one language, but $2x$ (twice as many) if they are presented bilingually to balanced bilinguals. This doubling of memory in the bilingual case is important because it falls halfway between monolingual and pictorial input in its power; the pictorial memory is nearly exactly $3x$ in this example. What is now coming to light is the fact that translation equivalents in lists are more powerful for memory than are synonyms in a single language, and the translation process itself may even promote imagery. That is, when a bilingual translates *church* to *église* or vice versa, the underlying concept may be made more vivid in imagery terms. This current line of research, which stretches far back in time, is getting hot, thanks mainly to Allan Paivio.

The neurological issue

McGill University has been just the right place to be to study bilingualism because of people like Donald Hebb, Wilder Penfield, Brenda Milner, and Peter Milner, who know so much about the brain and have all befriended us in our research endeavors. The aphasia study was a start, and the compound/coordinate business, although not thoroughly convincing to any of us, became a good reason to explore the neuropsychology of bilingualism. To sharpen up the distinction, we emphasized one main and easily categorized feature of compound/coordinate difference – early versus late bilingual development. Thus, in our more recent research, comparisons are made between early bilinguals (those who are bilingual from infancy on and who are more likely to develop compound linguistic systems) and late bilinguals (those who become bilingual in the childhood or adolescent years and who are most likely to develop coordinate systems). This turns out to be an extremely interesting and promising research domain because the behavioral distinctions, noted earlier, substantiate differences in the ways early (compounds) and late (coordinate) bilinguals think about and process verbal inputs.

The corresponding neuropsychological evidence on the early–late bilingual distinction is becoming convincing (see Vaid and Genesee 1980).

One McGill study dealt with young adults who had become perfectly bilingual in French and English in infancy, childhood, or adolescence (Genesee, Hamers, Lambert, Mononen, Seitz, and Starck 1978). These subjects were given very simple linguistic tasks to perform (such as to indicate whether the words they heard through earphones were English or French). At the same time, the electroencephalographic (EEG) activity in their left and right cerebral hemispheres was monitored and converted into average evoked reactions. It turned out that early bilinguals (those bilingual from infancy or childhood) processed the input information more quickly in their left than in their right hemispheres, while late bilinguals (the adolescent subgroup) processed the input information faster in their right than in their left hemispheres. We interpreted the results in terms of strategy differences. The early bilinguals apparently had a proclivity for a left-hemisphere strategy, one based more on semantic analysis, while the late bilinguals had a right-hemisphere proclivity, using a processing strategy based more on the gestaltlike or melodic properties of the input.

A second McGill study focused on the processing of meaning in early and late bilinguals, with verbal information presented through the left or right ear (Vaid and Lambert 1979). The assumption in this case too was that there is a more direct and efficient neurological route from one ear to the contralateral cerebral hemisphere. These findings also suggest that bilinguals tend to involve their right hemispheres more in the encoding and decoding of meaning than do monolinguals. But the degree of right-hemisphere involvement is determined by the sex of the subjects, as well as by the age of onset of their bilinguality. Thus, male monolinguals are more confined to the left hemisphere for the processing of meaning, whereas male bilinguals involve both right and left hemispheres if their bilinguality starts in infancy, and mainly the right hemisphere if the bilinguality dates from adolescence. Female monolinguals start with a balanced involvement of both right and left hemispheres, and bilinguality, whether early or late in its origin, shifts the control of meaning mainly to the right hemisphere.

Two recent studies outside McGill have come to similar conclusions; that is, greater right-hemisphere involvement in linguistic processing for late than for early bilinguals. One of these investigations was conducted by Hal Gordon, using a dichotic listening design, with Hebrew-English bilingual adults in Israel, and the other by Bella Kotik using the EEG design with Polish-Russian bilinguals in the Soviet Union (Gordon 1980; Kotik 1980).

Harvey Sussman and colleagues at the University of Texas have arrived at similar conclusions from a quite different probing approach (Sussman, Franklin, and Simon 1982). They have bilingual subjects tap on a table with a left- or right-hand finger while speaking in one or the other of their languages. Right-hand tapping, they find, is disrupted for mono-lingual controls when tapping is concurrent with speech, whereas both right- and left-hand tapping is disrupted for bilinguals. This presumed greater involvement of the right hemisphere is most pronounced for late bilinguals when using their non-native language. All told, then, there is a fairly solid accumulation of evidence for a relationship between early–late bilingualism and left-right hemisphere involvement; but as Vaid and Genesee (1981) mention, the concomitant influences of such factors as sex, formal versus informal modes of language acquisition, and stage of bilinguality have yet to be given appropriate attention in these studies (see also Hall and Lambert 1988). Nonetheless, we can now ask more penetrating questions about the different patterns of language acquisition experienced by bilinguals, especially the differences between early and late beginnings of bilingualism. Might there be some connections be-tween the cognitive processes of bilinguals, discussed earlier, and greater right-hemisphere involvement? Why are there such marked early–late differences in degree of right-hemisphere involvement among bilinguals? Why are male bilinguals so special? Because of these accumulating pieces of information, the next research probes into bilingualism will be more complex, but also much more exciting.

The issue of bilingualism's effect on intelligence

Does one pay a price in the development of language competence and thinking for being or becoming bilingual? The database for answering this question is still spotty in various ways and incomplete, even though serious attention has been given to the matter for nearly a century. However, enough data are available to conclude tentatively that under specified conditions, being bilingual can have tremendous advantages not only in terms of language competencies, but also in terms of cognitive and social development. The limiting condition is that the two (or more) languages involved in the bilingualism have enough social value and worth that *both* can be permitted to flourish as languages of thought and expression. This is the matter of balance and unbalance again, and we are interested in factors that hamper the development of balance. Jim Cummins (1978) puts the same idea another way: If both languages are given the opportunity to meet and pass some minimum threshold of competence, then one can realize the benefits of being bilingual. When these conditions are met, the evidence is very persuasive.

Our involvement at McGill with this research started in the early 1960s when we compared English-French bilingual and monolingual ten-year-olds, equated for social-class background, on a series of verbal and nonverbal tests of intelligence and tests of language competencies in each of the bilingual's two languages (Peal and Lambert 1962). A host of earlier studies from various world settings had turned up mainly deficits of various sorts associated with bilingualism. But we found the bulk of these inadequate in design; they had, for example, neglected to control for social-class background in their comparisons of bi- and monolingual groups, and they rarely measured degree of bilingualism.

To our surprise, our bilingual youngsters in Montreal scored significantly higher than did carefully matched monolinguals on both verbal and nonverbal measures of intelligence; they were further advanced in school grade than were the monolinguals; and they performed as well or better on various tests of competence in French (the language of schooling) than did the monolingual controls, at the same time as they outperformed the controls by far on all tests of competence in English. Furthermore, their pattern of test results indicated that, relative to monolinguals, they had developed a more diversified structure of intelligence and more flexibility in thought, those very features of cognition that very likely determine the depth and breadth of language competence.

Since that 1962 research, confirmations have emerged from carefully conducted research in different parts of the world, from Singapore, Switzerland, South Africa, Israel and New York, western Canada, and Montreal (Torrance, Gowan, Wu, and Aliotti 1970; Ianco-Worrall 1972; Ben Zeev 1972; Cummins and Gulutsan 1973). All these studies (and we have found no others in the recent literature to contradict them) indicate that bilingual young people, relative to monolingual controls, show definite cognitive and linguistic advantages as these are reflected in measures of cognitive flexibility, creativity, divergent thought, or problem solving. Ben Zeev's study, for example, involved Hebrew-English bilingual children in New York and Israel; her results strongly support the conclusion that bilinguals have greater cognitive flexibility in the sense that her bilinguals had greater skill at auditory reorganization of verbal material, a much more "flexible manipulation of the linguistic code," and more sophistication in "concrete operational thinking," as these were measured in her investigation. Ianco-Worrall's study involved Afrikaans-English bilingual children in Pretoria, South Africa, and it lends equally strong support for a somewhat different form of cognitive flexibility, an advantage bilinguals show over monolingual controls in separating word meaning from word sound. Ianco-Worrall's bilinguals were some two years more advanced in this feature of cognitive development, one that Leopold felt to be so characteristic of the liberated thought of bilinguals (Leopold 1949). Worrall also found a bilingual precocity in the realization of the arbitrariness of assignments of names to referents, a feature of thinking Vygotsky believed was a reflection of insight and sophistication (Vygotsky 1962).

The study by Scott (1973) of French-English bilinguals in Montreal is important because it involved a comparison of two groups of young children. One group had been given the opportunity to become bilingual over a period of years, while the second group had not been given this opportunity. Scott worked with data collected over a seven-year period from two groups of English-Canadian children, half of whom had become functionally bilingual in French during the time period through immersion schooling in French. The other half had followed a conventional English-language education program. Scott focused on the possible effects that becoming bilingual might have on divergent thinking, a special type of cognitive flexibility. Measures of divergent thinking provide the subject with a starting point for thought – "Think of a paper clip" – and ask the subject to generate a whole series of permissible solutions – "Tell me all the things one could do with it." Some researchers (Getzels and Jackson 1962) have considered divergent thinking to be an index of creativity, or at least an index of a rich imagination and an ability to scan a host of possible solutions rapidly. The results, based on a multivariate analysis, showed that the functionally bilingual youngsters were, at grades 5 and 6, substantially higher scorers than the monolinguals with whom they had been equated for IQ and social-class background at the grade 1 level. Although the numbers of children in each group are small, this study supports the causal link between bilingualism and flexibility, with bilingualism apparently the factor that enhances flexibility. Note also the possible tie-in with more right-hemisphere involvement among bilinguals.

There is, then, an impressive array of evidence accumulating that argues plainly against the common-sense notion that becoming bilingual – having two linguistic systems within one's brain – naturally divides a person's cognitive resources and reduces efficiency of thought or language. Instead, one now can put forth a very strong argument that there are definite cognitive and language advantages to being bilingual. Only further research will tell us how this advantage, assuming it is a reliable phenomenon, actually works. Perhaps it is a matter of bilinguals being better able to store information; perhaps it is the greater separation of linguistic symbols from their referents or the ability to separate word meaning from word sound; perhaps it is the contrasts of linguistic systems that bilinguals continually make that aids them in the development of general conceptual thought. My own working hypothesis is that bilingualism provides a person with a comparative, three-dimensional insight into language, a type of stereolinguistic optic on communication that the monolingual rarely experiences.

Bilingualism also helps protect a person against reification, the human tendency to attribute thing qualities to all non-things that happen to have names (like *soul, spirit, kindness*). The protection comes in the form of the bilingual person's better realization that names are essentially arbitrary assignments. This realization, along with the distance bilinguals can keep between names and referents, make them better able to play with words and their meanings – in other words, to be creative. Whatever the ultimate explanation, this new trend in research should give second thoughts to those who have used the bilingual-deficit notion as an argument for melting down ethnic groups. We hope, too, it will provide a new perspective for members of ethnolinguistic groups who may have been led to believe that bilingualism is nothing but a handicap. Kenji Hakuta's (1986) book on this topic presents a convincing set of arguments in favor of bilingualism's impact on cognitive development.

The sociology and politics of bilingualism

One feature of the studies just reviewed merits special attention. In each of the settings referred to (Singapore, South Africa, Switzerland, Israel, New York, Montreal), we are dealing with bilinguals for whom the two languages involved have social value and respect. Knowing Afrikaans and English in South Africa, Hebrew and English in New York and Israel, or French as well as English in Montreal would in each case be adding a second, socially relevant language to one's repertoire of skills. In none of these settings would the learning of the second language necessarily portend the slow replacement of the first, or home language, as would be the case for most linguistic minority groups in the United States and Canada who are pressured to develop high-level skills in English at the expense of their home languages. We refer to the former instances as examples of "additive" bilingualism, and we draw a sharp contrast with the "subtractive" form experienced by ethnolinguistic minority groups who, because of national educational policies and social pressures of various sorts, feel forced to put aside or subtract out their ethnic languages for a more necessary and prestigious national language. In the subtractive case, one's degree of bilinguality at any time would likely reflect a stage in the disuse of the ethnic home language and its associated cultural accompaniments, and its replacement with another, more "necessary" language. This form of bilingualism can be devastating because it usually places youngsters in a psycholinguistic limbo where neither language is useful as a tool of thought and expression – a type of "semi-lingualism," as Skutnabb-Kangas and Toukomaa (1976) put it.

The case of French and English in Montreal is interesting because both additive and subtractive features are involved. For anglophone Quebecers, learning French is clearly additive in nature, with no fear of a loss of identity or of French eradicating English competence. Since francophone Quebecers comprise some 80 percent of the population and have their own French-language school system from kindergarten to the most advanced professional institutions, learning English also might be thought of as additive. From a North American perspective, however, Quebec is a small French-speaking enclave continuously bombarded by English-language media, with pressures on its children to prepare themselves for life in an otherwise English-speaking semicontinent. For francophone Canadians outside Quebec, the chances of keeping French alive as a home, school, and work language are slim. This fear of subtractive loss of Frenchness is real for many French-speaking Quebecers as well: a too ardent move toward Englishness might well subtract out Frenchness.

In my mind, one important aim of education in North America should be to brighten the outlook for ethnolinguistic minority group children by preparing them to compete better in educational and occupational pursuits. As potential bilinguals, they certainly have the cognitive and linguistic potential, as shown by the research. The best way I can see to release the potential is to transform their subtractive experiences with bilingualism and biculturalism into additive ones. We already have a few research-based examples of how this transformation might work. The first is the case of Franco-Americans in northern New England who were recently given a chance to be schooled partly in their home language (see Dubé and Herbert 1975a, 1975b; Lambert, Giles, and Picard 1975; Lambert, Giles, and Albert 1976). Some 85 percent of the families in the northern regions of Maine have kept French alive as the home language or as one of the two home languages, even though traditionally all schooling has been conducted in English.

We participated in an experiment wherein a random selection of schools and of classes in the area were permitted to offer about a third of the elementary curriculum in French, and where a second sample of schools – with children of comparable intelligence scores and socioeconomic background – served as a control or comparison in that all their instruction was in English. After a five-year run, the children in the partial French classes clearly outperformed those in the control classes in various aspects of English-language skills and in academic content, such as math, learned partly in French. At the same time, French had become for them something more than an audiolingual language because of the reading and writing requirements. These results mean that the French-trained Franco-American children were given a better chance to compete in occupations or professions calling for high-level educational training; they had been lifted from the typical low standing on scholastic achievement measures that characterizes so many ethnolinguistic groups in North America.

An important element in this transformation was the change in the self-image of the French-trained youngsters who, we found, began to reflect a deep pride in being French as well as American and a realization that both languages were important media for education. Similar community-based studies are underway in the American Southwest, and these too are based on the belief that ethnolinguistic minorities need a strong educational experience in their own languages and traditions before they can cope in an "all-American" society or before they will want to cope in such a society.

A second example of a transformation of subtractive to additive bilingualism is provided by Carolyn Kessler and Mary Quinn (1980). In their study, Spanish-speaking grade 6 students were given the opportunity in elementary school to learn subject matters via Spanish while learning English; that is, like the Franco-Americans in the first example, to use their home language – the language through which their basic conceptual thinking developed in infancy – as one of the linguistic media for further conceptual growth. The Hispanic-American students were compared with a much-privileged sample of middle-class, white, monolingual English-speaking American pupils of the same age. Both groups were given an extensive training program in science inquiry through films and discussion of physical science problems and hypothesis testing. In tests given after the training, it was found that the Spanish-English bilinguals generated hypotheses of a much higher quality and complexity than did the monolinguals. This problem-solving quality was reflected also in the language used, as indexed by a syntactic complexity measure, so that the bilinguals clearly were using more complex linguistic structures as well. Kessler and Quinn also found substantial correlations between their measures of hypothesis quality and syntactic complexity, providing an important link between problem-solving capacity and linguistic skills.

The research by Kessler and Quinn jibes nicely with other findings. For example, Padilla and Long (1986 and 1970) found that Spanish-American children and adolescents can acquire English better and adjust more effectively to the educational and occupational demands of American society if their linguistic and cultural ties with the Spanish-speaking world are kept alive and active from infancy on. There are, in fact, numerous recent examples that point in the same direction (see Hanson 1979; McConnell 1980; Rosler and Holm 1980; Troike 1978). G. R. Tucker (1980) integrated these studies very intelligently and concluded that there is a "a cumulative and positive impact of bilingual education on all youngsters when they are allowed to remain in bilingual programs for a period of time greater than two or three or even five years and when there is an active attempt to provide nurturance and sustenance of their mother tongue in addition to introducing teaching via the language of wider communication."

The issue of immersion

It is one thing to get comfortable in the ivory tower while trying to figure out how the bilingual mind and the bilingual tongue work. But in doing so, one is continuously aware of the fact that one is studying bilingual people in a very demanding real world, making the social aspects of bilingualism an inseparable part of the endeavor. We were aware from the mid–1950s on of the social and political psychology of bilingualism, of the background tensions between francophones and anglophones in Quebec and Canada, and of the stereotypes each major ethnic group held toward their own group and the other group (Lambert 1967). Gardner and Lambert (1972) also started linking attitudes and stereotypes of own group and other group with the second language learning process, using high school and college students, a facet of research that Gardner and his colleagues have since developed splendidly (e.g., Gardner and Lambert 1972; Gardner and Kalin 1981).

It is quite a different thing to get out of the ivory tower and put research ideas into practice. This urge to do something about bilingualism led us into immersion education. We have learned much about the developmental course of language acquisition and the sociology of ethnolinguistic minority and majority groups from our longitudinal studies of early immersion programs in elementary schools. We have also profited enormously from our collaboration with Merrill Swain and Jim Cummins, who got immersion out of Quebec and made it a Canadian issue.

In North America, immersion programs are intended mainly for English-speaking children who, as representatives of the major ethnolinguistic group, are ready to add a second language with no fear of losing their footing in English. From their first day in kindergarten or grade 1, they find themselves with a teacher who speaks only some foreign language (French, Ukrainian, Hebrew, Spanish, German) and who starts conversing and interacting, slowly and considerately, in that language. The foreign language (L1) is used as the sole medium of instruction for kindergarten and grades 1 and 2, and only then is English introduced, in the form of English language arts. By grades 5 and 6, half of the curriculum is taught via L2 and half via L1.

The rather dramatic results of early immersion schooling have been described elsewhere (see Lambert and Tucker 1972; Swain 1974; Genesee 1978). Briefly, we find that by the end of elementary school, students in immersion have developed a functional bilinguality in L2, which is learned mainly in an incidental fashion through its use as a language of instruction. The functional bilinguality attained by grades 5 and 6 does not impair in any way the development of language skills in L1. In fact,

L1 competencies generally are enriched when comparisons are made with carefully matched control (nonimmersion) groups. Immersion pupils who learn to read via L2 keep up with the nonimmersion controls in English-language reading as well as all other aspects of English. Likewise, skills in content matter (such as math, science, social studies) taught through L2 are as well developed for immersion as for control pupils.

Thus, much transfer from L2 to L1 seems to take place naturally in these programs, as though what is learned through L2 with regard to content matters and with regard to reading skills and language development percolates down to the first language. The immersion children seem to attack the L2 demands of the program with all the thinking and language abilities they have, and this apparently promotes a continuous, mutually beneficial interplay between L2 (the instructional code) and L1 (the basic language of thought and expression for the children at the start of the experience). This fascinating transfer of skills from L2 to L1 and vice versa holds also for Jewish youngsters whose only home language is English and who follow a double-immersion program where Hebrew and French are used by separate teachers as the sole media of instruction from kindergarten through grade 3 (see Genesee and Lambert 1981). The interplay in this case is among L2-H, L2-F, and L1. The main finding here is that language acquisition can proceed at a normal pace even though it involves one or more second languages, for these can interact supportively with first language development.

It has also been found that those with early immersion experiences are more anxious to learn a third language than are the controls who have experienced mainly French as a second language training (see Cziko, Lambert, Sidoti, and Tucker 1980). Apparently because they have had a successful experience in mastering one foreign language, they are confident and inquisitive about learning others. It is also true that because linguistic majority group children are interested enough in minority group languages to learn them through immersion, this fact can have a powerful supportive effect on increasing the value and status of minority languages in the United States and Canada. Furthermore, parents love the idea because they quickly see the advantages of additive bilingualism in the lives of their children.

But here's the important point: immersion education conducted in a second or foreign language is not meant for the linguistic minority child. It fuels the subtractive process and places the minority child into another form of psycholinguistic limbo, where his/her infant language is suppressed and his/her cultural heritage and its language is subtly stigmatized as a handicap to be washed away. Richard Tucker and I argued this point as strongly as we could in our 1972 book on immersion but some, with a form of cultural myopia, missed this critical distinction.

Our remedy for the language minority child is to root him/herself thoroughly in the likely to be bypassed heritage language, bringing the infant language-thought connections to fruition, and when solidly literate in the first language then, and only then, start the transformation from a subtractive to a thoroughly additive outlook on being bilingual.

So here is what I conclude from all this: Bilingualism is by its nature a very hot topic of study; it touches many other fields of study, from neurology to politics and sociology; it is a fun topic; it has a good start; only the surface has been scratched; and there is a splendidly educated cadre of young people who are taking over the direction of the field. They are certain to make it even hotter and even more fun.

CONCLUSION

17 *The project in perspective*

G. Richard Tucker

The research orientation

This volume derived from the Development of Bilingual Proficiency symposium has focused on the presentation and analysis of careful, complex, well-implemented theory-driven research, as opposed to practice-driven research. This observation is, I believe, important because the theoretical orientation colors the perceived utility of the DBP findings and our discussions for various audiences. It is important to understand that when one is examining the outcomes and potential implications of theory-driven as opposed to practice-driven research, one brings certain predispositions, certain ways of organizing information, and certain ways of asking questions to the research setting. Would there have been a different set of questions, analyses, or outcomes if the research had been practice-driven? Probably. Would such research have been as likely to be funded? Probably not.

The nature of proficiency

The discussion of the nature of language proficiency in Part I of this volume was a rich one. It was an intellectually engaging debate on the nature of construct validation and the choice of hypotheses; on the role of traits versus methods; on the form and the content of tests; and on what would constitute an adequate sample of behavior so it could be said that something which reflected grammar ability, discourse ability, or sociolinguistic ability was being tapped. The debate, although lively, nevertheless engendered a gnawing fear that even if there was agreement that we should or should not do exploratory factor analysis before confirmatory factor analysis, or should use one type of factor rotation rather than another, somehow we still would not be able to inform and improve educational practice. It may well be that such a worry is not particularly relevant. Perhaps this particular set of activities is important in its own right if looked at from the broader perspective of trying to understand the nature of language proficiency in a Canadian context; but it is certainly the case that a good deal more discussion is warranted.

One research priority identified in the discussion was the need to replicate a basic series of studies with a larger number of French immersion students, a larger number of native speakers, and so on. I would also propose as a research priority to seek out and retest the original cohort of sixth graders. I think that there are different contributions to be made by the most imaginative of cross-sectional studies and by longitudinal studies in which one has an opportunity to follow the same subjects over time – with the caveat that one needs to know a good deal about what goes on during that time.

It seems to me that a major contribution of the original St. Lambert immersion experiment (Lambert and Tucker 1972) was that we had an opportunity not only to look at one or two groups of children who participated in early immersion programs at one or two grade levels, but were also able to follow a group of subjects through their entire educational experience and then ask them, with all the data that we had accumulated at yearly intervals as a backdrop, to reflect on the experience, and to share with us what it meant for them, how their lives were different (if at all), and so on. Although effects do not necessarily show themselves at the end of one or two years, the cumulative impact of an educational innovation may be quite large, and one needs to take a step back to look at that impact. During the symposium, the issue of effect over time was raised in a slightly different way when a participant asked what had happened to the D in DBP. The question, of course, was how much attention had been paid to the children's development.

In Chapter 11, d'Anglejan reminds us of the importance of mother-tongue assessment for both majority and minority language children. She concludes that mother-tongue assessment is particularly important for minority children both because it gives us a benchmark against which to examine other findings, and because of the symbolic value of such assessment in according legitimacy to the use of the language. The importance of further qualitative analyses of existing data for an understanding of proficiency development is pointed out by Schachter (Chapter 3), who argues that additional descriptive analyses of the data would have implications for the improvement of educational practice in second language teaching.

A further issue that may be raised within the context of the DBP studies concerns the appropriate goals or objectives for students who participate in innovative language training programs. Is the goal to score 3 + on the ILR (Interagency Language Roundtable) Oral Proficiency Interview Scale? Is the goal to acquire sufficient facility in French so that in a matched guise experiment an individual would be evaluated favorably? An interesting feature of the data was that native speakers varied so greatly in their control of their mother tongue. What exactly should that mean to us? Why do native French-speaking children not score 90 percent + on sociolinguistic tests? Should their behavior be regarded as normative? D'Anglejan raised the related question of whether there is explicit transmission of anticipated normative language behavior through participation in French immersion programs. She implied strongly that there was not. It might also be asked whether there is consensus about what the norm should be. Again, probably there is not. It seems quite clear that we must have some better understanding of what is to be achieved by participating in innovative language education programs than we do at the present time.

Classroom treatment

The discussion in Part II of this volume focuses on COLT and classroom observation. Clearly, it is important that we have some scheme to observe, to capture and to characterize what goes on in the classroom, because teachers are always in dynamic interaction with their students, their materials, and their programs. In Chapter 14, Handscombe is concerned specifically about the implications of DBP for teacher education – both in-service and pre-service – and asserts that COLT would be particularly useful in this context. Can one capture what goes on in the classroom using an observation schedule such as COLT? It is difficult, as those who have worked with COLT or any of its derivatives have found out. In fact, researchers have only begun to mine some of the data that are there.

During the symposium it emerged that some dynamic patterns have not yet been captured in the coding scheme. The question arises as to whether on the basis of the so-called COLT studies we would be justified in suggesting that curricula, in general, move in a more experiential direction. Should the traditional grammatical focus be abandoned or should we return to a more grammatical focus? Should we include some mixture of experiential and analytic activities? Would any change be warranted, and if so, how are we to know what change? How can we accurately describe what happens in classroom settings? COLT certainly is an exciting tool. But the consensus of those attending the symposium was that a good deal more work needs to be done before we are ready to change classroom practice.

In her discussion paper (Chapter 6), Lightbown asks a very simple question, but one that is intriguingly difficult to answer. In what cases are statistically significant differences educationally and pedagogically relevant? This is a crucial question for those of us who are charged with responsibility for modifying curricula, adapting materials, recommending differential treatments for children, and so on. Paulston, in Chapter 15, calls our attention to the importance of individual variation in the classroom. If children learn differently, then there should be a wide variety of activities in the class. We should be able to reflect the broad differences in strategies preferred or typically used by children, and involve children in relevant and challenging tasks within the language learning environment regardless of their own preferred strategies.

Social and individual variables

McLaughlin (Chapter 12) is also concerned with the importance of individual variables, in particular of language aptitude. I was left with the impression from the discussion of aptitude and language learning strategies that the set of abilities may develop early and that they are mutable. There are important differences in the ways in which children behave, in the ways in which they interact with material, with their environment, and with their teachers, that may have a very special significance we need to be able to account for. How can teachers facilitate the emergence of strategies, of metacognitive skills? How can they help children to use the strategies they prefer, as opposed to gearing instruction to the children's weaknesses?

An important area for further investigation is the way in which various aspects of proficiency and language development are differentially related to the personal characteristics of students. Do students merely have different profiles on tests, or are they really different? They are, of course, in some sense really different, but what does this mean? How do we get at what it means? How do we examine effectively the relationship between the types of questions we ask and how students reveal themselves by performance?

McLaughlin referred to the implications of expert-novice systems and similar paradigms for informing us about the various dynamics involved in language learning. I was struck by the fact that there are anecdotal accounts which are at least tangentially relevant to this concern. These are the recollections many of us have culled from individuals such as Charles Ferguson and Joseph Greenberg – each of whom would fall into the category of expert second or other-language learner. They have each been called on many times to reflect on their experiences as to what it was that constituted the difficulties in adding yet another language to their repertoire. What were the strategies they used? What worked well? What did not? What was difficult? One might rethink some of this information within the context of a systematic study of successful second language learners. (This is analogous to work that was done at the Modern Language Centre in the 1970s and to work currently being undertaken by McGroarty at the Center for Language Education and Research (CLEAR).) How might one bring such observations into the laboratory using some kind of expert/novice paradigm, as McLaughlin suggested?

Finally, I would like to comment on the paper by Bourhis (Chapter 13). His contribution was particularly helpful in calling our attention to other models or theoretical frameworks such as those of Clément (1980) and Gardner (1983). I think it is particularly useful to examine the very rich data collection and theorizing that have been carried out in the DBP project in relation to that of other Canadian researchers and indeed to that of researchers in other parts of the world.

Key individuals

Let me now say a word about two outstanding contributors to this volume. It was both appropriate and indeed absolutely necessary that Wallace Lambert participate in the DBP symposium. The magnitude of his contributions can best be captured by paraphrasing Barry Mc-Laughlin who, after listening to Lambert's public lecture, commented that some of the studies he was just now planning were quite similar to those that had already been done by Lambert thirty years ago. That may be a slight exaggeration, but it does seem to me to capture the essence of the catalytic influence Wallace Lambert has had on the field, and it shows how fortunate we were to have had him with us at the symposium.

Second, I particularly appreciated the symposium presentation by Mari Wesche of David Stern's discussion paper. This struck me as important for several reasons. His contributions, as we know, have been many; his influence, on the field of English language teaching and French language teaching, has been enormous; the legacy he left has been profound. But perhaps the most important factor was his continual insistence that research must inform educational practice.

Conclusion

At the end of a volume such as this we need to ask whether one of Canada's goals is the development of a bilingual citizenry and, if so, whether one can enhance the opportunity individuals have to achieve it by systematically varying language education policy. I believe the answer to that question is that one can; by systematically varying language education policy it is possible to manipulate contingencies in such a way that we enhance for some children their opportunity to acquire facility in a second language. Obviously, a great deal still needs to be done to match child to program, program to teacher, program and teacher and child to available resources and opportunities. But the research that has been carried out during these past five years, particularly within the context of the DBP project, leads us to answer "yes" to the question. Second, the question needs to be asked: If *de facto* or *de jure* one must test, as a measure of entrance to a particular occupation, qualification for premium pay, program graduation, can we do it better tomorrow than we did it yesterday? I am not as confident about responding positively to this second question as I was to the first. I raise this issue because I am doubtful whether on the basis of our work we will be able to test more accurately tomorrow without fear of misclassifying or misassigning individuals than we have done for the past twenty-five years.

Let me end with a personal view. The question has often been raised about why an early start, that is, early immersion, does not produce greater advances in terms of second language learning. This is an interesting question, but it seems to me that in some sense it is almost a trivial one. From my perspective, we start early because second language study is an important part of a core curriculum. If we start early, then study via the second language can become a key component of the curriculum. Likewise, the reasons for starting early are symbolic and political. There are a variety of reasons in countries such as Canada for advocating the early start of second language study that do not have very much to do with age of arrival, length of residence, or other permutations of the data.

In conclusion, I should say that for many years now I have appreciated very much indeed the magnitude of the work that has been undertaken and has now been reported by the DBP researchers. It is my firm belief that such research must inform educational practice, and that one of the tasks remaining to the team over the months ahead is to extract and to make tangible the implications of the present findings for the improvement of educational programs. We all eagerly await the next steps to be taken.

References

Adelson, B. 1981. Problem solving and the development of abstract categories in programming languages. *Cognition* 9:422–33.

Allen, P. 1983. A three-level curriculum model for second language education. *Canadian Modern Language Review* 40/1:23–43.

Allen, P., Bialystok, E., Cummins, J., Mougeon, R., and Swain, M. 1982. *The development of bilingual proficiency: interim report on the first year of research*. Toronto: Modern Language Centre, O.I.S.E.

Allen, P., Carroll, S., Burtis, J., and Gaudino, V. 1987. The core French observation study. In Harley, Allen, Cummins, and Swain, Vol. II.

Allen, P., Cummins, J., Mougeon, R., and Swain, M. 1983. *The development of bilingual proficiency: second year report and appendices*. Toronto: Modern Language Centre, O.I.S.E.

Allen, P., Fröhlich, M., and Spada, N. 1984. The communicative orientation of language teaching: an observation scheme. In J. Handscombe, R. A. Orem, and B. P. Taylor (eds.), *On TESOL '83*. Washington, D.C.: TESOL.
1987. COLT observation scheme: development and validation. In Harley, Allen, Cummins, and Swain, Vol. II.

Allen, P., Howard, J., and Ullmann, R. 1984. Module making research. In Allen and Swain (eds.).

Allen, P., and Swain, M. (eds.) 1984. *Language issues and educational policies*. ELT Documents 119. Oxford: Pergamon.

Anderson, J. R., Greeno, J. G., Kline, P. J., and Neves, D. M. 1981. Acquisition of problem-solving skill. In J. R. Anderson (ed.), *Cognitive skills and their acquisition*. Hillsdale, N.J.: Lawrence Erlbaum.

Anthony, E. M. 1972. Approach, method and technique. In H. Allen and R. Campbell (eds.), *Teaching English as a second language*. New York: McGraw-Hill.

Bachman, L. F. 1990. *Fundamental considerations in language testing*. Oxford: Oxford University Press.

Bachman, L. F., and Mack, M. 1986. A causal analysis of learner characteristics and second-language proficiency. Paper presented at the 1986 TESOL Convention, Anaheim, California.

Bachman, L. F., and Palmer, A. S. 1982. The construct validation of some components of communicative proficiency. *TESOL Quarterly* 16/4:449–65.
1983. The relationship between background and learner variables and aspects of communicative proficiency. Paper presented at the 1983 TESOL Convention. Toronto.

Balakrishnan, T., and Kralt, J. 1987. Segregation of visible minorities in Montreal, Toronto and Vancouver. In L. Drieger (ed.), *Ethnic Canada*. Toronto: Copp Clark Pitman.

Balkan, L. 1970. *Les effets du bilinguisme français-anglais sur les aptitudes intellectuelles*. Brussells: Aimav.

Barnes, D. 1976. *From communication to curriculum*. Harmondsworth, England: Penguin.

Ben Zeev, S. 1972. The influence of bilingualism on cognitive development and cognitive strategy. Ph.D. dissertation, University of Chicago.

Berry, J., Kalin, R., and Taylor, D. 1977. *Multiculturalism and ethnic attitudes in Canada*. Ottawa: Minister of Supply and Services.

Bialystok, E. 1978. A theoretical model of second language learning. *Language Learning* 28:69–83.

Bialystok, E., Fröhlich, M., and Howard, J. 1979. Studies on second language learning and teaching in classroom settings: strategies, processes and functions. Toronto: Ontario Institute for Studies in Education, unpublished report.

Bibeau, G. 1984. No easy road to bilingualism. In Stern (ed.).

Blalock, H. M. 1964. *Causal inferences in nonexperimental research*. Chapel Hill: University of North Carolina Press.

Bley-Vroman, R. 1986. Hypothesis testing in second-language acquisition theory. *Language Learning* 36/3:353–76.

Bourhis, R. Y. 1979. Language in ethnic interaction: a social psychological approach. In H. Giles and B. Saint-Jacques (eds.), *Language and ethnic relations*. Oxford: Pergamon Press.

   1987. Social psychology and heritage language research: a retrospective view and future trends in Canada. In J. Cummins (ed.), *Heritage language research in Canada*. Ottawa: Minister of Supply and Services.

Bourhis, R. Y., Giles, H., and Rosenthal, D. 1981. Notes on the construction of a "Subjective Vitality Questionnaire" for ethnolinguistic groups. *Journal of Multilingual and Multicultural Development* 2:144–55.

Bourhis, R. Y., and Sachdev, I. 1984. Vitality perceptions and language attitudes: some Canadian data. *Journal of Language and Social Psychology* 3:97–125.

Bredimas-Assimopoulos, N. 1975. Intégration civique sans acculturation: les Grecs à Montréal. *Sociologie et Société* 7/2:129–40.

Britton, J. 1970. *Language and learning*. Harmondsworth, England: Penguin Books.

Brown, J. S., and Burton, R. R. 1978. Diagnostic models for procedural bugs in basic mathematical skills. *Cognitive Science* 2:155–92.

Brown, R. 1973. *A first language: the early stages*. Cambridge, Mass.: Harvard University Press.

Brumfit, C. 1987. Concepts and categories in language teaching methodology. In *Linguistics as applied linguistics*, AILA Review 4. Amsterdam: Free University Press.

Campbell, D. T., and Fiske, D. W. 1959. Convergent and discriminant validation by the multitrait-multimethod matrix. *Psychological Bulletin* 56:81–105.

Canale, M. 1983. From communicative competence to communicative language pedagogy. In J. C. Richards and R. W. Schmidt (eds.), *Language and communication*. London: Longman.

Canale, M., and Swain, M. 1980. Theoretical bases of communicative approaches to second language teaching and testing. *Applied Linguistics* 1: 1–47.

Carroll, J. B. 1967. Foreign language proficiency levels attained by language majors near graduation from college. *Foreign Language Annals* 1:131–51.

1975. *The teaching of French as a foreign language in eight countries.* New York: Wiley.

1981. Twenty-five years of research on foreign language aptitude. In K. C. Diller (ed.), *Individual differences and universals in language learning aptitude.* Rowley, Mass.: Newbury House.

1983. Psychometric theory and language testing. In J. W. Oller Jr. (ed.), *Issues in language testing research.* Rowley, Mass.: Newbury House.

Cattell, J. 1877. Experiments on the association of ideas. *Mind* 12:68–74.

Cattell, R. B. 1966. The scree test for the number of factors. *Multivariate Behavioral Research* 1:245–76.

Cazden, C. 1986. ESL teachers as language advocates for children. In P. Rigg and D. S. Enright (eds.), *Children and ESL: integrating perspectives.* Washington, D.C.: TESOL.

Chapelle, C., and Roberts, C. 1986. Ambiguity tolerance and field dependence as predictors of proficiency in English as a second language. *Language Learning* 36:27–45.

Chase, W. C., and Simon, H. A. 1973. Perception in chess. *Cognitive Psychology* 4:55–81.

Chaudron, C. 1977. Teachers' priorities in correcting learners' errors in French immersion classes. *Working Papers on Bilingualism* 12:21–33.

1988. *Second language classrooms: research on teaching and learning.* Cambridge: Cambridge University Press.

Chi, M., Glaser, R., and Rees, E. 1981. Expertise in problem solving. In *Advances in the psychology of human intelligence,* Vol. 1. Hillsdale, N.J.: Lawrence Erlbaum.

Chomsky, N. 1980. *Rules and representations.* Oxford: Basil Blackwell.

Clark, H., and Clark, E. 1977. *Psychology and language: an introduction to psycholinguistics.* New York: Harcourt Brace Jovanovich.

Clay, M. M. 1981. *The early detection of reading difficulties: a diagnostic survey.* 2nd ed. London: Heinemann.

Clay, M. M., Glynn, E. L., McNaughton, A. H., and Salmon, K. W. 1976. *Record of oral language.* Wellington: New Zealand Educational Institute.

Clément, R. 1980. Ethnicity, contact and communicative competence in a second language. In H. Giles, P. Robinson, and P. Smith, (eds.), *Language: social psychological perspectives.* Oxford: Pergamon.

1986. Second language proficiency and acculturation: an investigation of the effects of language status and individual characteristics. *Journal of Language and Social Psychology* 5:271–290.

Clément, R. and Kruidenier, B. G. 1985. Aptitude, attitude and motivation in second language proficiency: a test of Clément's model. *Journal of Language and Social Psychology* 4:21–38.

Collier, V. P. 1987. Age and rate of acquisition of cognitive academic second language proficiency. Paper presented to the annual conference of the American Educational Research Association.

Comrie, B. 1976. *Aspect.* Cambridge: Cambridge University Press.

Cronbach, L. J., Gleser, G., Nanda, H., and Rajaratnam, N. 1972. *The dependability of behavioral measurements: the theory of generalizability for scores and profiles.* New York: Wiley.

Cummins, J. 1978. Educational implications of mother tongue maintenance in minority-language groups. *The Canadian Modern Language Review* 34:395–416.

1979. Linguistic interdependence and the educational development of bilingual children. *Review of Educational Research* 49:222–51.

1980. The cross-lingual dimensions of language proficiency: implications for bilingual education and the optimal age question. *TESOL Quarterly* 14:175–87.

1981a. The role of primary language development in promoting educational success for language minority students. In California State Department of Education, ed., *Compendium on bilingual-bicultural education.* Sacramento: California State Department of Education.

1981b. Age on arrival and immigrant second language learning in Canada: a reassessment. *Applied Linguistics* 2:132–49.

1984. *Bilingualism and special education: issues in assessment and pedagogy.* Clevedon, England: Multilingual Matters.

Cummins, J., and Gulutsan, M. 1973. Some effects of bilingualism on cognitive functioning. Unpublished ms., University of Alberta, Edmonton.

Cummins, J., Lopes, J., and King, M. L. 1987. The language use patterns, language attitudes, and bilingual proficiency of Portuguese Canadian children in Toronto. In Harley, Allen, Cummins, and Swain, Vol. III.

Cummins, J., Lopes, J., and Ramos, J. 1987. The development of bilingual proficiency in the transition from home to school: a longitudinal study of Portuguese-speaking children. In Harley, Allen, Cummins, and Swain, Vol. III.

Cummins, J., and Nakajima, K. 1987. Age of arrival, length of residence, and interdependence of literacy skills among Japanese immigrant students. In Harley, Allen, Cummins, and Swain, Vol. III.

Cummins, J., Swain, M., Nakajima, K., Handscombe, J., Green, D., and Tran, C. 1981. *Linguistic interdependence among Japanese and Vietnamese immigrant students.* Arlington, Va.: National Clearinghouse for Bilingual Education.

Cziko, G., Lambert, W. E., Sidoti, N., and Tucker, G. R. 1980. Graduates of early immersion: retrospective views of grade 11 students and their parents. In R. St. Clair and H. Giles (eds.), *The Social and Psychological Contexts of Language.* Hillsdale, N.J.: Lawrence Erlbaum.

Daoust-Blais, D. 1979. Corpus and status planning in Quebec. In J. Cobarrubias and J. Fishman (eds.), *Progress in language planning: international perspectives.* Amsterdam: Mouton.

de Groot, A. D. *Thought and choice in chess.* The Hague: Mouton.

Dillon, W. R., and Goldstein, M. 1984. *Multivariate analysis: methods and applications.* New York: Wiley.

Dodson, C. J. 1978. The independent evaluator's report. In Schools Council Committee for Wales.

Dubé, N. C., and Herbert, G. 1975a. *St. John Valley bilingual education project.* Washington, D.C.: U.S. Department of Health, Education and Welfare.

1975b. Evaluation of the St. John Valley Title VII bilingual education program 1970–1975. Unpublished ms., Madawaska, Maine.

Dunkel, H. B. 1948. *Second-language learning*. New York: Ginn.

Duran, R. P. 1985. Discourse skills of bilingual children: precursors of literacy. *International Journal of the Sociology of Language* 53:99–114.

Ellis, R. 1984. Can syntax be taught? a study of the effects of formal instruction on the acquisition of WH-questions by children. *Applied Linguistics 5/* 2:138–55.

Enright, D. S. 1984. The organization of interaction in elementary classrooms. In J. Handscombe, R. A. Orem, and B. P. Taylor (eds.), *On TESOL '83: the question of control*. Washington, D.C.: TESOL.

Enright, D. S., and McCloskey, M. L. 1988. *Integrating English: developing English language and literacy in the multilingual classroom*. Reading, Mass.: Addison-Wesley.

Ervin, S. M., and Osgood, C. E. 1954. Second language learning and bilingualism. *Journal of Abnormal and Social Psychology* 49:139–46.

Fanselow, J. F. 1977. Beyond Rashomon – conceptualizing and describing the teaching act. *TESOL Quarterly* 11/1:17–39.

1987. *Breaking rules – generating and exploring alternatives in language teaching*. New York: Longman.

Fouly, K. A. 1985. A confirmatory multivariate study of the nature of second language proficiency and its relationship to learner variables. Ph.D. dissertation, University of Illinois.

Gardner, R. C. 1983. Learning another language: A true social psychological experiment. *Journal of Language and Social Psychology* 2:219–30.

1985. *Social psychology and second language learning*. London: Edward Arnold.

Gardner, R. C., and Kalin, R. (eds.) 1981. *A Canadian social psychology of ethnic relations*. Toronto: Methuen.

Gardner, R. C., Lalonde R. N., and Pearson, R. 1983. The socio-educational model of second language acquisition: an investigation using LISREL causal modeling. *Journal of Language and Social Psychology* 2/1:1–16.

Gardner, R. C., and Lambert, W. E. 1972. *Attitudes and motivation in second language learning*. Rowley, Mass.: Newbury House.

Genesee, F. 1976. The role of intelligence in second language learning. *Language Learning* 26:267–80.

1978. Scholastic effects of French immersion: an overview after ten years. *Interchange* 9:20–29.

1981. A comparison of early and late second language learning. *Canadian Journal of Behavioral Science* 13:115–27.

Genesee, F., and Hamayan, E. 1980. Individual differences in second language learning. *Applied Psycholinguistics* 1:95–110.

Genesee, F., Hamers, J., Lambert, W. E., Mononen, L., Seitz, M., and Starck, R. 1978. Language processing in bilinguals. *Brain and Language* 5:1–12.

Genesee, F., and Lambert, W. E. 1981. Trilingual education for the majority language child. Unpublished ms., Psychology Department, McGill University.

Getzels, J. W., and Jackson, P. W. 1962. *Creativity and intelligence*. New York: Wiley.

Giles, H., and Byrne, J. 1982. An intergroup approach to second language acquisition. *Journal of Multilingual and Multicultural Development* 3:17–40.

Giles, H., Bourhis, R. Y., and Taylor, D. 1977. Towards a theory of language in ethnic group relations. In H. Giles (ed.), *Language, ethnicity and intergroup relations*. New York: Academic Press.

Giles, H., Garrett, P., and Coupland, N. 1987. Language acquisition in the Basque country: invoking and extending the intergroup model. Second World Basque Congress, San Sebastian.

Giles, H., and Johnson, P. 1981. The role of language in ethnic group relations. In J. C. Turner & H. Giles (eds.), *Intergroup behaviour*. Oxford: Basil Blackwell.

Gordon, H. W. 1980. Cerebral organization in bilinguals: lateralization. *Brain and Language* 9:255–68.

Gumperz, J. 1982. *Discourse strategies*. Cambridge: Cambridge University Press.

Guntermann, G., and Phillips, J. K. 1981. Communicative course design: developing functional ability in all four skills. *The Canadian Modern Language Review* 37/2:329–43.

Hakuta, K. 1986. *Mirror of language: the debate on bilingualism*. New York: Basic Books.

Hall, B., and Gudykunst, W. 1986. The intergroup theory of second language ability. *Journal of Language and Social Psychology* 5:291–302.

Hall, G., and Lambert, W. E. 1988. French immersion and cerebral lateralization: a dual task study. *Canadian Journal of Behavioural Science* 20/1: 1–14.

Halliday, M. A. K. 1978. *Language as social semiotic: the social interpretation of language and meaning*. London: Edward Arnold.

Hamers, J., and Blanc, M. 1982. Towards a social-psychological model of bilingual development. *Journal of Language and Social Psychology* 1:29–50.

Hansen, L. 1984. Field dependence-independence and language testing: evidence from six Pacific island cultures. *TESOL Quarterly* 18:311–24.

Hanson, G. 1979. *The position of the second generation of Finnish immigrants in Sweden: the importance of education in the home language*. Report presented at the Symposium on the Position of the Second Generation of Yugoslav Immigrants in Sweden, Split, Yugoslavia, October 29–November 1, 1979.

Harley, B. 1984. How good is their French? In Stern (ed.).

    1987. The relationship between starting age and oral second language proficiency in three groups of classroom learners. In Harley, Allen, Cummins, and Swain, Vol. III.

    1989a. Transfer in the written compositions of French immersion students. In H. W. Dechert and M. Raupach (eds.), *Transfer in language production*. New York: Ablex.

    1989b. Functional grammar in French immersion: a classroom experiment. *Applied Linguistics* 10/3:331–359. (Also in Harley, Allen, Cummins, and Swain, Vol. II.)

    1989c. Second language proficiency and classroom treatment in early French immersion. In R. Freudenstein (ed.), *Error in foreign languages: analysis and treatment*. Marburg: Informationszentrum für Fremdsprachenforschung der Philipps-Universität. (Also in Harley, Allen, Cummins, and Swain 1987, Vol. II.)

Harley, B., Allen P., Cummins, J., and Swain, M. 1987. *The development of bilingual proficiency: final report. Volume I: The nature of proficiency;*

Volume II: *Classroom treatment*; Volume III: *Social context and age*. Toronto: Modern Language Centre, O.I.S.E. [ED 291248]

Harley, B., and King, M. L. 1989. Verb lexis in the written compositions of young L2 learners. *Studies in Second Language Acquisition*. 11: 415–39.

Harley, B., King, M. L., and Burtis, J. 1987. Perspectives on lexical proficiency in a second language. In Harley, Allen, Cummins, and Swain, Vol. I.

Harley, B., and Swain, M. 1978. An analysis of the verb system used by young learners of French. *Interlanguage Studies Bulletin* 3/1:35–79.

Harley, B., and Swain, M. 1984. The interlanguage of immersion students and its implications for second language teaching. In A. Davies, C. Criper, and A. P. R. Howatt (eds.), *Interlanguage*. Edinburgh: Edinburgh University Press.

Harmon, H. H. 1976. *Modern factor analysis*. 3rd ed. Chicago: University of Chicago Press.

Harris, D. B. 1963. *Children's drawings as measures of intellectual maturity: a revision and extension of the Goodenough draw-a-man test*. New York: Harcourt, Brace and World.

Head, H. 1926. *Aphasia and kindred disorders of speech*. London: Cambridge University Press.

Heath, S. B. 1983. *Ways with words*. Cambridge: Cambridge University Press.

Hebb, D. O. 1958. *A textbook of psychology*. Philadelphia: Saunders.

Heller, M. 1983. The social meaning of French and English in a Toronto French-language school. In Allen et al., Appendices.

1984. Language and ethnic identity in a Toronto French language school. *Canadian Ethnic Studies* 16/2:1–14.

Higgs, T. V., and Clifford, R. 1982. The push toward communication. In T. V. Higgs (ed.), *Curriculum, competence and the foreign language teacher*. Skokie, Ill.: National Textbook Company.

Hudson, R. A. 1980. *Sociolinguistics*. Cambridge: Cambridge University Press.

Hulstijn, J. 1983. Communicative skills of young second language learners: issues in coding speech data from face-to-face conversations. In Allen et al., Appendices.

Humphreys, L. G., and Montanelli, R. G., Jr. 1975. An investigation of the parallel analysis criterion for determining the number of common factors. *Multivariate Behavioral Research* 10:193–206.

Hymes, D. H. 1970. On communicative competence. In J. Gumperz and D. H. Hymes (eds.), *Directions in sociolinguistics*. New York: Holt, Rinehart and Winston.

Ianco-Worrall, A. D. 1972. Bilingualism and cognitive development. *Child Development* 43:1390–1400.

Jakobovits, L. A. 1968. Implications of recent psycholinguistic developments for the teaching of a second language. *Language Learning* 18:89–109.

1972. Authenticity in FL teaching. Introduction to Savignon.

Jakobovits, L. A., and Lambert, W. E. 1961. Semantic satiation among bilinguals. *Journal of Experimental Psychology* 62:576–82.

James, L. R., Mulaik, S. A., and Brett, J. M. 1982. *Causal analysis: assumptions, models and data*. Beverley Hills, Calif.: Sage.

Johnson, J. 1987. The developmental growth of metaphor comprehension in children's first and second language. In Harley, Allen, Cummins, and Swain, Vol. I.

Johnson, P., Giles, H., and Bourhis, R. Y. 1983. The viability of ethnolinguistic vitality: A reply. *Journal of Multilingual and Multicultural Development* 4:255–69.

Jöreskog, K. G. 1971. Statistical analysis of sets of congeneric tests. *Psychometrika* 36:109–34.

Jöreskog, K. G., and Sörbom, D. 1978. *Lisrel IV – Analysis of linear structural relationships by the method of maximum likelihood*. Chicago: National Educational Resources.

Kessler, C., and Quinn, M. 1980. Bilingualism and science problem-solving ability. Paper presented at the 14th Annual International Convention of Teachers of English to Speakers of Other Languages, San Francisco.

Kloss, H. 1969. *Research possibilities on group bilingualism: a report*. Quebec: International Center for Research on Bilingualism.

Kochman, T. 1981. *Black and white styles in conflict*. Chicago: University of Chicago Press.

Kotik, B. S. 1980. Investigation of speech lateralization in multilinguals. Rostov State University, Rostov, USSR. (Unpublished personal communication of additional research findings.)

Krashen, S. D. 1981. *Second language acquisition and second language learning*. Oxford: Pergamon.

    1982. *Principles and practice in second language acquisition*. Oxford: Pergamon.

    1984. Immersion: why it works and what it has taught us. In Stern (ed.).

    1985. *The input hypothesis: issues and implications*. London: Longman.

Krashen, S. D., and Terrell, T. D. 1983. *The Natural Approach: language acquisition in the classroom*. Oxford: Pergamon.

Lambert, W. E. 1955. Measurement of the linguistic dominance of bilinguals. *Journal of Abnormal and Social Psychology* 50:197–200.

    1967. A social psychology of bilingualism. *Journal of Social Issues* 23:91–109.

    1969. Psychological studies of the interdependencies of the bilingual's two languages. In J. Puhvel (ed.), *Substance and structure of language*. Los Angeles: University of California Press.

    1974. Culture and language as factors in learning and education. In F. Aboud and R. Meade (eds.), *Cultural factors in learning and education*. Bellingham: Fifth Western Washington Symposium on Learning.

Lambert, W. E., and Fillenbaum, S. 1959. A pilot study of aphasia among bilinguals. *Canadian Journal of Psychology* 13:28–34.

Lambert, W. E., Giles, H., and Albert, A. 1976. Language attitudes in a rural city in northern Maine. *La Moda Lingvo-Problemo* 5/15:129–92. The Hague: Mouton.

Lambert, W. E., Giles, H., and Picard, O. 1975. Language attitudes in a French-American community. *International Journal of Sociology of Language* 4:127–52.

Lambert, W. E., Havelka, J., and Crosby, C. 1958. The influence of language acquisition contexts on bilingualism. *Journal of Abnormal and Social Psychology* 56:239–44.

Lambert, W. E., Havelka, J., and Gardner, R. C. 1959. Linguistic manifestations of bilingualism. *American Journal of Psychology* 72:77–82.

Lambert, W. E., Ignatow, M., and Krauthamer, M. 1968. Bilingual organization in free recall. *Journal of Verbal Learning and Verbal Behavior* 7:207–14.

Lambert, W. E., and Jakobovits, L. 1960. Verbal satiation and changes in the intensity of meaning. *Journal of Experimental Psychology* 60:376–83.

Lambert, W. E., and Rawlings, C. 1969. Bilingual processing of mixed-language associative networks. *Journal of Verbal Learning and Verbal Behavior* 8:604–09.

Lambert, W. E., and Tucker, G. R. 1972. *Bilingual education of children: the St. Lambert experiment*. Rowley, Mass.: Newbury House.

Leopold, W. F. 1949. *Speech development of a bilingual child*. Evanston, Ill.: Northwestern University Press.

Levine, N. 1981. History. In M. Torbe (ed.), *Language teaching and learning*. London: Ward Lock Educational.

Levinson, S. L. 1983. *Pragmatics*. Cambridge: Cambridge University Press.

Lewis, C. 1981. Skill in algebra. In J. R. Anderson (ed.), *Cognitive skills and their acquisition*. Hillsdale, N. J.: Lawrence Erlbaum.

Lightbown, P. M. 1983. Acquiring English in Quebec classrooms. In S. Felix and H. Wode (eds.), *Language development at the crossroads*. Tübingen, West Germany: Gunter Narr.

1985. Great expectations: second-language acquisition research and classroom teaching. *Applied Linguistics* 6/2:173–89.

Lindblad, T., and Levin, L. 1970. *Teaching grammar: an experiment in applied linguistics, assessing three different methods of teaching grammatical structures in English as a foreign language*. Gothenburg, Sweden: Gothenburg School of Education.

Long, K. K., and Padilla, A. M. 1970. Evidence for bilingual antecedents of academic success in a group of Spanish-American college students. Unpublished ms., Western Washington State College, Bellingham.

Long, M. 1980. Inside the "black box": methodological issues in classroom research on language teaching. *Language Learning* 30:1–42.

1983. Does second language instruction make a difference? *TESOL Quarterly* 17/3:359–82.

1988. Instructed interlanguage development. In L. Beebe (ed.), *Issues in second language acquisition: multiple perspectives*. Cambridge, Mass.: Newbury House.

Long, M. H., and Sato, C. J. 1983. Classroom foreigner talk discourse: forms and functions of teachers' questions. In H. W. Seliger and M. H. Long (eds.), *Classroom-oriented research in second language acquisition*. Rowley, Mass.: Newbury House.

MacNab, G. L. 1979. Cognition and bilingualism: a reanalysis of studies. *Linguistics* 17: 231–55.

Macnamara, J. 1973. Nurseries, streets and classrooms: some comparisons and deductions. *Modern Language Journal* 57/5/6:250–54.

Martin, N., D'Arcy, P., Newton, B., and Parker, R. 1976. *Writing and learning across the curriculum 11–16*. London: Ward Lock Educational.

McConnell, B. B. 1980. Effectiveness of individual bilingual instruction for migrant students. Ph.D. dissertation, Washington State University, Pullman.

McConnell, D., Daoust-Blais, D., and Martin, A. 1979. Language planning and language treatment. Unpublished ms. cited in Daoust-Blais.

McKeithen, K., Reitman, J. S., Rueter, J., and Hirtle, S. C. 1981. Knowledge organization and skill differences in computer programmers. *Cognitive Psychology* 13:307–325.

McLaughlin, B. 1984. *Second-language acquisition in childhood*, Vol. 1, *Pre-school children*. Hillsdale, N.J.: Lawrence Erlbaum.

1985. *Second-language acquisition in childhood*. Vol. 2, *School-age children*. Hillsdale, N.J.: Lawrence Erlbaum.

1987. *Theories of second language learning*. London: Edward Arnold.

McLaughlin, B., and Baker, C. 1985. Are poor readers all the same? a comparison of monolingual and bilingual readers in the upper elementary grades. University of California, Santa Cruz.

McLaughlin, B., Rossman, T., and McLeod, B. 1983. Second language learning: an information-processing perspective. *Language Learning, 33,* 135–58.

Milner, P. M. 1957. The cell assembly: Mark II. *Psychological Review, 64,* 242–52.

Mitchell, R., Parkinson, B., and Johnstone, R. 1981. *The foreign language classroom: an observational study*. Stirling, Scotland: Department of Education, University of Stirling, Educational Monographs, 9.

Moffett, J. 1968. *A student-centered language arts curriculum, grades K–13: a handbook for teachers*. Boston: Houghton Mifflin.

Mohan, B. A. 1986. *Language and content*. Reading, Mass.: Addison-Wesley.

Montanelli, R. G., Jr., and Humphreys, L. G. 1976. Latent roots of random data correlation matrices with squared multiple correlations on the diagonal: a Monte Carlo study. *Psychometrika* 41/3:207–45.

Morgan, J. L., and Newport, E. L. 1981. The role of constituent structure in the induction of an artificial language. *Journal of Verbal Learning and Verbal Behavior* 20:67–85.

Moskowitz, G. 1970. *The foreign language teacher interacts*. Chicago: Association for Productive Teaching.

Naiman, N., Fröhlich, M., Stern, H. H., and Todesco, A. 1978. *The good language learner*. Toronto: OISE.

Nation, R., and McLaughlin, B. 1986. Experts and novices: An information-processing approach to the "good language learner" problem. *Applied Psycholinguistics* 7:41–56.

Nayak, N., Hansen, N., Krueger, N., and McLaughlin, B. 1987. *Language-learning strategies in monolingual and multilingual subjects*. University of California, Santa Cruz.

Neustupny, J. 1970. Basic types of treatment of language problems. *Linguistic Communications* 1:77–98.

Newmark, L., and Reibel, D. A. 1968. Necessity and sufficiency in language learning. *IRAL: International Review of Applied Linguistics in Language Teaching* 6/2:145–64.

O'Bryan, K. G., Reitz, J., and Kuplowska, D. 1976. *Non-official languages: a study in Canadian multiculturalism*. Ottawa: Minister of Supply and Services.

Oller, J. W., Jr. 1976. Evidence for a general language proficiency factor: an expectancy grammar. *Die Neueren Sprachen* 2:165–74.

1981. Language as intelligence? *Language Learning* 31:465–92.

(ed.). 1983. *Issues in language testing research*. Rowley, Mass.: Newbury House.

Olton, R. M. 1960. Semantic generalization between languages. M.A. thesis, McGill University.

Omaggio, A. C. 1986. *Teaching language in context: proficiency-oriented instruction.* Boston: Heinle & Heinle.

Ortiz, A. A., and Yates, J. R. 1983. Incidence of exceptionality among Hispanics: implications for manpower planning. *NABE Journal* 7:41–54.

Oxford, R. L. 1986. *Second language learning strategies: current research and implications for practice.* Los Angeles: University of California Center for Language Education and Research.

Padilla, A. M., and Long, K. K. 1969. An assessment of successful Spanish-American students at the University of New Mexico. Paper presented at the Annual Meeting of the American Association for the Advancement of Science, Rocky Mountain Division, Colorado Springs, Colo.

Paivio, A., Clark, J. M., and Lambert, W. E. 1988. Bilingual dual-coding theory and semantic repetition effects on recall. *Journal of Experimental Psychology: Learning, Memory, and Cognition* 14/1:163–172.

Paivio, A., and Lambert, W. E. 1981. Dual-coding and bilingual memory. *Journal of Verbal Learning and Verbal Behavior* 20:532–39.

Pak, A., Dion, K. L., and Dion, K. K. 1985. Correlates of self-confidence with English among Chinese students in Toronto. *Canadian Journal of Behavioural Sciences* 17:369–78.

Paulston, C. B. 1970. Structural pattern drills: a classification. *Foreign Language Annals* 4/1:187–93.

—— 1980. *Bilingual education: theory and issues.* Rowley, Mass.: Newbury House.

—— 1982. *Swedish research and debate about bilingualism: A report to the National Swedish Board of Education.* Stockholm: Skolöverstyrelsen.

—— 1983. Language planning. In C. Kennedy (ed.), *Language planning and language education.* London: Allen & Unwin.

—— 1984. Second language acquisition in school settings. In *Significant bilingual instructional features study.* San Francisco. Far West Laboratories.

Peal, E., and Lambert, W. E. 1962. The relation of bilingualism to intelligence. *Psychological Monographs* 76:1–23.

Pedhazur, E. J. 1982. *Multiple regression in behavioral research.* 2nd ed. New York: Holt, Rinehart and Winston.

Penfield, W., and Roberts, L. 1959. *Speech and brain mechanisms.* Princeton, N.J.: Princeton University Press.

Philips, S. 1983. *The invisible culture.* London: Longman.

Pica, T. 1987. Second language acquisition, social interaction, and the classroom. *Applied Linguistics* 8/1:3–21.

Pienemann, M. 1985. Learnability and syllabus construction. In K. Hyltenstam and M. Pienemann (eds.), *Modelling and assessing second language acquisition.* Clevedon, England: Multilingual Matters.

Purcell, E. T. 1983. Models of pronunciation accuracy. In J. W. Oller, Jr. (ed.).

Raleigh, M. 1981. *The languages book.* London: ILEA English Centre.

Ramsey, R. M. G. 1980. Language-learning approach styles of adult multilinguals and successful language learners. *Annals of the New York Academy of Sciences* 345:73–96.

Reitz, J. G. 1980. *The survival of ethnic groups.* Toronto: McGraw-Hill.

Richards, J. C. 1972. Social factors, interlanguage, and language learning. *Language Learning* 22/2:159–88.

Rivers, W. 1972. Talking off the tops of their heads. *TESOL Quarterly* 6/1:71–81. (Also in Rivers, W. 1983. *Communicating naturally in a second language.* Cambridge: Cambridge University Press.)

Rosen, C., and Rosen, H. 1973. *The language of primary school children.* Harmondsworth, England: Penguin Books.

Rosenshine, B., and Furst, N. 1973. The use of direct observation to study teaching. In R. Travers (ed.), *Second handbook of research on teaching.* Chicago: Rand McNally.

Rosler, P., and Holm, W. 1980. *Saad naaki bee na'nitin: teaching by means of two languages – Navajo and English – at Rock Point Community School.* Washington, D.C.: Center for Applied Linguistics.

Rubin, J. 1973. Language planning: discussion of some current issues. In J. Rubin and R. Shuy (eds.), *Language planning: current issues and research.* Washington, D.C.: Georgetown University Press.

———. 1975. What the "good language learner" can teach us. *TESOL Quarterly* 9:41–51.

———. 1981. Study of cognitive processes in second language learning. *Applied Linguistics* 11:117–31.

Sang, F., Schmitz, B., Vollmer, H., Baumert, J., and Roeder, P. M. 1986. Models of second language competence: a structural equation approach. *Language Testing* 3/1:54–79.

Savignon, S. J. 1972. *Communicative competence: an experiment in foreign-language teaching.* Philadelphia: Center for Curriculum Development.

Schachter, J. 1984. A universal input condition. In W. E. Rutherford (ed.), *Language universals and second language acquisition.* Philadelphia: John Benjamins.

Schachter, J., and Celce-Murcia, M. 1977. Some reservations concerning error analysis. *TESOL Quarterly* 11/4:441–51.

Schieffelin, B., and Ochs, E. 1986. *Language socialization across cultures.* Cambridge: Cambridge University Press.

Schmid, J., and Leiman, J. M. 1957. The development of hierarchical factor solutions. *Psychometrika* 22:53–61.

Schmitt, N., Coyle, B. W., and Saari, B. B. 1977. A review and critique of analyses of multitrait-multimethod matrices. *Multivariate Behavioral Research* 12:447–78.

Schumann, J. H. 1978. Social and psychological factors in second language acquisition. In J. C. Richards (ed.), *Understanding second and foreign language learning.* Rowley, Mass.: Newbury House.

Scott, S. 1973. The relation of divergent thinking to bilingualism: cause or effect? Unpublished ms., Psychology Department, McGill University.

Scovel, T. 1988. *A time to speak: a psycholinguistic inquiry into the critical period for human speech.* New York: Newbury House.

Seliger, H. 1979. On the nature and function of language rules in language teaching. *TESOL Quarterly* 13:359–70.

Skehan, P. 1986. The role of foreign language aptitude in a model of school learning. *Language Testing* 3/2:188–221.

Skutnabb-Kangas, R., and Toukomaa, P. 1976. *Teaching migrant children's mother tongue and learning of the language of the host country in the context of the socio-cultural situation of the migrant family.* Helsinki: The Finnish National Commission for UNESCO.

Smith, P. D. 1970. *A comparison of the cognitive and audiolingual approaches to foreign language instruction: the Pennsylvania foreign language project.* Philadelphia: Center for Curriculum Development.

Snow, C. E., and Hoefnagel-Höhle, M. 1978. Age differences in second language acquisition. In E. Hatch (ed.), *Second language acquisition: a book of readings.* Rowley, Mass.: Newbury House.

Spada, N., and Lightbown, P. 1989. Intensive ESL programmes in Quebec primary schools. *TESL Canada Journal* 7/1.

Stern, H. H. 1981. The formal-functional distinction in language pedagogy: a conceptual clarification. In J. G. Savard and L. Laforge (eds.), *Proceedings of the 5th Congress of L'Association internationale de linguistique appliquée.* Quebec: Les Presses de l'Université Laval.

1983. *Fundamental concepts of language teaching.* Oxford: Oxford University Press.

(ed.) 1984. *The immersion phenomenon.* Special issue, No. 12 of *Language and Society.* Ottawa: Commissioner of Official Languages.

Swain, M., McLean, L.D., Friedman, R. J., Harley, B., and Lapkin, S. 1976. *Three approaches to teaching French.* Toronto: Ministry of Education, Ontario.

Strong, M. 1983. Social styles and the second language acquisition of Spanish-speaking kindergarteners. *TESOL Quarterly* 17/2:241–58.

Stubbs, M. 1983. *Discourse analysis: the sociolinguistic analysis of natural language.* Chicago: University of Chicago Press.

Sussman, H. M., Franklin, P., and Simon, T. 1982. Bilingual speech: bilateral control? *Brain and Language* 15:125–42.

Swaffar, J. K., Arens, K., and Morgan, M. 1982. Teacher classroom practices: redefining method as task hierarchy. *Modern Language Journal* 66:24–33.

Swain, M. 1974. French immersion programs across Canada. *Canadian Modern Language Review* 31:117–28.

1985. Communicative competence: some roles of comprehensible input and comprehensible output in its development. In S. Gass and C. Madden (eds.), *Input in second language acquisition.* Rowley, Mass.: Newbury House.

1988. Manipulating and complementing content teaching to maximize second language learning. *TESL Canada Journal* 6/1:68–83. (Also in Harley, Allen, Cummins, and Swain 1987, Vol. II).

Swain, M., and Carroll, S. 1987. The immersion observation study. In Harley, Allen, Cummins, and Swain, Vol. II.

Swain, M., and Lapkin, S. 1982. *Evaluating bilingual education: a Canadian case study.* Clevedon, England: Multilingual Matters.

Swain, M., and Lapkin, S. In press. Aspects of the sociolinguistic performance of early and late French immersion students. In R. Scarcella, E. Anderson, and S. D. Krashen (eds.), *On the development of communicative competence in a second language.* Cambridge, Mass.: Newbury House. (Also in Harley, Allen, Cummins, and Swain 1987, Vol. II.)

Swan, M. 1985. A critical look at the communicative approach. *ELT Journal* 39/1:2–12; 39/2:76–87.

Tizard, B., and Hughes, M. 1984. *Young children learning.* London: Fontana.

Torbe, M., and Medway, P. 1981. *The climate for learning.* Montclair, N.J.: Boynton/Cook.

Torrance, E. P., Gowan, J. C., Wu, J. M., and Aliotti, N. C. 1970. Creative functioning of monolingual and bilingual children in Singapore. *Journal of Educational Psychology* 61:1–23.

Troike, R. C. 1978. Research evidence for the effectiveness of bilingual education. *NABE Journal* 3:13–24.

Tucker, G. R. 1980. Comments on proposed rules for nondiscrimination under programs receiving federal financial assistance through the Education Department: 5–6. Unpublished ms., Center for Applied Linguistics, Washington, D.C.

Ullmann, R., and Geva, E. 1984. The target language observation scheme (TALOS). York Regional Board of Education Core French Evaluation Project. Toronto: Modern Language Centre, O.I.S.E., unpublished report.

Vaid, J., and Genesee, F. 1980. Neuropsychological approaches to bilingualism: A critical review. *Canadian Journal of Psychology* 34:417–45.

Vaid, J., and Lambert, W. E. 1979. Differential cerebral involvement in the cognitive functioning of bilinguals. *Brain and Language* 8:92–110.

VanPatten, B. 1987. Can learners attend to form and content while listening to the L2? Unpublished ms., University of Illinois.

Vygotsky, L. S. 1972. *Thought and language.* Cambridge, Mass.: MIT Press.

Wang, L.-S. 1987. A comparative analysis of cognitive achievement and psychological orientation among language minority groups: A linear structural relations (LISREL) approach. Ph.D. dissertation, University of Illinois.

Warshaw, J. 1934. Automatic reactions in practical foreign language work. *Modern Language Journal* 9:151–58.

Waugh, L. R., and Monville-Burston, M. 1986. Aspect in discourse function: the French simple past in newspaper usage. *Language* 62/4:846–77.

Weinreich, U. 1953. *Languages in contact.* New York: Linguistic Circle of New York.

Wells, G. 1981. *Learning through interaction.* Cambridge: Cambridge University Press.

1982. *Language development in the pre-school years.* Cambridge: Cambridge University Press.

Wenden, A. 1985. Learner strategies. *TESOL Newsletter* 19/5:1, 4–5, 7.

White, L. 1985a. Is there a "logical problem" of second language acquisition? *TESL Canada Journal* 2/2:29–41.

1985b. Island effects in second language acquisition. Paper presented at the Workshop on Linguistic Theory and Second Language Acquisition, MIT, October.

1987a. Against comprehensible input: The input hypothesis and the development of second-language competence. *Applied Linguistics* 8/2:95–110.

1987b. Implications of learnability theories for second language learning and teaching. Paper presented at the Eighth World Congress of AILA in the Symposium: the role in second language acquisition of explicit metalinguistic knowledge or instruction, Sydney, August.

Widdowson, H. G. 1978. *Teaching language as communication.* Oxford: Oxford University Press.

Wigginton, E. 1985. *Sometimes a shining moment: the Foxfire experience.* Garden City, N.Y.: Anchor/Doubleday.

Wong Fillmore, L. 1985. When does teachers' talk work as input? In S. Gass and C. Madden (eds.), *Input in second language acquisition.* Rowley, Mass.: Newbury House.

Author index

241

Subject index

245